Leadership
Maps

Leadership Maps

Stephen H. White, Ed.D.

LEAD+
LEARN
PRESS

The Leadership and Learning Center
317 Inverness Way South, Suite 150
Englewood, Colorado 80112
Phone 1.866.399.6019 | Fax 303.504.9417
LeadandLearn.com

Published by Lead+Learn Press, a division of Advanced Learning Centers, Inc.

All Web links in this book are correct as of the publication date below but may have become inactive or otherwise modified since that time. If you notice a deactivated or changed link, please notify the publisher and specify the Web link, the book title, and the page number on which the link appears so that corrections may be made in future editions.

Lead+Learn Press also publishes books in a variety of electronic formats. Some content that appears in print may not be available in electronic books.

11 10 09 08 01 02 03 04 05 06 07 08 09

ISBN 978-1-933196-93-0

Library of Congress Cataloging-in-Publication Data

White, Stephen H., 1949–
  Leadership maps / Stephen H. White.
       p. cm.
  Includes bibliographical references.
  ISBN 978-1-933196-93-0
  1. Educational leadership. 2. Student achievement. I. Title.
  LB2805.W477 2009
  371.2'07—dc22
                                        2009024008

Contents

List of Exhibits

About the Author

 **Stephen H. White, Ed.D.**

Dr. Stephen White is an internationally known educational consultant whose expertise in data analysis, systems, leadership assessment, and school improvement is helping to change the way educators view themselves and manage data in an era of high-stakes accountability and testing.

He is the author of several books, including the award-winning *Beyond the Numbers*, *Show Me the Proof*, and *School Improvement for the Next Generation* (in press 2010). He has authored numerous articles and two invited chapters for bestselling authors, including "Data on Purpose" in *Ahead of the Curve* (2007). As a former superintendent and high school principal, Dr. White brings more than thirty-five years of experience at all levels and has worked with Dr. Douglas Reeves at The Leadership and Learning Center since 2003. He is the primary author of the PIM™ school improvement framework and the *Leadership Map*, and he has reviewed more than 2,300 school improvement plans since 2005. He is active in his church, The Rock, and lives with his lovely wife, Linda, and the youngest of eight children, Jonathan.

Dr. White can be reached at:

Stephen White, Ed.D.
The Leadership and Learning Center
317 Inverness Way South, Suite 150
Englewood, CO 80112
303.504.9312 Ext. 518
720.219.1628 Mobile
swhite@leadandlearn.com

Introduction

The literature on school leadership is saturated with conceptual models about how to improve student achievement and teacher effectiveness (DuFour, Eaker, and DuFour 2005; Schlechty 2000; Lezotte and McKee 2002; Fullan, Hill, and Crevola 2006). Others have extrapolated evidence over time from the literature to identify leadership characteristics and successfully quantify the impact of leadership on student achievement (Sanders and Horn 1998; Wenglinsky 2002; Marzano, Waters, and McNulty 2005; Hoy and Smith 2007). Scholars across professions have consistently identified the need to move from vision to execution, from strategy to implementation, and from knowing to doing (Pfeffer and Sutton 2000; Elmore 2000; Collins 2001; Fullan, Hill, and Crevola 2006; Schmoker 2006; Reeves 2006; Heath and Heath 2007).

Despite this wealth of research, school improvement plans are often frameworks associated less with leadership than with compliance and stakeholder participation. Most school improvement plans are more apt to maintain the status quo rather than transform it, and rarely do school improvement plans focus the real work of school leaders or leadership teams. *Leadership Maps* connects the personal and organizational characteristics that leaders must demonstrate to create concise school improvement frameworks for novice leaders and seasoned veterans alike.

The Leading-Learning (L^2) Matrix developed by Douglas Reeves (2002) represents a compelling theoretical construct that presumes a relationship between what adults do in schools and resulting student achievement. Based on field research with school improvement plans at The Leadership and Learning Center, Dr. Reeves' *The Learning Leader* (2006) enhanced the theoretical by introducing the need to examine implementation through a candid and comprehensive self-assessment system. *Leadership Maps* provides that self-assessment framework by examining professional values and beliefs as well as their impact on program implementation and school improvement.

Research for *Leadership Maps* represents more than 2,300 school improvement plans across North America since 2005 and offers an empirical application of this framework. *Leadership Maps* has also been informed by more than 140 authors and researchers. Chapter 1 describes the genesis for *Leadership Maps*, while Chapters 2 through 10 describe the eight domains associated with standards and leadership in the context of school improvement. *Leadership Maps* concludes in Chapter 11 with three guiding principles for school improvement and leadership at all levels: communicate, replicate, and celebrate.

By distinguishing performance from knowledge and values, *Leadership Maps* will accomplish four major goals:

1. Provide a responsive and safe self-assessment of leadership practices.

2. Provide leaders with a real-time diagnostic tool to assess leadership in practice.

3. Provide a comprehensive array of measurable indicators of best practices to drive improvement strategies and tactics.

4. Provide a thorough background of elements of leadership in a standards-based environment.

Readers will be better able to make strategic and focused school improvement decisions in selecting goals, monitoring current practice, and determining levels of effectiveness. Essential questions and big ideas at the end of every chapter will assist leaders as they reflect upon leadership practice. Hopefully, as a result, they will take action to improve schools.

Leadership Maps helps leaders examine effectiveness from a new paradigm, characterized by solid standards-based dimensions of leadership. It represents a shift from focusing on test scores to drive strategies to focusing on antecedent adult actions to drive student achievement. It represents a second-order level of change, where the focus shifts from the leader alone to the leader's ability to influence others and build capacity in school and school district practices that work. *Leadership Maps* is designed for school leaders at all levels—superintendents, central-office officials, site administrators, and teacher leaders. It is hoped that this simple tool will become a valued resource that stretches the most successful among us while guiding the next generation of school leaders.

CHAPTER 1

Background and Genesis of Leadership Maps

*"If you don't know where you are going,
any road will get you there."*
LEWIS CARROLL, 1832–1898

Leadership Maps is fundamentally about discovering what works and what doesn't. It is an attempt to provide a map of one's leadership that can allow leaders to determine not only their target for achievement, but how to achieve it and what results indicators can assure them that they are on the right path. The Leading-Learning Matrix (L^2) developed by Dr. Douglas Reeves (2002) provided a conceptual framework linking student achievement results to professional practices. It was premised on the assumption that understanding the practices that produce gains in student achievement is a prerequisite to sustaining and extending such gains. This approach challenges the premise that student achievement is primarily a function of family income or parent education levels, and it shifts the emphasis from what students do in completing assessments to what professionals do to impact student learning.

Wenglinsky (2002) found that teaching practices had an equal or greater effect on student achievement than family income, race, or parent education levels, and a mountain of evidence is now available that demonstrates how students from poor families, immigrant families, and families of color can achieve at high levels. The L^2 Matrix captured the reality that student and school success is a function of what adults know and how they put that knowledge into action. The 90/90/90 schools provide a case in point, where hundreds of schools across the country with 90 percent of their students from high-poverty families and 90 percent being students of color also witness more than 90 percent of students meeting or exceeding high academic standards in math or reading. These results are based on independently conducted state assessments of academic achievement (Reeves 2003; Reeves 2004, pages 185–186; Kannapel and Clements 2005; School Matters 2008; Haycock 2008). Based on the Texas Assessment of Knowledge and Skills (TAKS), the Houston Independent School

District alone had twenty-seven 90/90/90 schools in 2007 in terms of students who were proficient on the TAKS in math, reading, or both (White, Crouse, and Burcham, *et al.* 2008, page 9).

Actions of adults impact achievement. Some professional practices are so highly correlated with school improvement that they become predictors of improved achievement, such as posting of objectives or collaborative meetings where teacher teams examine student work and design interventions. Such antecedents of excellence need to be measured and monitored in each setting to determine their impact and the fidelity with which such actions are implemented. The L^2 Matrix helped educators see the need to capture and analyze data about teaching and leading as readily as we currently examine data about learning. Exhibit 1.1 illustrates how schools can have the appearance of success but struggle to maintain their successes, while other schools have lower achievement but are much better poised for sustained and continuous improvement.

EXHIBIT 1.1

The Leadership and Learning Matrix (L^2)

Achievement of Results		
	Lucky High Results, Low Understanding of Antecedents Replication of Success Unlikely	**Leading** High Results, High Understanding of Antecedents Replication of Success Likely
	Losing Ground Low Results, Low Understanding of Antecedents Replication of Mistakes Likely	**Learning** Low Results, High Understanding of Antecedents Replication of Mistakes Unlikely

Understanding of the Antecedents of Excellence

Lucky

When achievement is high but understanding and application of antecedents is low, the leaders' responses fall within the lucky quadrant. This is a common occurrence, where student achievement occurs at high levels but educators are at a loss to explain why. How often have you heard the comment, "We had a great class of kids this year"? Lucky schools are often found in affluent neighborhoods where students come from families that value education, introduce children to print-rich environments early, and provide a range of life experiences that encourage and foster cognitive development and learning. These schools simply have not taken the time to focus on professional practices and high-yield instructional strategies because they have not been faced with the need to do so. If educators don't know what led to success, it is almost certain that they will not be able to replicate the practice. Lucky schools are the most vulnerable to changing demographics.

Losing Ground

When achievement is low and school officials are equally at a loss as to the reasons for that low achievement, clearly education at that school is losing ground. Not only is it unlikely that any successes will be replicated, it is highly likely that the conditions that led to poor performance will continue. When you overhear educators attribute poor performance to students or their parents, watch out. That perspective avoids the kind of reflection needed to learn from mistakes and find a better way. At this point, it is useful to note that educators everywhere engage in a very people-intensive business full of complexity, ambiguity, and nonstop activity. It is entirely possible to exhaust oneself in the day-to-day operation of a school but fail to learn from the experience in the process. Educators who find themselves in the lower left quadrant are losing ground.

Learning

When achievement is low but the leaders' understanding and application of antecedents is high, the responses fall within the learning quadrant. The ability to discern what needs to be done (understanding) and the ability to act on that knowledge (application) are attributes of learners that rarely replicate mistakes and often learn from them to improve practice and, ultimately, student achievement. Knowledge of antecedents of excellence includes knowledge of best practices and high-yield instructional strategies, but there are many other antecedents, such as "enabling administrative structures" (Hoy and Smith 2007), how leaders schedule time, how leaders commit resources, and how leaders provide feedback.

Leading

Leading school practitioners have high student achievement and understand why. For example, Maplewood Elementary School in the Metropolitan School District of Wayne Township, Indiana, was once a low-performing, high-poverty school. When the principal, Janet Ham, began to analyze data, institute collaborative teams, and monitor best instructional practices, scores improved until Maplewood became one of the highest-performing elementary schools in Indiana. Ham's understanding and application of what works resulted in improved student achievement, as best practices were replicated and obsolete or ineffective practices ("mistakes" in Exhibit 1.1) were eliminated or diminished. When school teams understand what actions are needed to produce high student achievement, they are more apt to be able to replicate them and refine them in the process. Because educators like Janet Ham and her staff understand the research and apply their knowledge to daily practice, it is more likely they will experience positive gains, applying lessons learned at each juncture.

Antecedents of Excellence

The application of the L^2 Matrix to *Leadership Maps* is simply the identification of variables (adult actions) that distinguish leaders who experience success from the actions of those leaders who do not. *Leadership Maps* are based on the notion that those who understand the conditions and structures that are predictive of success (antecedents of excellence) and know how to avoid antecedents that perpetuate mediocrity or static student performance will be able to sustain improvement year after year, despite staffing and program changes. Exhibit 1.2 provides examples of three distinct types of antecedent actions and invites the reader to determine which action is representative of each type.

Classroom walk-throughs (CWTs) are administrative structures that have the potential to influence student achievement by influencing the quality of instructional strategies provided. Scheeler, Ruhl, and McAfee (2004; pages 396–407) found that the most effective feedback to improve teacher performance was immediate feedback—something that CWTs are designed to provide. Common formative assessments are also administrative structures that enable proven instructional strategies and all kinds of improved teaching practices to occur.

Data displays are powerful teaching practices that predict student achievement gains, even though displaying data is not a specific instructional strategy. It nonetheless represents a practice that can supplement any strategy the teacher selects.

EXHIBIT 1.2

Antecedent Type Definitions and Examples

Antecedent Type	Definition	Example
Instructional Strategies	Teacher-to-student interactions that **engage students in thinking**, require **professional development** to acquire, and require **practice** to achieve proficiency	Reciprocal teaching
Teaching Practices	Practices of teachers that improve efficiency, classroom management	Opening activities
Administrative Structures	Systematic provision of time, opportunity, and resources	Common planning time

Your Turn	Instructional Strategies	Teaching Practices	Administrative Structures
Classroom Walk-Throughs?			X
Common Formative Assessments?		X	
Data Displays?		X	
Use of Metaphors and Analogies?	X		

Daily use of metaphors and analogies is an instructional strategy because it engages students in thinking, requires professional development to understand fully, and needs to be practiced and refined to establish proficiency.

Distinguishing adult actions by antecedent type allows the practitioner to explicitly define actions in ways that lend themselves to measures that can be monitored. Use of metaphors is a measure that can be monitored by individual teachers, grade-level teams, or department teams, and it may be monitored in one class period or every period. The strategy can be measured as a proportion of teachers who introduce metaphors and analogies three days a week, or as a proportion of class periods where the strategy is introduced and students respond in writing during those class periods. Walk-throughs can be measured in terms of percentage of classrooms visited weekly or percentage of classroom teachers who receive the same-day feedback. Data displays might be measured in terms of quantity created each month or serve as a measure of quality by monitoring the number of teams or teachers who initiate the next steps determined as a result of the data display. The possibilities are as numerous as classroom conditions and teacher or administrator expertise. Many school data teams or professional learning communities struggle with data analysis simply because they examine only student achievement data and neglect the data of teaching or data of leading. Data about adult practices are essential to determine what is working and what is not (White 2007). All other analysis is speculation at best, even when the data is disaggregated by subgroup.

Leadership Maps as Antecedents of Excellence

Leadership Maps offers 100 factors that have been demonstrated to be antecedents of improved student achievement driven by acts of leadership. Research indicates that leaders who are cognizant about the effect that new initiatives have on staff wisely limit the number of school improvement initiatives at their school (Collins 2001; Lencioni 2004; White 2005a, page 93; Fullan 2008, page 2; Pfeffer and Sutton 2006, page 38). We also know that structures that promote collaboration among teachers help distribute leadership, increase ownership in a reform initiative, and produce new solutions and ideas through synergy realized from collaborative reflection (DuFour, Eaker, and DuFour *et al.* 2005). Ron Edmonds noted a generation ago:

> We can, whenever and wherever we choose, successfully teach all children whose schooling is of interest to us. We already know more than we need to do that. Whether or not we do it must finally depend on how we feel about the fact that we haven't so far.
> — Ron Edmonds, 1982 (Lezotte and McKee 2002, page 2)

Edmonds's statement applies not only to teaching but also to leading. We have enough knowledge about what works. The real task of leadership is to determine how to make it happen, how to implement it, and how to empower teachers and staff to protect the focus and translate intentions into reality. The *Leadership Map* is designed to promote that transformation with a safe, reflective self-assessment of what works.

Exhibit 1.3 represents the *Leadership Maps* for eighty-five administrators in a metropolitan school district of 33,000 students in the Southeast. Each dot represents that point where the mean student achievement scores intersect with the administrator's total score for understanding and applying antecedents in their area of responsibility. The result is a graphic depiction of the entire district in terms of its knowledge of leadership practices and collective impact on student achievement.

The large shaded diamond in Exhibit 1.3 provides the district with a composite score for all of its leaders across district student achievement

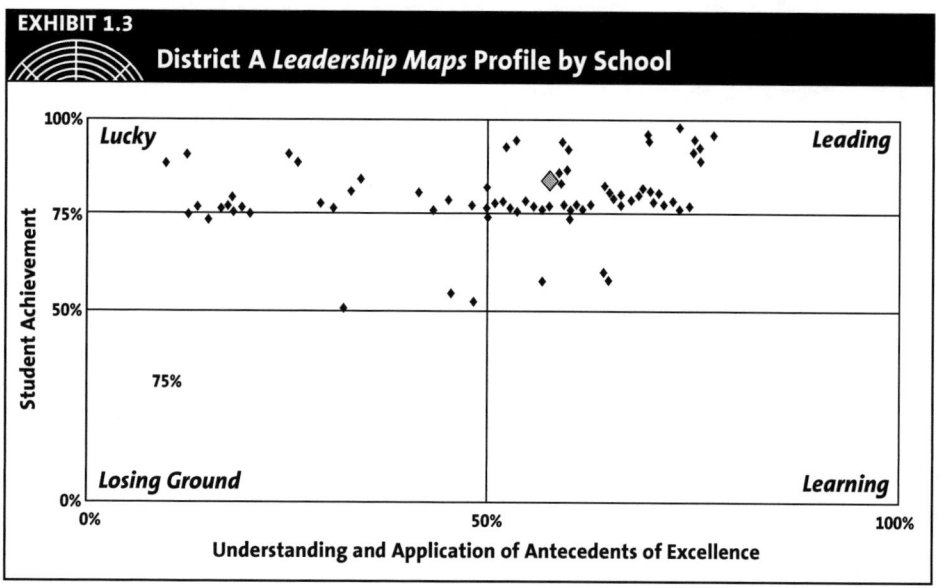

EXHIBIT 1.3

District A *Leadership Maps* Profile by School

assessments. Note how all schools have at least 50 percent of their students at standard (Y horizontal access), and a majority of schools have more than 75 percent of students at standard. The *Leadership Map* invites participants to identify the point at which they will be satisfied with student achievement, and for District A, that point represents 75 percent proficiency or higher. Against its own standard for performance, District A found itself in the *leading* quadrant (fifty-two schools) with four schools in the *learning* quadrant, six schools in the *losing ground* quadrant, and twenty-three schools in the *lucky* quadrant.

In this way, District A has detailed, empirical information to guide decisions to differentiate professional development for administrators and to identify leadership practices that need to be replicated across the district. *Leadership Maps* offers districts, schools, and individual leaders a wealth of data to help develop personal growth goals, determine school improvement targets, and select strategies and tactics to achieve them. When leaders complete their own personal leadership map, they also have a ready source of reliable antecedent conditions or practices to measure and monitor within the context of their own school, district, or department, all of which will be addressed in subsequent chapters. The remainder of this chapter will provide the rationale and methodology employed in the *Leadership Map*, introduce its eight domains, and illustrate a number of strategies that leaders can employ to get the most out of this reflective, standards-based self-assessment. We will begin with safety.

Safety and Self-Assessment

Leadership Maps is first and foremost a self-assessment of leadership beliefs and practices. A safe and candid assessment is required for the results to be helpful to each participant. Many leaders, especially at the central office, are apt to view implementation of district initiatives at higher levels simply because they are proven improvements that have been budgeted and supported through professional development and district goals.

In a study of more than 1,000 teachers in North Thurston, Washington, both principals and central-office administrators were much more apt to view reforms such as systematic lesson planning or data teams (DTs) as being fully implemented than their faculty (Belmonte 2006). North Thurston administrators redoubled their efforts in 2007 and 2008 to firmly establish these key practices by focusing professional development and improvement planning primarily on these two long-standing district initiatives. In reality, the change process is often much more difficult than anticipated, and one person's goal can be another's obligation. For this reason, it is imperative that each leader be able to safely assess not only his or her own performance but the influence of his or her leadership in terms of classroom or school implementation.

The *Leadership Map* process is guided by a simple commitment: **No individual *Leadership Map* is shared with a leader's supervisor, period.** Even when the district purchases the *Leadership Map*, the district receives only the district summaries, such as that depicted in Exhibit 1.3. The summaries are sufficient for planning and differentiation, but the onus and responsibility to take advantage of related training, coaching, or support reside with the participant.

This commitment to honor the confidentiality of *Leadership Maps* does not preclude leaders from sharing results or asking for assistance or introducing findings into their work with colleagues or supervisors, and we hope that occurs—and that it occurs frequently. Because our purpose is primarily self-assessment, however, it is critical that leaders are able to access their *Leadership Map* frequently and use it to guide their own growth and development.

Dichotomies and Savvy Test Takers

Leadership Maps is a 100-factor assessment of leadership values, beliefs, and perceived levels of practice. Accessible online at LeadandLearn.com, *Leadership Maps* is designed to allow respondents to select the response most representative of their leadership along a continuum of ten radio button alternatives. Most factors are presented in terms of a dichotomy, with polar ends of that continuum. For example, for many implementation items, the choices range from less than 10 percent of teachers in one's school (staff for central-office departments) to more than 90 percent of teachers in one's school. In this way, respondents are encouraged to reflect on the reality at their campus and select their best estimate of current practice. At times, one end of the continuum represents the preferred response, and for other factors, the preferred response is at the midpoint of the continuum. Every effort has been made to make all responses plausible so that savvy test takers are unable to inflate their scores through guessing, and to emphasize the reflective nature of the self-assessment.

Stretch Items

All 100 factors are representative of best practices in the literature, and the assessment is updated at least annually to ensure that a number of "stretch" items are included—items that defy the conventional wisdom but that reflect emerging and best leadership practices. At the time of this writing, version 2.0 of *Leadership Maps* has been introduced, and subsequent versions are anticipated as educational leadership is articulated and refined more precisely in the literature and in the field.

Reliability and Validity

To draw inferences from *Leadership Maps* about current practice or to guide decisions that commit resources or pursue a course of action requires that the 100-factor self-assessment be both reliable and valid. Reliability is the degree to which an assessment is consistent and repeatable, and validity is the degree to which *Leadership Maps* measures what it purports to measure, in this case leadership. There are a number of excellent measures of leadership charac-teristics, values, and dispositions (Covey 1989; Lencioni 1998; Buckingham and Clifton 2001; Bradberry and Greaves 2003; Boyatzis and McKee 2005; Marzano, Waters, and McNulty 2005). The Hallmarks of Excellence® (2007) is a recent addition to quality leadership assessments that draws from a number of these instruments to integrate personal qualities, personal competencies, and emotional intelligence. All of these tools add to one's understanding of leadership through reflection and candor. *Leadership Maps,* however, examines leadership from two different, well-defined, and limited perspectives: (1) leadership actions, and (2) the degree to which those actions are implemented to improve schools and classroom practice. Appendix A describes technical aspects for development of *Leadership Maps,* but a brief review of reliability and validity is provided here.

Reliability

Two measures have been applied to determine the degree to which *Leadership Maps* is consistent and repeatable—the Pearson's *r* coefficient of correlation and the standard error of measurement. The first demonstrated the ability of the *Leadership Map* to yield consistent results across multiple administrations (repeatability), and the second helped establish confidence that the items and domains of the *Leadership Map* met accepted probability levels.

Reliability is essential as a characteristic of *Leadership Maps*, and as the number of administrations increase, *Leadership Maps* lends itself to continued review for test-retest, equivalent test forms, and split-half reliability.

Validity

Since its creation in March 2006, the *Leadership Map* has been completed by more than 900 administrators. While this is a relatively small sample, we have been able to document construct, content, and, to a lesser degree, criterion-related validity. We will now examine the degree to which *Leadership Maps* as a self-assessment meets the standard for validity. Validity is often defined by the question: Are we measuring what we think we are measuring? Three forms of evidence comprise the overall concept of validity: construct, content, and criterion-related validity (see Appendix A for technical aspects).

Construct validity. Earlier, the L^2 Matrix was cited as the conceptual framework that forms the basis of *Leadership Maps* and is premised on the assumption that understanding what works to produce gains in student achievement is critical to sustaining and extending such gains. The research clearly supports this notion (Hernandez 2006; Elmore 2000; Schmoker 2001; Sparks 2004). Richard Elmore found that faculties in the highest performing schools not only knew how to implement proven strategies and protocols—they also knew what strategies and protocols to apply to specific situations and why. Kenneth Hernandez found that the quality of school improvement research-based practices, monitoring, and implementation serve as predictors of improved achievement. Mike Schmoker discovered that deliberate selection (knowledge) and implementation (application) of discrete instructional strategies dramatically improves student achievement, and Dennis Sparks offers a compelling rationale for applying proven professional development strategies to improve student achievement. *Leadership Maps* is premised on the assumption that knowledge and application of acts of leadership result in improved student achievement. Is there evidence to support that hypothesis?

Marzano, Waters, and McNulty (2005) conducted an oft-cited meta-analysis of leadership practices that unequivocally demonstrates that twenty-one key leadership responsibilities are powerfully related to improved student achievement. Reeves (2004a) and Schmoker (2006) addressed the weak relationship between leadership behaviors and leadership evaluation. Research in the larger context of business, industry, and education also affirms the validity of leadership practices (Weick 1976; Covey 1989; Senge 2000; Collins 2001). Exhibit 1.4 identifies leadership actions applied to the research basis for content validity in *Leadership Maps* from my own work on data analysis.

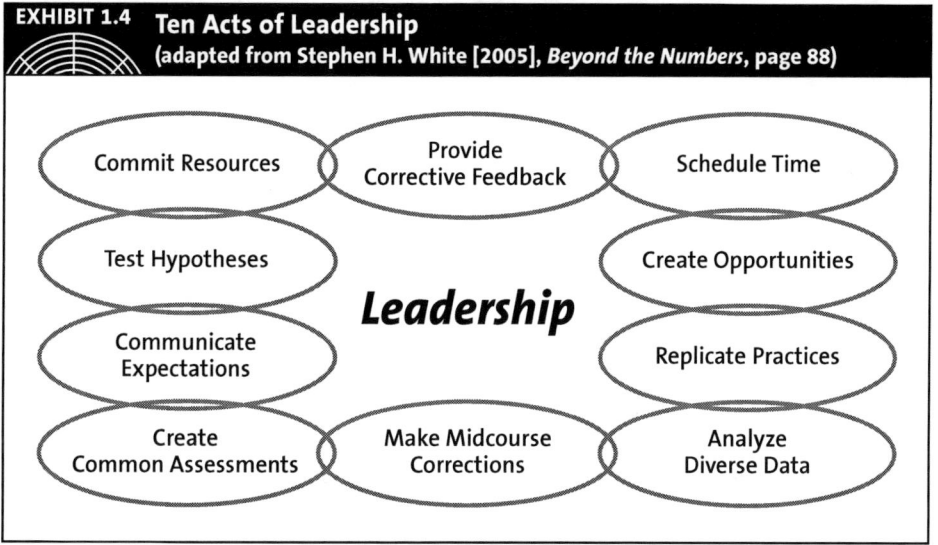

EXHIBIT 1.4   Ten Acts of Leadership
(adapted from Stephen H. White [2005], *Beyond the Numbers*, page 88)

- Commit Resources
- Provide Corrective Feedback
- Schedule Time
- Test Hypotheses
- Create Opportunities
- **Leadership**
- Communicate Expectations
- Replicate Practices
- Create Common Assessments
- Make Midcourse Corrections
- Analyze Diverse Data

Leadership Maps provides readers the opportunity to reflect on their own acts of leadership by responding to items across eight distinct leadership domains, with an emphasis on values representative of breakthrough, transformational leadership (Lencioni 2002; Boyatzis and McKee 2005; Rushkoff 2005; Fullan, Hill, and Crevola 2006; Reeves 2006). Those domains include:

- Data analysis
- Standards at work
- Accountability in action (AIA)
- Leading change
- Content expertise
- Powerful instructional strategies (HYS)
- Planning, implementation, and monitoring (PIM™)
- Leadership attributes

Many acts of leadership are, in fact, antecedents of excellence (see Exhibit 1.2), and *Leadership Maps* items were carefully selected across these domains based on the research of no fewer than fifty-six thought leaders and educational researchers. Correlations with achievement add to our understanding by demonstrating insightful connections, as depicted in Exhibit 1.5.

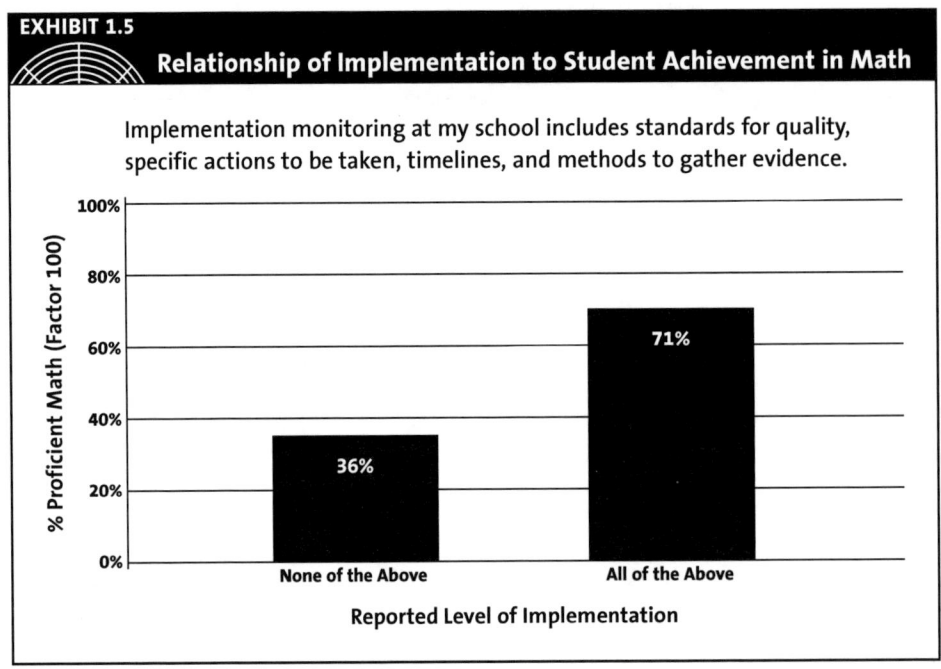

EXHIBIT 1.5

Relationship of Implementation to Student Achievement in Math

Implementation monitoring at my school includes standards for quality, specific actions to be taken, timelines, and methods to gather evidence.

% Proficient Math (Factor 100)

Reported Level of Implementation

Schools with explicit monitoring achieved at higher levels than schools where monitoring was assumed or implied. Other strong correlations included the use of essential questions and big ideas in science (standards at work); the use of metaphors and analogies across content areas (HYS); and alignment of curriculum, instruction, and assessments to standards (standards at work). A powerful correlation regarding teacher assignments is depicted in Exhibit 1.6.

Leaders who are courageous enough to engage faculty around student needs in order to make teacher assignments demonstrate the impact that discrete acts of leadership have on resulting student achievement. *Leadership Maps* builds upon a powerful theoretical concept, is supported by an exhaustive body of leadership research, and in its infancy, has a number of empirical, criterion-related findings that collectively meet high standards for validity.

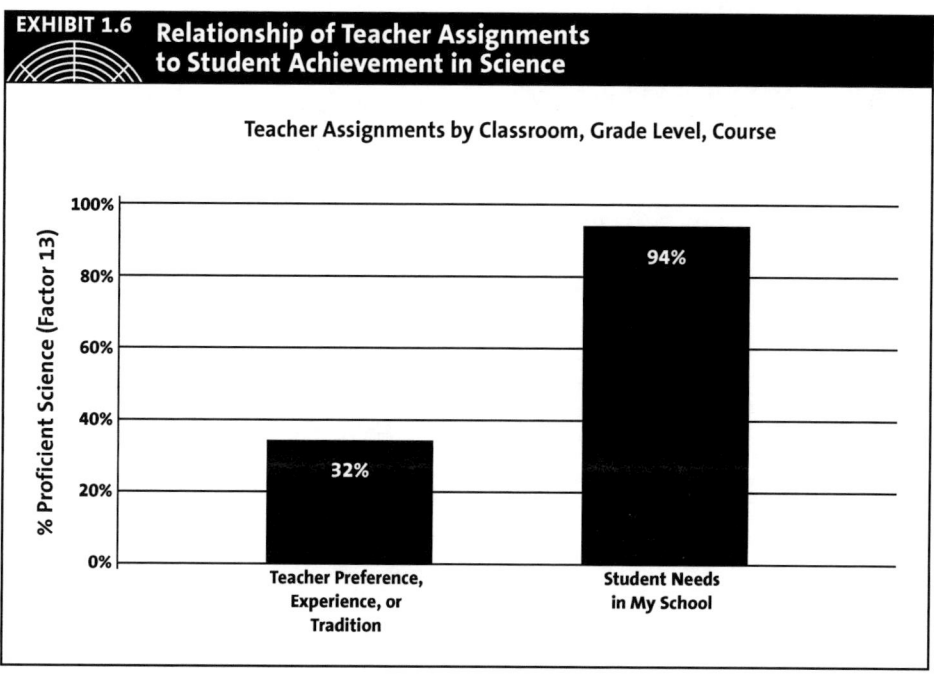

EXHIBIT 1.6 Relationship of Teacher Assignments to Student Achievement in Science

Teacher Assignments by Classroom, Grade Level, Course

% Proficient Science (Factor 13)

- Teacher Preference, Experience, or Tradition: 32%
- Student Needs in My School: 94%

Leadership Domains and Realities of Leading Schools

Each *Leadership Map* is divided into eight related domains of leadership: data analysis; standards at work; accountability in action; leading change; content expertise; high-yield strategies; planning, implementation, and monitoring; and attributes of leadership. These domains do not presume to capture all of the nuances and realities of leadership in today's schools. Instead, they focus on the area most neglected—implementation. *Leadership Maps* examines the language and practice of standards by assessing quality across eight key domains associated with standards and leadership. Chapters 2 through 9 are devoted to a deeper understanding of these domains and their central role for leadership in a post–No Child Left Behind (NCLB) era. They represent the domains of the work of leading that challenge each school leader. By providing a comprehensive array of measurable indicators of best practices, *Leadership Maps* offers the leaders of tomorrow an important tool to identify, monitor, and replicate practices that are predictive of continuous, sustained, improved student achievement.

Reflection

Essential Questions

How does the knowing–doing gap apply to school leaders today?

What are the actions that leaders need to take to close the gap between vision and implementation?

To what degree do school leaders need a road map in today's climate?

Big Ideas

Leadership is more about what gets done than about what we say we will do.

Leadership needs to be measured, monitored, and celebrated.

Leadership development requires a viable, empirical assessment of leadership in action for seasoned veterans and novices alike.

Consider addressing these conceptual ideas and questions collaboratively in reflective study groups or opportunities that present themselves whenever school leaders meet.

CHAPTER 2

Data Analysis

"I can't do what ten people tell me to;
so I guess I'll remain the same."

OTIS REDDING, 1969
Sitting on the Dock of the Bay

Data analysis is a central tenet of leadership, especially for schools post–No Child Left Behind (NCLB). Achievement data determines the school rankings that are broadcast to the general public, and the ability to create a sense of urgency as a leadership responsibility is well documented in the literature (Hall and Hord 1987; Collins 2001; Reeves 2004a; Marzano, Waters, and McNulty 2005; DuFour, Eaker, and DuFour *et al.* 2005; Fullan, Hill, and Crevola 2006; Schmoker 2006). Data provides leaders the ingredients for persuasion, and data mitigates the emotional attachment to the status quo when it reveals a sense of urgency. The most effective leaders serve data to those whom they supervise and those whom they represent, revealing insights that are not apparent without the story that data tells. Data analysis is much more about analysis than data, and this chapter provides examples of how leaders might leverage data to increase a sense of efficacy for staff, faculty, and students, and create a "culture of evidence" in the process. Readers will be challenged to assess their current level of data analysis and to recognize the need to use data to focus and prioritize initiatives, as well as communicate expectations.

Assessments and Response

In *Beyond the Numbers* (2005), I described how responding to the data before us is as much a matter of ethics as it is an opportunity to improve student achievement. Aggregating and even disaggregating data is meaningless unless a response follows that applies lessons learned from the data. Consider Bill's situation:

> Bill is principal of Data High School, and the district benchmark assessment results were just returned for the second trimester. Next month, Bill's ninth-, tenth-, and

eleventh-graders will take the state assessments in math, reading, and science, and the benchmark results are not particularly encouraging. Ninth- and eleventh-graders actually lost ground in terms of percent proficient, while tenth-graders improved from 43 percent proficient to 59 percent. When he reviewed results with his department heads and leadership team, comments like, "We didn't cover that content this term; we get to quadrilateral equations next month," conveyed less than the sense of urgency he had hoped for. Even Carol, his assistant for curriculum, commented, "Of course, our results slipped. We don't emphasize drawing conclusions from text until the final quarter in ninth grade, and eleventh-graders focus on literature in English." While the team was comforted by Carol's comments as a former English teacher, Bill was uncomfortable with the tendency to explain away the data rather than learn from it. He quietly determined that next week's meeting would somehow create a breakthrough that he could build on—and quickly.

"Thanks for coming, everyone. Please take some time before next week's meeting to reflect on these results and bring one recommendation we could implement right away that would improve the likelihood of better results, even if it is outside of your department. We'll be scratching our heads to identify possible changes we need to make schoolwide, so Thursday next will be an important meeting. Expect a ninety-minute meeting."

There were a few glances across the room to assess the reaction of peers to this charge, and even Bill knew that he was stepping out of character. Still, it felt good, because he knew that Data High School needed to take some time to learn from this data. Bill had no idea how he would shape and facilitate the next leadership team meeting. He just knew that he had to do something different.

At the very least, Bill exercised courageous leadership in leaving his comfort zone. He also focused on what needed to happen to move staff from dispassionate observers of data to engaged, responsible, accountable school leaders. They had to see what he saw, embrace a vision of a better future, and identify steps to achieve that better future. Leadership also means hosting the conversation, and while Bill communicated clearly his intent to use data to change current practice at Data High School, his frustration was as much a result of his failure to be proactive as of his leadership team's tendency to manufacture excuses.

A common trap that many educators fall into is relying solely on student achievement data to guide decisions—a phenomenon I refer to as the "rearview mirror" effect (White 2005). Achievement data alone is woefully inadequate for school leaders, because the information describes the results of our efforts and never the causes. Bill could have modeled powerful data analysis with his staff by introducing patterns or trends associated with teaching practices, behavior referrals, curriculum alignment, or practices in the classroom that impact achievement. Undoubtedly, at Bill's next meeting, his leadership team will contribute a number of insights, supported by their own deeper investigation, but without a deliberate, proactive effort to make meaning of student achievement results, his impact will be minimal. Post–NCLB, leaders need to have dramatic rather than minimal impact on teaching practices and on student achievement.

Seven principles of data analysis are provided to prevent dilemmas like the one facing Bill. They will help the most data-phobic leader to improve decision-making, instructional focus, and resource allocation to yield second-order changes of sufficient magnitude to change school practices and transform school cultures. Data-driven decision making is much more about leadership than it is about numbers.

Analysis Over Data

The first principle of data analysis is simply a set of parameters to assist leaders as they pursue that transformation. These parameters can be summed up in five leadership actions that I have described as the five Rs (White 2005):

- Recognize the negative impact of relying on single, high-stakes, annual assessments of learning as the primary source of data (the rearview mirror effect).

- Realize that data opportunities require thoughtful analysis, infusion of our own experience and insights, and decisions that change how we practice the craft of teaching.

- Reflect on available data with other professionals, engaging the power of collaboration to examine student work, implement and monitor insightful changes, and improve student achievement.

- Respond to urgent challenges.

• Replicate practices that work to share the wealth of knowledge and expertise that exists in every school in America.

Our profession is much more complex than the general public or practitioners typically recognize (Darling-Hammond 1997), and this is especially true regarding the methods used to gather, disseminate, and report data. When teachers are provided summative assessment data in late May, is it any wonder that schools devote very little time to analysis of results? Even when teams of teachers and principals attempt to make sense of state assessments, the distinctions between content area subtests or between variations in performance of student subgroups are difficult to translate sufficiently to inform changes in classroom or school practice. W. James Popham (2003) notes "What teachers and administrators need to know about testing, at least for purposes of educational accountability, relies on common sense more than statistical exotica" (page 83).

Leadership will only alter that reality by providing time and training in the process of data analysis. Isn't it about time educators are as deliberate in developing this skill as they are in developing lesson plans?

Quality Over Quantity in Data Analysis

The second principle is like apple pie: Everyone likes the idea of quality over quantity. *The Knowing-Doing Gap* (Pfeffer and Sutton 2000) documented just how extensive the gap was between professional knowledge of what is best practice and the change in current practice to achieve best practice. One need only examine school improvement plans or district strategic planning documents to realize that the difference between knowing and doing is nowhere more pronounced than in the number of initiatives launched in schools every year. Three forces work against getting to quality.

Initiative Glut and Fatigue

There are many well-intentioned reasons for attempting to do more. As a principal described to me several years ago, "If I can save one student by adopting the newest best practice, it will be worth it." We don't want to miss out. When a good idea comes along that has our faculty buzzing about its potential, it is very tempting for leaders to make it available to their faculties. As a professional, I am amazed at the volume of work that educators everywhere heap on themselves to make sure that they are doing all they can to help each and every child. Unfortunately, underestimating the time, resources, and emotional impact that change initiatives have on educators rarely accomplishes that end. It is not unusual for school improvement plans across the continent to layer change initiatives on top of prior changes that are only in the early awareness stages of change. Evans (2001) describes this reality as one where educators routinely "over-promise and under-deliver," contrasting attempts to simultaneously initiate numerous large-scale changes with the physician who is careful not to promise a successful surgery even when advancements in technology and innovative practices make success for the most complex procedure almost routine. Quality will always be subservient to quantity as long as educators attempt to do too much with limited time, limited resources, and unrealistic timelines and expectations.

EXHIBIT 2.1

Routine Subtraction Protocol

Subtracting Obsolete or Ineffective Practices

1. Does the practice yield data about teaching or learning?	Yes	No
2. Does the practice address specific content standards?	Yes	No
3. Does the practice/resource provide diagnostic data about student achievement?	Yes	No
4. Does the practice invite collaboration with colleagues?	Yes	No
5. Is there data supporting the need for or value of the practice or resource to improve student achievement in my classroom?	Yes	No

Yes to three or fewer questions, the practice or resource should be subtracted in some measure. Yes to four or more questions, the practice or resource should be retained or possibly replicated.

6. Can the same practice/resource be accomplished through other means, such as improved technology?	Yes	No
7. Can the practice be omitted and achieve the same result?	Yes	No
8. Can the same result be accomplished in less time?	Yes	No
9. Can the same result be accomplished with less preparation time?	Yes	No
10. Can the same result be accomplished with less expense in time, talent, and resources?	Yes	No

Yes to three or fewer questions, the practice or resource should be replaced at some time. Yes to four or more questions, the practice or resource should be replaced as soon as possible.

Leadership in data analysis requires a thorough needs assessment to determine whether our ambitions are matched by time and resources to implement well. As an auditor of more than 2,000 school improvement plans since 2005, I distinctly remember reviewing the high school improvement plan for Southwest Allen High School in Fort Wayne, Indiana. The plan had a single schoolwide strategy that students in every classroom would write in every class every day. The plan was a simple recognition of the data before them and a savvy understanding about the change process. Exhibit 2.1 describes a system for routinely subtracting practices.

The Independent Contractor

To the degree that educators invite individual teachers to pursue innovations with almost complete autonomy, to that same degree it is virtually impossible to determine which practices work. For principals, the conventional wisdom of allowing individual discretion over adoption of programs and instructional strategies has the negative impact of diluting focus and resources, as well as the empirical conundrum of having little capacity to determine what is working well and why. This does not mean that administrators should limit teacher leadership. On the contrary, taking the time necessary to engage in rich, passionate dialogue and debate about schoolwide practices not only encourages a schoolwide focus, but requires candid collaboration that builds capacity and teacher leadership through informed, reflective, evidence-based, professional dialogue. This requires a sea change in our thinking.

Assumptions and Presumptions

The third force working for quantity and against quality is a culture of loosely coupled systems. Weick (1976) described schools as loosely coupled structures where a presumption of competence exists like few other professions. Weick observed that administrators viewed their role as primarily one of support for teacher autonomy and innovation rather than as a leader of that innovation for the school. Administrators were reluctant to inquire into the arena of teaching and learning, occupying their time with the smooth operation of the school. The accountability era has had a significant change in recoupling leading and learning, as evidenced by instructional leadership as an expectation for principals, the rise of data teams and professional learning communities, and classroom walk-throughs. However, the presumption remains that selection of curriculum content and delivery of instruction are the prerogative of individual teachers, and that the details of both instruction and curriculum are the primary responsibility for individual teachers. Ask any first-year teacher who is responsible for lesson design, delivery, and selection of content, as most are keenly aware of that obligation. The relationship is loosely coupled with limited involvement in classroom practice by administrators and limited involvement in the management of schools by teachers.

Ted Sizer took Weick's notion a step further in *Horace's Compromise* (1992). He describes a type of truce between educators, where administrators refrain from inspecting or providing substantive feedback to teachers in exchange for limited conflict and confrontation on issues of management. Teachers, in turn, negotiate a compromise with students, where students agree, implicitly, to allow teachers to deliver instruction without confrontation if the students are compliant and courteous. Sizer viewed this reality in the 1980s and 1990s as an albatross that inhibits reform. Richard Elmore (2004) built on both Weick's notion and Sizer's research by describing the current reality in terms of a general "circling of the wagons" mentality, brought on at least in part by a growing dissatisfaction with government institutions by a skeptical public. In Elmore's loosely coupled scenario, administrators not only have negotiated a mutually beneficial compromise with teachers, but they presume the highest level of competence and proficiency for their teachers and defend it as a matter of course. This is equally true for school boards and for activist parents and realtors at the local school who proudly proclaim their schools, principals, and teachers as the "best" without any knowledge of how they apply the art and science of the profession.

Elmore, like Weick and Sizer before him, viewed this unspoken, loosely coupled culture as a serious drain on reform efforts that failed to adhere to Jim Collins' (2001) admonition to "confront the brutal facts." This reality is most evident in the narratives of both teacher and administrator evaluation reports. Any administrator engaged in a dismissal hearing will tell you that the bane of that process is historical accolades and glowing commendations for a very small proportion of teachers who would benefit from a career change. In the standards era, it is increasingly common for teacher associations to be proactive in counseling marginal teachers out themselves, and in today's high-stakes environment, courageous educators are trying to tighten up the couplings and make staff responsible for improvements in teaching and learning. Quality will always be subservient to quantity until there is deliberate alignment of effort around teaching, learning, and leading. This requires data analysis that is transparent and thorough in the examination of student achievement, teaching practice, and acts of leadership.

Data on Purpose

It is hard to imagine that as recently as 1997, less than 10 million people accessed the Internet, and that most mobile phones were large, cumbersome units requiring a permanent power-access plug such as an automobile cigarette lighter. There were virtually no DVDs and absolutely no MP-3s or I-phones. Today, it is rare to find a school system without a data warehouse that is accessible by teachers at their desktops. It is common to find classroom teachers with SMART boards and Palm Pilots capable of gathering significant, real-time data about teaching and learning. If anything, there is a glut of information—an avalanche of data. Leadership in data analysis requires that the selection of data from that glut of information be purposeful, focused, and on point. It means that data is gathered on important factors that help us discover antecedents of excellence in real time that can be used to predict improved achievement and improved professional practice. Unfortunately, these powerful tools of technology rarely examine teacher practice or leadership actions, or gather data about the context of learning. By and large, data warehouse systems gather mountains of data about students, achievement results, demographics, and behavior history. Data about teaching practices is strangely absent from data management software. This reality only affirms the loosely coupled culture observed for a generation by Weick, Sizer, and Elmore. *Leadership Maps* anticipates a different reality—one where schools gather information *on purpose*.

Data on purpose refers to accepted protocols that represent practices agreed upon by teachers and administrators as powerful predictors of improved performance (antecedents). One school may determine that the sheltered instruction observation protocol (SIOP) would be implemented schoolwide, both for students who are taking English as a second language and for students who are at risk. Another may determine that classroom teachers would adhere to the Four-Block Reading Model, or to the Five Dimensions of Reading Program, or to the Six Plus Traits of Writing Program, or to the Five Easy Steps to a Balanced Math Program. Each of these six well-known frameworks has a strong research basis and a prescribed protocol for delivering instruction, and each one offers schools meaningful data about the degree of implementation and effective teaching. A dozen other approaches could be delineated, but the point is that educators need to exercise their best judgment about which data will provide them with the most powerful insights into the learning process. Schools will differ as to which intervention or instructional strategy to measure, but all should agree that in this era of increasingly sophisticated technology, data needs to be purposeful and schools must augment achievement data about learning with data about teaching. Even better, consider gathering data about the impact of leadership decisions regarding resources, time, and capacity building.

How leaders design budgets, how they designate opportunities for growth or collaboration, and how they provide feedback have a great impact on student achievement. Data on purpose requires that such leadership actions be monitored and that the data be included in any thorough analysis of learning and teaching. In *Ahead of the Curve* (Reeves 2007), I describe the importance of triangulating data of learning, teaching, and leading to determine with greater precision which classroom or school practices work and which practices do not.

Data on purpose is reflected in a number of *Leadership Map* items, but to be purposeful and meaningful, it must also be data on point. Quality in data analysis means identifying indicators of teacher-friendly results that communicate to us two basic realities that should be evident when powerful, research-based approaches are undertaken: (1) progress toward our stated goal in terms of student achievement, and (2) progress in building capacity that improves instruction. Both of these concepts are simple and straightforward, and data on point is best represented by high-quality results indicators, a key step in The Leadership and Learning Center's data team process (step 5). Results indicators become laser-like data on point when they probe for progress and capacity building. Consider these examples:

- **Progress toward stated SMART goals**. If the target goal is math proficiency demonstrated by a multiple-step response writing prompt, a results indicator might be solving an algebraic problem of the week, with a written summary that describes the step-by-step process utilized. Results indicators can be routine assessments that take very little additional time to administer but offer data on point because they reveal progress linked to our desired outcome.

- **Degree of implementation**. This results indicator examines the actions of adults in terms of consistency, accuracy, and adherence to protocols. If the SMART goal is math-related, a quality results indicator might be the frequency with which the entire data team administers Five Easy Steps weekly. This provides the team with information to determine the impact of the selected strategy, and it does so in time to make instructional adjustments.

Data on point means that we select key progress or results indicators to inform us about our efforts and student progress toward a desired outcome. *Leadership Maps* anticipates strategic, careful selection of data points from the universe of numbers and measures available through technology. Leaders add value to the data whenever they apply their best professional judgment to make decisions.

Formative Over Summative Assessments

Common formative assessments (Ainsworth and Viegut 2006) enrich the quality and range of assessments by informing instructional decisions for teams of teachers. The more frequent the assessments, the greater the likelihood of improved student achievement (Bangert-Drowns, Kulik, and Kulik 1991). Common formative assessments are closely related to a number of accepted reform initiatives, including differentiated instruction, curriculum mapping, and even the process of leading school change and impacting culture (Fisher and Frey 2007).

Common formative assessments are assessments for learning that are used to: (1) diagnose student learning difficulties, (2) set individual teacher goals and team goals for student improvement, (3) identify and share effective teaching strategies, and (4) plan ways to differentiate instruction so that all students can succeed on subsequent summative assessments (Ainsworth and Viegut 2006, page 24). These four purposes distinguish common formative assessments from the notion of assessments as accountability tools that verify the degree to which learning has occurred. Both forms of assessments are essential, but unlike the summative state assessments, which will occur by statute, common formative assessments will occur only when leaders provide the resources, expertise, and structures to make them part of the school culture. *Leadership Maps* anticipates leadership that is disciplined to establish common formative assessments that routinely adhere to four basic principles for powerful assessments of student achievement:

1. Embed assessments into the instructional process in such a way that they do not interrupt instruction.

2. Drive instructional decisions.

3. Inspire confidence in those who use them by being accurate, valid, and reliable.

4. Assist students in learning to achieve proficiency targets.

Tools Over Serendipity

Many criticize NCLB because its short history has not significantly altered the landscape in terms of student achievement. On a national level, poor students of color continue to achieve at much lower levels than their affluent White or Asian counterparts, despite a growing number of schools that are succeeding across subgroups, even for students from families in poverty (School Matters 2008). However, most educators will agree that there has been a quantum leap in the amount of time and energy devoted to collaboration among teachers and among school leaders. These collaboration sessions have had an enormous influence on school practice and have been instrumental in building capacity one school, one grade, and one department at a time. Whether schools label teams professional learning communities, data teams, whole-faculty study groups, or something altogether different, collaborative teams that examine data to improve student achievement have become the rule that was a definite exception just a few short years ago. In Concord, Indiana, Assistant Superintendent Wayne Stubbs and a

EXHIBIT 2.2

Data Analysis Tools for Leaders

Data Tool	Purpose of Tool	Capacity for Action Resulting from Tool
Forest and Trees "Fishbone"	Identify current cause-and-effect relationships	• Identify causes for success within current resources • Design foundation for action research projects • Promote replication of internal best practices • Identify factors within educator control or influence
Triangulation	Examine patterns and trends across context of teaching and learning	• Anticipate otherwise unseen obstacles and opportunities • Perform due diligence around data • Increase confidence in team decision • Perform comprehensive rather than one-dimensional data analysis • Systematically examine learning, teaching, and leading
"Wagon Wheel"	Determine interaction of multiple antecedents	• Conduct multivariate analyses across an unlimited range of antecedents important to educators • Establish priorities • Determine fidelity of implementation
Critical Incident	Identify needs for data gathering	• Provide informed starting point for data gathering and monitoring based on judgment of educators in the field • Triage educational challenges • Illuminate hidden problems
Clarification Analysis	Keep important change initiatives on track	• Respond quickly to difficulties associated with implementing a wide range of change initiatives • Provide clarity when new initiatives meet cultural operating procedures and habits
Assessment Calendar	Create a pacing guide for key assessments	• Distribute limited time for reflection and analysis • Identify assessment redundancy and assessment gaps

very enlightened teachers association set a new standard by institutionalizing data teams in their negotiated agreement. Many systems assume that merely creating the opportunity for collaboration will result in quality, informed, effective data analysis. It will not happen by accident or serendipity. Teams need data tools to dig deeper, to systematically "unpack" or "unwrap" data just as carefully as curriculum teams unwrap standards and identify power standards to leverage and reduce achievement gaps. Exhibit 2.2 illustrates the data analysis tools for leaders.

Leadership Maps invites leaders to examine the degree to which the tools in Exhibit 2.2 and others are operational. It invites leaders to examine the effectiveness of data analysis and guides leaders to establish protocols for continuous improvement. Your *Leadership Map* provides a number of methods to distribute leadership and pursue that elusive elixir for schools—"buy-in."

Due Diligence

Examine some authentic state assessment results for fourth grade in Exhibit 2.3. What should the team do with the achievement results?

Such results reflect state and provincial reports across the English-speaking world, but the distinctions between literacy standards provide little direction regarding what to do next. Educators understand the difference between significant and meaningful and seek the latter. If this were a large urban district with 30,000 fourth-graders, even a 1 percent distinction between writing applications

EXHIBIT 2.3

Hypothetical School Literacy Results on State Assessment

Year	Standard	Points Possible	Test Type	Passing Score	Mean	Percent Mastery
2006-07	Reading Vocabulary	9	MC*	74	71.6	52
2006-07	Reading Composition	14	MC, OE	62	64.6	57
2006-07	Literary Response, Analysis	18	MC, OE	59	61.5	60
2006-07	Writing Process	10	MC	69	70.8	58
2006-07	Writing Applications	12	MC, OE	54	56.4	59
2006-07	Language Conventions	13	MC, OE	72	73.1	58

*MC = multiple choice; OE = open-ended

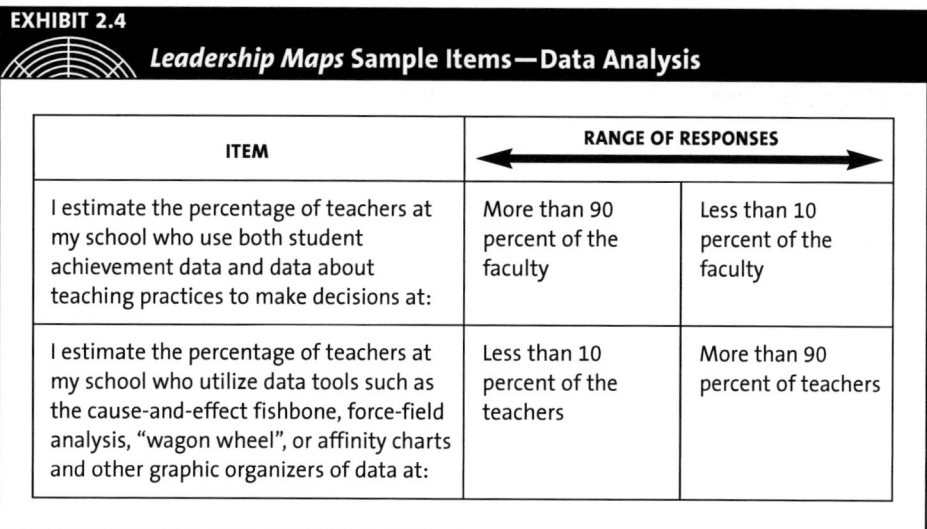

EXHIBIT 2.4

Leadership Maps Sample Items—Data Analysis

ITEM	RANGE OF RESPONSES	
I estimate the percentage of teachers at my school who use both student achievement data and data about teaching practices to make decisions at:	More than 90 percent of the faculty	Less than 10 percent of the faculty
I estimate the percentage of teachers at my school who utilize data tools such as the cause-and-effect fishbone, force-field analysis, "wagon wheel", or affinity charts and other graphic organizers of data at:	Less than 10 percent of the teachers	More than 90 percent of teachers

and language conventions is statistically significant. Does Exhibit 2.3 mean that schools should now devote more time to vocabulary than to literary response and analysis or other sub skills? My guess is that each reader has attended more than one collaborative meeting where the data failed to provide clear direction. That doesn't mean we should throw our hands up and revert to what we've always done. It *does* mean that we need to stop assuming that collaborative opportunities lead to quality decisions. Today's schools need viable tools that help us dig deeper in systematic ways. Exhibit 2.4 presents sample *Leadership Maps* items for data analysis to challenge leaders to new levels.

Due diligence in data analysis occurs when leaders examine student achievement data *and* inquire about the relationship between key professional practices and improvements in achievement. Due diligence examines: (1) the degree of fidelity in the implementation of instructional strategies, (2) the degree to which effective collaboration is prevalent, and (3) effective accountability structures, such as corrective feedback, transparency in communication, and follow-through. Due diligence is deliberate about gathering data across these key aspects of professional practice to inform our understanding about student achievement.

Insights Over Information

Basic data analyses gather and categorize information. Advanced data analyses provide insights to make difficult decisions. Most schools do an admirable job of disaggregating assessment results for patterns and trends in student achievement. What is needed is leadership that applies data tools to reveal insights about the causes of those results and the relationship between our actions as professionals and improved performance. Leaders investigate such correlations in order to challenge faculty to glean insights and form hypotheses for the next steps. *Leadership Maps* invites leaders to reflect on the degree to which their schools, their departments, and their districts utilize data analysis tools such as the six tools described in Exhibit 2.2.

Summary

Adherence to the seven leadership principles communicates a systematic approach to data that is responsive and practical. *Leadership Maps* inquires about the degree to which these principles have been applied, providing leaders a snapshot of how well their skills in leveraging data have impacted teaching practices, and, in turn, influenced and improved student achievement. Leaders who create transparent, collaborative structures for teacher-to-teacher dialogue are much more apt to see classroom practices respond to the needs of individual learners (DuFour, Eaker, and DuFour *et al.* 2005; Murphy and Lick 2001; Surowiecki 2004). Ample evidence suggests that leaders who introduce the five Rs of data analysis into their culture will be on solid ground for changing school practice and improving student achievement (Schmoker 2006; Fullan, Hill, and Crevola 2006; Rogers 1995).

Leadership Maps as a self-assessment of leadership skills in data analysis will reveal to leaders the degree to which they lead through loosely coupled assumptions or through verified evidence of deep and effective implementation. The need for improved student achievement is reason enough to lead with data analysis, and leaders who embrace these principles will be well positioned to build capacity to create and sustain a culture of evidence.

Reflection

Essential Questions

Why is analysis more important than methods to collect and aggregate data in today's schools?

What is involved to ensure that data is on point and on purpose?

Describe one situation within the past year where the utilization of data tools would have provided clarity and improved the quality of the decisions made.

Big Ideas

Basic data analyses gather and categorize information.
Advanced data analyses provide insights to make difficult decisions.

Data about achievement is instructive, but triangulating learning data with data about teaching and leading yields discoveries about learning.

Leaders add value each time they apply their best professional judgment to inform and direct decisions based on data.

CHAPTER 3
Standards at Work

"Priority is a function of context."
STEPHEN COVEY, 1994

Standards at work is all about responding to the right work in the right way at the right times. *Leadership Maps* is designed to capture the essential components of a standards-based educational framework in a reflective self-assessment. The standards movement was in part a response to the catalyst 1983 study "Nation at Risk," commissioned by the National Commission on Excellence in Education. It framed the need for educational reform in terms of economic competitiveness at a time when employment was stagnant and the United States was losing market share in major industrial markets to both Europe and Asia. The question raised most frequently was, "What do students need to learn and be able to do to be successful and competitive in the twenty-first century?" Because children born in 1983 were likely to graduate in the new millennium, the timing of "Nation at Risk" was perfect to engage a debate about schools and shift that debate from what we do to what students learn. The timing also coincided with the Effective Schools Movement, which defined effectiveness across seven correlates in the research. Rigorous standards for students were proposed and adopted across content areas by professional associations and states, and most of these rigorous outcomes have guided the development of state-level assessments that form the basis for accountability systems in the United States.

Standards describe expectations for learning that include not only *acquisition of knowledge* but also *application of that knowledge.* Standards have radically altered testing and assessment, launched the focus on accountability and results, and dramatically changed the development of curriculum and materials.

Standards represent a foundation for teaching and learning in virtually every state, province, or English-speaking locale on the planet, but translating standards into classroom practice is anything but easy. The proliferation of standards in the 1980s and 1990s resulted in a new set of problems. Marzano and Kendall (1996) identified four challenges in designing standards-based educational systems: multiple documents, varying definitions, varying levels of generality, and varying levels of subordination. Subordination, or subdividing of standards, is illustrated by national standards in a major content area where topics are divided into standards, standards into understandings, understandings into components by grade levels, and components into examples of achievement. Consider the impact of such subordination across no fewer than twelve major subject content areas, from kindergarten to grade 12, and across states and localities (Marzano and Kendall 1996, pages 19–25). The volume alone illustrates the conundrum of the move to standards. The same conundrum exists in terms of generality, definitions, and literally hundreds of source documents. What document describes the "official" set of standards? Are standards content standards or curriculum standards? These issues continue to challenge educators in the twenty-first century, although the question regarding which document serves as the "official" document has largely been resolved by individual states and provinces. State and provincial assessments are almost always based on their own established standards.

Challenges to effective implementation of a standards-based educational system require an informed leadership response to make standards work. Standards require leadership to prioritize resources, time, and actions on the basis of those standards, and always within the context of local expectations, cultures, and obligations. *Leadership Maps* is designed to provide a quality self-assessment of that leadership in action. The seven characteristics of a standards-based education assessed through each leadership map include:

- High expectations and fixed standards
- Focus on the essential: powering and unwrapping standards
- Scoring guide rubrics
- Authentic performance assessments
- Big ideas and essential questions
- Multiple opportunities for success
- Varied time and opportunity

Standards and *Leadership Maps* are inextricably linked by the fact that each Leadership Map probes not only for the leader's knowledge but also for the application of that knowledge where it counts— in the schools and classrooms where teaching and learning take place. This chapter will identify in more detail the above seven characteristics of standards and offer examples of *Leadership Maps* items that capture that knowledge, disposition, or skill.

High Expectations and Fixed Standards

Consult virtually any mission statement since the turn of the century, and districts and schools will almost certainly proclaim their commitment to all students. As Larry Lezotte often remarks, "Fix the standards; vary time and opportunity." Dr. Lezotte's research revealed that many subgroups of students who traditionally underachieve when compared to their peers also receive less exposure to challenging curriculum, experience less time devoted to instruction in core areas, and have less access to the most highly trained teachers (Lezotte and McKee 2002). Readers need only examine the course schedules at their local high school. How large are the advanced placement and honors classes compared to ninth-grade English or Algebra I? Do teachers of the advanced classes also teach classes of students in need of remediation or skill building? Many districts like that of Minnetonka, Minnesota, insist that International Baccalaureate (IB) teachers also teach beginning English and Algebra I. Districts are beginning to recognize that struggling students need to be exposed to teachers who have the expertise to teach the most rigorous classes. Leadership makes the difference in terms of high expectations. Where do you fall on the continuum in Exhibit 3.1 for these two distinct items in order to make standards work?

Focus on the Essential: Powering and Unwrapping Standards

A major aspect of a standards-based education is the how, what, and why of curriculum selection. Given the challenge of an almost unlimited avalanche of content during an era where information doubles every sixty minutes (Mangan 2000), the need to prioritize and focus is evident. In fact, EMC^2 estimates that Internet information expands at a rate of 100 trillion bytes every ten seconds! (retrieved December 3, 2007 from http://www.emc.com/about/destination/digital_universe).

Focusing on the essential is a key act of leadership. It is more efficient, more effective, and more necessary than ever. One outgrowth of the standards movement is a recognition of the problem of volume and a very smart process to address that at the classroom level. Teachers who learn to "power" their standards (Ainsworth 2003) focus their work on standards that provide enduring understanding (Wiggins and McTighe 1998), a foundation for the next environment, and opportunity to leverage or integrate that standard in other content areas. Exhibit 3.2 provides example *Leadership Maps* items.

EXHIBIT 3.1 *Leadership Maps* **Sample Items—Expectations and Fixed Standards**

ITEM	RANGE OF RESPONSES	
In my school or school system, procedures are in place to ensure that all teachers teach all students, with the exception of licensure requirements for IEP and LEP/ESL students.	True of my leadership now in more than 90 percent of teaching assignments	True of my leadership now in less than 10 percent of teaching assignments
In regard to aligning curriculum, assessment, instruction, and professional development to standards:	I have yet to align each of these to standards	I align each of these to standards

The first item in Exhibit 3.2 refers to the degree to which power standards have been applied and extended to the classroom, while the second item refers to the leader's own personal acquisition of important knowledge and readiness to teach others. Both aspects of standards are critical to leadership, knowledge, and application.

Unwrapping Power Standards

The notion of prioritizing standards to manage curriculum and deliver instruction is so central to leadership that leaders need to know how to analyze

EXHIBIT 3.2 *Leadership Maps* **Sample Items—Power Standards**

ITEM	RANGE OF RESPONSES	
The proportion of my faculty who choose to emphasize essential power standards in core subjects rather than cover every subject or every topic is estimated at:	More than 90 percent of the faculty	Less than 10 percent of the faculty
In regard to teaching the criteria for developing power standards for any curriculum area to my faculty and staff (leverage, endurance, foundation), I:	Am currently unable to teach the criteria	Am comfortable teaching the criteria

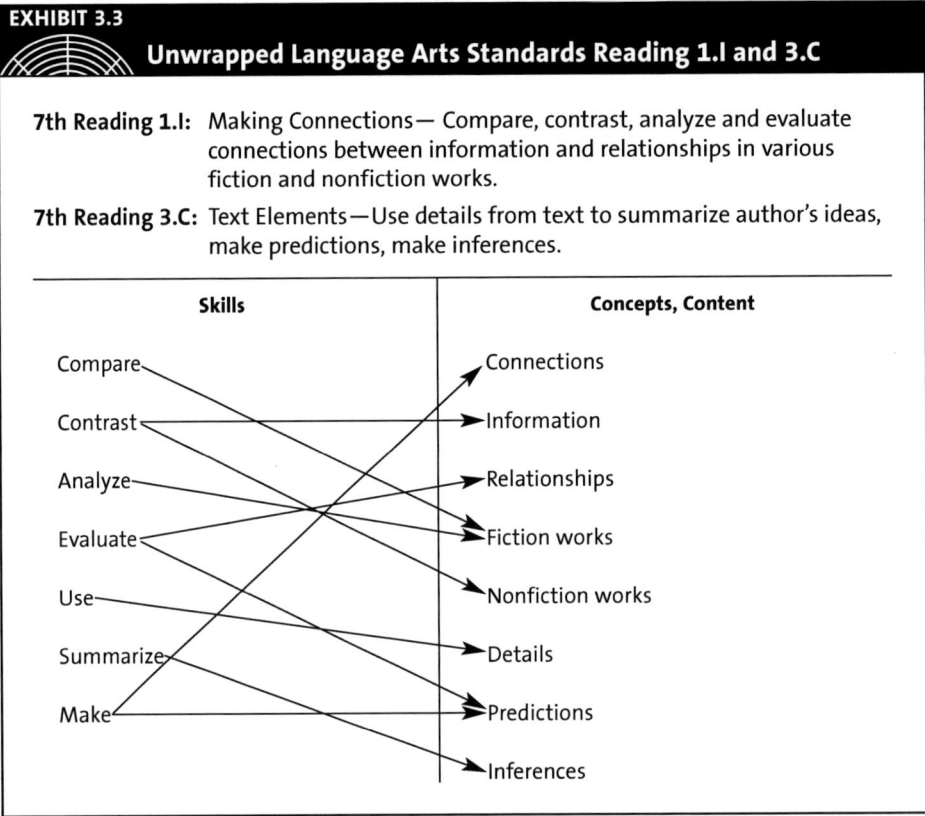

EXHIBIT 3.3

Unwrapped Language Arts Standards Reading 1.I and 3.C

7th Reading 1.I: Making Connections— Compare, contrast, analyze and evaluate connections between information and relationships in various fiction and nonfiction works.

7th Reading 3.C: Text Elements—Use details from text to summarize author's ideas, make predictions, make inferences.

Skills	Concepts, Content
Compare	Connections
Contrast	Information
Analyze	Relationships
Evaluate	Fiction works
Use	Nonfiction works
Summarize	Details
Make	Predictions
	Inferences

those standards to deliver instruction wisely. Unwrapping (Ainsworth 2003a), or "unpacking" standards (Wiggins and McTighe 1998), refers to the process of identifying the knowledge to be learned (concepts and content) and the skills needed to apply that knowledge (skills) for each standard. Larry Ainsworth developed a powerful and very user-friendly process to conduct that analysis. By identifying the nouns and noun phrases to represent content or concepts of the standard, and by identifying the verbs that represent the actions or skills required to achieve proficiency, teacher teams can quickly identify a myriad of possibilities for units and lessons to implement the curriculum powerfully. Exhibit 3.3 offers one such seventh-grade standard, unwrapped with common formative assessment possibilities, for illustration. Arrows indicate possible assessments or lesson plan options for the standard.

Consider the positive impact on student achievement if entire school faculties analyzed standards as carefully and designed instruction with so many powerful possibilities. Exhibit 3.4 provides sample *Leadership Maps* items related to this powerful example of instructional leadership.

EXHIBIT 3.4

Leadership Maps **Sample Items—Unwrapping Standards**

ITEM	RANGE OF RESPONSES	
Unwrapping of standards to design and implement more focused, standards-based lessons is something I teach my faculty by identifying the concepts, skills, and context needed to master specific standards:	Not yet	Routinely
Unwrapping of policies and procedures to design and implement focused improvements is something I teach my team by aligning practices with policy and goal targets:	Not yet	Routinely

The first item in Exhibit 3.4 examines the readiness and knowledge of the leader in terms of unwrapping power standards, while the second extends the practice to the analysis of policies and procedures and their alignment.

Scoring Guide Rubrics

Scoring guides provide evidence of a standards-based framework. Each time a scoring guide continuum is utilized, instructors, parents, teachers, and the general public are informed as to what is expected in terms of knowledge and how that knowledge will be applied. Rubrics are standards-based in other ways as well, including the transparent and public display of expectations—something that increases focus on the knowledge and skills required to demonstrate proficiency. The continuum of skill and knowledge described in each scoring guide provides clarity, with no surprises as to what success looks like. Rubrics are not uncommon in schools today, but it is less common that school leaders model the use of rubrics in their work as leaders. *Leadership Maps* includes items that assess how well leaders leverage this powerful, standards-based tool. Exhibit 3.5 provides two examples.

Scoring guides and rubrics are often developed as an assessment tool to guide students in their learning and to describe proficiency on a nontraditional performance assessment. The next section describes the many benefits of authentic performance assessments.

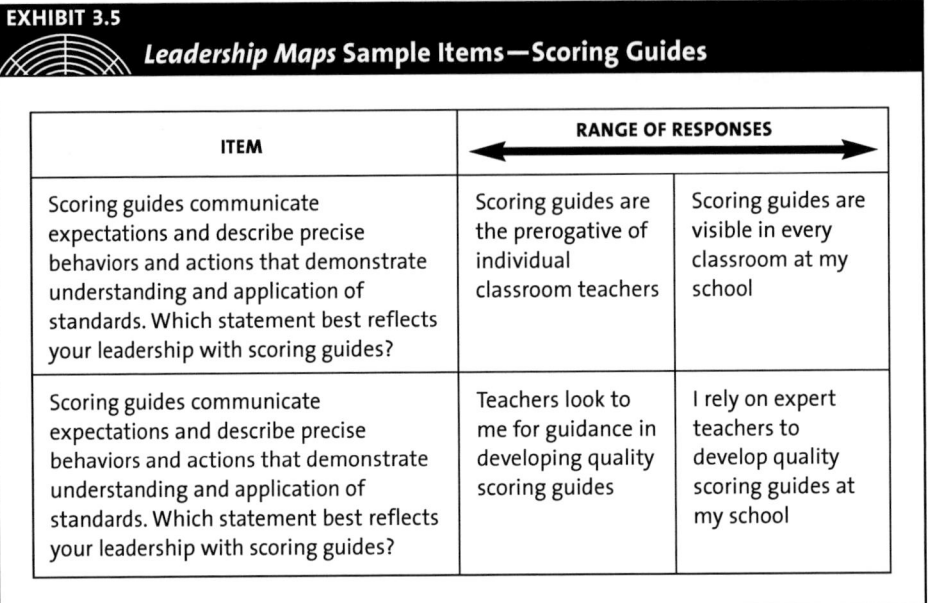

EXHIBIT 3.5

Leadership Maps **Sample Items—Scoring Guides**

ITEM	RANGE OF RESPONSES	
Scoring guides communicate expectations and describe precise behaviors and actions that demonstrate understanding and application of standards. Which statement best reflects your leadership with scoring guides?	Scoring guides are the prerogative of individual classroom teachers	Scoring guides are visible in every classroom at my school
Scoring guides communicate expectations and describe precise behaviors and actions that demonstrate understanding and application of standards. Which statement best reflects your leadership with scoring guides?	Teachers look to me for guidance in developing quality scoring guides	I rely on expert teachers to develop quality scoring guides at my school

Authentic Performance Assessments

As standards were developed in the 1980s and 1990s, a corresponding, parallel effort to develop authentic assessments gained momentum. Because standards required both demonstration of knowledge and application of skills, the assessments needed to be authentic and reflect the ability to apply knowledge that would address challenges of real life. Educators therefore endeavored to create assessments that were not only reliable and valid but engaging as well. Performance assessments represented the means to demonstrate proficiency on standards, and their design and implementation addressed the many benefits that standards were developed to generate: engagement, motivation, curriculum integration, and real-world issues of the day. Authentic performance assessments were those that resulted in enduring understandings (Wiggins and McTighe 1998) that would be so powerful that learners would apply them throughout their lives. This was a tall order for testing and a dramatic departure from traditional assessments that were designed to sort students on the basis of linguistic and mathematical understandings only. Authentic performance assessments opened the door to embracing other attributes of learning, such as learning styles, interest inventories, or Howard Gardner's eight multiple intelligences (Heacox 2002), and to a deeper application of Benjamin Bloom's

EXHIBIT 3.6 *Leadership Maps* Sample Items— Authentic Performance Assessments		

ITEM	RANGE OF RESPONSES	
I estimate the proportion of teachers at my school who create classroom environments that stimulate engagement by posting standards, displaying excellent student work, and making sure essential questions are evident at:	More than 90 percent of the teachers	Less than 10 percent of the teachers
I estimate the proportion of teachers at my school who implement at least one interdisciplinary performance assessment each quarter at:	Less than 10 percent of the teachers	More than 90 percent of the teachers

higher-order thinking (Anderson *et al.* 2001). Various authentic performance assessment definitions include:

- Assessment activities that require students to construct a response, create a product, or perform a demonstration (Ainsworth and Viegut 2006, page 57).

- "… Engaging and worthy problems or questions of importance, in which students must use knowledge to fashion performances effectively and creatively. The tasks are either replicas of or analogous to the kinds of problems faced by adult citizens and consumers or professionals in the field"(Wiggins 1993, page 229).

Rick Stiggins summed it up with this simple statement about authentic assessments: "Performance assessments call upon the examinee to demonstrate specific skills and competencies, that is, to apply the skills and knowledge they have mastered" (Stiggins 1987, page 34).

Authentic assessments allow students to apply their knowledge in novel settings to meet established criteria, cross academic disciplines, approach current real-world issues, and develop a deeper, more enduring understanding of the standards being taught. *Leadership Maps* examines the degree to which leaders promote the use of authentic assessments, provide support in their development, and address the components of authentic performance assessments in their communication and expectations. Exhibit 3.6 provides examples.

Big Ideas and Essential Questions

Perhaps no other aspects are more reflective of a standards-based educational framework than big ideas and essential questions. Both require educators to select critical elements of the curriculum from which essential questions are derived, and from which students are guided to discover big ideas. Essential questions are open-ended, higher-order cognitive questions that pique student curiosity and invite them into the learning process through discovery, research, and dialogue. Big ideas represent the core of learning units—the key "take-aways"' for students that are both practical and applicable to their lives and their futures.

Each essential question invites a range of big ideas. Each big idea answers the essential question without being prescriptive or merely restating the essential question. Workable definitions for these key components of a standards-based educational framework are as follow:

- Essential questions stimulate inquiry, debate, and further questions that can be reexamined over time (Piercy 2006, page 144).

- Essential questions cultivate a sense of curiosity and motivate students to seek answers (Fisher and Frey 2007, page 74).

- A big idea can be described in two ways: as involving an enduring conception or principle that transcends its origins, subject matter, or place in time; and as a linchpin idea that is crucial to a student's ability to understand a subject (Wiggins and McTighe 1998, page 113).

- Big ideas represent the kernels of understanding we want students to comprehend independently and remember indefinitely (Ainsworth 2003, page 28).

Big ideas answer essential questions, and *Leadership Maps* includes items that assess how well leaders leverage this powerful, standards-based concept. Exhibit 3.7 provides two examples.

Note how the second item in Exhibit 3.7 asks leaders to reflect on their own skill level with these concepts, while the first item asks leaders to estimate the degree of implementation for their staff. The final two areas of a standards-based education deviate from the prior focus on what is taught (curriculum) by focusing on opportunities to learn that curriculum.

Multiple Opportunities for Success

Standards are premised on the notion that rigorous, challenging expectations for learning can be described in terms of both acquiring knowledge and demonstrating that knowledge by applying specific skills through authentic

EXHIBIT 3.7	*Leadership Maps* **Sample Items—** **Essential Questions and Big Ideas**

ITEM	RANGE OF RESPONSES	
I estimate the proportion of teachers at my school who use the concept of Big Ideas as part of their unit or lesson planning at:	Less than 10 percent of my faculty	More than 90 percent of my faculty
At what level are you comfortable teaching Essential Questions to your faculty (the process of inviting students into the learning process and preparing them to answer the questions at the end of the lesson, unit, semester)?	I am comfortable teaching Essential Questions	I am not at all comfortable teaching Essential Questions currently

performance assessments. Standards mean that the standard itself (learning expectation) will remain fixed, while the opportunities to learn, apply, and demonstrate that standard will vary so that all students, or a majority of students, will achieve proficiency on critical power standards as described earlier in this chapter. Reeves (2002a) identified provision of multiple opportunities as a key predictor or antecedent of excellence for high-performing, high-poverty schools.

Having multiple opportunities for success means that grading systems are based more on a continuous-improvement J curve than the traditional bell-curve system, where grades during the grading period are averaged. The latter penalizes any student who does not meet the grading standard early in the term, while standards recognize that achievement at standard is worthy of celebration whenever that standard is achieved. A standards-based system, while challenging, is fundamentally fair and equitable. A fixed standard also offers educators the opportunity to design creative curricular approaches and multiple creative assessment opportunities for students.

Providing multiple opportunities for success offers benefits beyond creativity for teachers. It communicates to students and their parents that "it isn't over until it's over"—that additional effort can result in additional learning—and it communicates that there is more than one way to achieve and demonstrate proficiency. As in other areas reviewed in this chapter, the actions of leaders are critical in making multiple opportunities for success a reality. For this reason,

EXHIBIT 3.8	*Leadership Maps* **Sample Items— Multiple Opportunities for Success**

ITEM	RANGE OF RESPONSES ← →	
I estimate the proportion of staff in my department who agree on a specific standard for acceptable work at:	More than 90 percent of my staff	Less than 10 percent of my staff
As a leader, I expect industry standard best practices to be evident in procedures and practices in:	Less than 10 percent of staff	More than 90 percent of staff
I estimate the proportion of faculty who provide multiple assessments of key standards during each grading period at:	More than 90 percent of classroom teachers	Less than 10 percent of classroom teachers

Leadership Maps includes a wide range of items related to this variable. Exhibit 3.8 provides three examples, the first two from the perspective of central-office administrators and the third from that of building principals.

Varied Time and Opportunity

The final aspect of a standards-based education is the need to vary time and opportunity for students to achieve proficiency. Similar to providing multiple opportunities for success, varying time and opportunity has three basic aspects: (1) provision of additional time for instruction to struggling students through a variety of times and structures, (2) open access to the entire curriculum to as many students as possible, and (3) mixed-ability grouping of students.

Opportunities for tutoring from teachers and peer tutoring during, before, and after school are common interventions for struggling students. One of the most powerful interventions is student-to-student tutoring. A second form of tutorial is as simple as differentiating homework assignments to provide students novel opportunities to master material rather than assuming that one size fits all.

Open access presents a number of challenges to the status quo, particularly in terms of access to honors and advanced-placement (AP) classes. Traditionally, enrollment in such classes has been restricted to students with higher grade-point averages or higher aptitude scores on standardized, norm-referenced assessments. As the standards movement has advanced, however, more and more schools have embraced fixed standards and varied time and opportunity to improve achievement for all students. In fact, AP programs welcome students with disabilities and home-schooled students and allow students to take AP exams multiple times. Programs like Advancement Via Individual Determination (AVID) now serve more than 120,000 middle school and high school students who traditionally have not had access to rigorous, college-bound curricula (Gira 2002). Since 1980, the mission of AVID has been to ensure that all students, especially middle-performing students, will:

- Succeed in the most rigorous curriculum
- Enter the mainstream activities of the school
- Increase their enrollment in four-year colleges
- Become educated, responsible participants and leaders in a democratic society

AVID, like a growing number of accelerated educational approaches, including AP and IB programs, have moved away from aptitude or scholarship requirements to holistic requirements based on motivation and access. Programs like the Ben Davis High School credit-recovery program, directed by David Nagel under the tutelage of Principal Joel McKinney, have dramatically reduced high school dropout rates without reducing performance standards or high expectations simply by targeting time and opportunity to specific students in need. Credit recovery and ninth-grade academies are prevalent across North America as schools modify time and opportunity to raise achievement levels for all students.

To make standards work, time and opportunity are critical elements for reform and ones where leadership is almost always the primary variable for action. *Leadership Maps* recognizes the fact that decisions about resources, course sequences, entrance requirements, and access are fundamental to expanding the proportion of students who succeed in demonstrating rigorous performance standards. Exhibit 3.9 provides example items associated with time and opportunity, the first two for central-office administrators and the final two items for building principals.

It is no accident that time and opportunity are presented as the last elements of leadership practices focused to make standards work. Power standards, unwrapping, essential questions, scoring guides, big ideas, and authentic performance assessments are fundamental to a standards-based educational framework. However, until leaders facilitate multiple opportunities for success by strategically resourcing time and opportunity to increase rigor and increase access to challenging curriculum, standards at work will remain an elusive goal rather than an established reality of school cultures.

EXHIBIT 3.9

Leadership Maps Sample Items—Time and Opportunity

ITEM	RANGE OF RESPONSES	
In my department or district, staffing patterns match the most experienced and capable teachers with students of both high and low ability or motivation.	More than 90 percent of school leaders specify teachers of both groups in core content	Less than 10 percent of school leaders specify teachers of both groups in core content
In my department or district, resources are distributed to increase participation in the most rigorous course offerings.	True in specific ways for more than 90 percent of schools	True in specific ways for less than 10 percent of schools
Class sizes are never larger for beginning course sequences than for advanced or honors courses.	True in all content areas at my school	Not true for any content areas at my school
Advanced and honors courses at my school are encouraged for average-ability students with multiple support structures in place to increase the likelihood of successful completion.	Not true for any content areas at my school	True in all content areas at my school

Each of these characteristics invites a deeper knowledge of curriculum (content expertise) and a deeper application of strategies (high-yield strategies), which are addressed more thoroughly in Chapters 5 and 6, respectively.

Reflection

Essential Questions

How does a reliance on standards differ from a process of standardization?

Are there elements of teaching and learning that need to be standardized? Why or why not?

What is the rationale behind providing multiple opportunities for students to demonstrate success on the same standard or indicator?

Big Ideas

Standards enhance the opportunity for teacher creativity to engage all students more effectively.

Leaders add value when time and opportunity are directed to increase access to rigorous and challenging curricula.

Having multiple opportunities for success recognizes students and increases the proportion of students meeting standards without compromising quality or rigor.

CHAPTER 4

Accountability in Action

> *"Accountability: the quality or state of being accountable; esp: an obligation or willingness to accept responsibility or to account for one's actions."*
>
> *Merriam-Webster's Collegiate Dictionary* 2003, page 8

Accountability can be either an obligation or a willing acceptance of responsibility, but to educators, it is too often viewed as an obligation—a reality the profession tolerates, rather than an opportunity. In *Beyond the Numbers* (2005), I tell the story of the anxious superintendent who waited on pins and needles for release of the state assessments. Accountability for results is hardly something celebrated or enjoyed in schools and is most often associated with the annual high-stakes assessment results. This chapter changes the perception of accountability from "gotcha" to "with you," and from something that must be endured to something that can be celebrated.

Accountability is more than being held to account. Accountability is being transparent about expectations and outcomes, individuals being responsible for results, and improving performance and results. As in previous chapters, the key variable in changing such perceptions is leadership, and *Leadership Maps* items examine school practices across seven principles of accountability.

The Need for Accountability

Accountability systems alone rarely transform educational practices, and while changes have resulted from the increased scrutiny on results from NCLB, school reform continues to be challenged by a number of unspoken cultural assumptions about education. These barriers are perhaps best represented by a characterization of schools as loosely coupled organizations.

Schools As Loosely Coupled Organizations

Loosely coupled systems (Weick 1976) have ambiguous goals, unclear technologies, and autonomy that result in uncoordinated activities—a unique blend of both professional autonomy and bureaucracy. Weick viewed schools as particularly problematic because there is such loose control over how well the work is done. As professionals, teachers are allowed considerable latitude in determining not only what is taught, but how it is taught as well. It is not uncommon for negotiated agreements between teachers and school boards to require that observations are scheduled in advance if they are to be used as part of the evaluation process. This reality clearly reveals the loosely coupled nature of schools, and a comparable reality is experienced in terms of supervision of principals. Educators are afforded extraordinary latitude regarding how they ply their craft—something that standards, pacing guides, classroom walk-throughs, and transparent data analyses push against. In fact, the loosely coupled nature of schooling directly contradicts the notion of accountability or responsibility for results, as there is a presumption of competence that is almost sacred.

Richard Elmore (2000, page 11) elaborates on loosely coupled systems by describing three deep cultural barriers to educational reform: (1) the inviolability of teaching and learning, (2) the sanctity of local preferences in the governance of schools, and (3) the generally positive support of local schools by their elites.

The inviolability of teaching to which Elmore refers is simply the tendency at all levels of the profession to protect the profession from scrutiny. Schmoker (2006) is even more direct, viewing the tendency as a buffer—a culture of privacy and non-interference. The result of failing to examine the schools has inadvertently led to society's perception that instruction and supervision are relatively effective.

Schmoker attributes much of the problem to a historical tendency toward isolation, while Elmore points to a culture that expects the bulk of learning for teachers to occur prior to entering the classroom and a corresponding axiom that, once certified, licensed, and hired, teacher A on his or her first day is just as qualified and competent as teacher B, who has eleven years of experience. As educators, few subscribe to such a naïve viewpoint, but that is exactly how our legal system views teaching. The fact that both teachers A and B are licensed by the state, screened and hired by the district, and selected by the principal, designates both as equally, if not minimally, competent to fulfill their jobs. We have nothing of the differentiated career ladders to proficiency in medicine or architecture, or even automobile technicians who acquire levels of expertise over time.

Elmore cites the sanctity of local preferences as the second challenge to the profession in terms of loosely coupled systems. This belief permeates all levels of decision-making, from legislatures to local school boards, and from principals to teachers. It is as if an unspoken compact has been struck that confers respect and autonomy to each level one step removed. States assume that good intentions translate into desired results for districts, districts accept school improvement plans as blueprints for success, and principals assume that quality professional development is followed by quality implementation and changes in classroom practice. These assumptions rarely are borne out, as Auman and Young (2004) found in a comprehensive study of 1,500 brief classroom walk-throughs in U.S. urban, rural, and suburban schools, where a very small fraction of classrooms reflected district-wide professional development initiatives that had been present for years. My own research on planning, implementation, and monitoring (see Chapter 9) consistently points out that most school, region, or district improvement documents rarely reflect the level of desired implementation, and that *assignment of individuals responsible for completing action steps (accountability) is a key predictor of achievement gains.* Granting complete autonomy to those we serve and supervise is a recipe for inconsistency and fragmented implementation, not improvement.

The third attribute of loosely coupled systems is the positive support that local elites ascribe to their local schools. Ask your local realtor where the best schools are, and the answer provided will be specific, swift, and confident. Ask the follow-up question about what makes school A the best school and the platitudes begin, with maybe a reference to an award won sometime in the recent past. We shouldn't expect the realtor to know the nuts and bolts of teaching and learning, but often the same response is made by school board officials or even by principals about their faculty with little or no evidence of how they teach or what makes them successful. Our pluralistic political system contributes to that reality, as candidates are quick to praise local school officials and very slow to ask questions about results or accountability. Schmoker challenges us to consider whether maintaining harmony is of greater value to stakeholders than improving instruction (Lortie 1975; Powell, Farrar, and Cohen 1985). Ted Sizer's *Horace's Compromise* (1992) describes the profession in terms of compromises between teachers and students, teachers, and administration, and between the administration and the school board. Elmore (2004) describes uncoupled systems as contrary both to standards and to reform, and Schmoker describes them as the "best friend the status quo could ever ask for" (2006, page 14).

There is a much greater recognition of the power of collaboration and the need to drive decisions based on data than there was a decade ago, but plenty of evidence remains to suggest that loosely coupled systems are alive and well. *Leadership Maps* assists leaders in self-assessing whether their actions advance holistic accountability or sustain the status quo of loosely coupled systems. Seven principles of accountability guide our discussion with example *Leadership Map* items for each.

Architecture of Accountability

All accountability systems need a framework to communicate expectations, record goal targets, implement change initiatives, apply lessons learned, and, when possible, celebrate gains. Growth models, or accountability frameworks that focus on cohort year-to-year growth, as opposed to comparing this year's third-graders with last year's third-graders, are gaining in popularity (Hoff 2007, pages 22–25). Growth models contrast with the status model, which evaluates school progress from year to year and has characterized state responses to NCLB since its inception. Growth models focus on student gains from year to year, and while this is commendable for attention to student cohort gains, growth models fail to describe a holistic accountability system where sustaining success and capacity-building are part and parcel of achieving ambitious targets.

Holistic accountability focuses on more than test scores and monitors improvement targets in five critical, holistic areas: (1) academic achievement, (2) personal responsibility, (3) community engagement, (4) fiscal stewardship, and (5) capacity-building. The Leadership and Learning Center has assisted a number of award-winning districts such as Norfolk Public Schools (Virginia), the Metropolitan School District of Wayne Township (Indiana), Hazelwood School District (Missouri), Pueblo School District (Colorado), and Savannah–Chatham County Schools (Georgia) to establish a three-tier framework of holistic accountability. The model incorporates the five areas of accountability through three levels of implementation.

Tier 1 Indicators

The first level identifies systemwide, or Tier 1, indicators. Districtwide tests and assessments are Tier 1 indicators used by almost every state accountability system, but they are only part of a holistic accountability framework. In addition, Tier 1 gathers data that is indicative of the degree to which the system responds to and welcomes its constituencies, the degree to which the system is rigorous and focused in its academic content, and the degree to which it indicates the quality of its fiscal stewardship. It also examines whether the system is building the capacity of its faculty and staff. Exhibit 4.1 describes examples of Tier 1 indicators.

Indicators often begin as easily accessible measures such as attendance rates, but over time they mature into very explicit and focused targets that represent the district's vision and mission. Holistic accountability systems are all about continuous improvement that yields greater clarity and responds to local conditions and data over time. Some Tier 1 indicators may address facility issues within community engagement, and personnel practices almost always address

EXHIBIT 4.1

Potential System Level (Tier 1) Indicators

	TIER 1 INDICATORS		
Academic Achievement	State assessment scores	Percent completing on time	Percent graduating from college in five years
Personal Responsibility	Attendance rates by student group, grades	Number of cohort dropouts, ninth grade, twelfth grade	Number of suspensions and expulsions
Community Engagement	Number of parents participating in school-based adult education annually	Complaint resolution rates/time for central office	Number of schools with established multifaceted listening systems
Fiscal Stewardship	Budget balances, reserves	Return on investment, such as professional development dollars to achievement gains	Trend analyses about efficiency; return on investment, exemplar practices
Capacity-Building	Percent of highly qualified teachers hired by May; teacher tenure; opportunity to lead	Aligned professional development with curriculum, percent aligned to improve-ment initiatives	Number or percent of teacher participation in mentoring, coaching

capacity-building, but virtually all needs can be nested within the five Tier 1 areas described in Exhibit 4.1. Examine the sample *Leadership Maps* items in Exhibit 4.2 as they relate to Tier 1 indicators.

The items in Exhibit 4.2 describe the depth of implementation, clarity in understanding the vision, and the degree to which educators accept responsibility (a key measure of accountability) for achieving district or school goal targets.

Tier 2 Indicators

Tier 2 indicators focus primarily on how Tier 1 targets will be achieved, and they are informed by data about the individual school or department as a distinct

EXHIBIT 4.2

Leadership Maps Sample Items—Accountability Architecture

ITEM	RANGE OF RESPONSES	
The proportion of my direct reports that is fluent with a three-tiered accountability system that I can verify is:	More than 90 percent of my direct reports	Less than 10 percent of my direct reports
The proportion of my staff that can describe our vision for the future and defend it to others is estimated at:	More than 90 percent of staff	Less than 10 percent of staff
Vision and mission statements at my school/department/district are:	Visible, and form the basis of our decision-making	Necessary, but have little to do with the decisions required to lead

unit. If we consider Tier 1 data as a combination of what we want to achieve and why, Tier 2 indicators reveal *how we will accomplish those focused targets.* Tier 2 indicators should monitor two aspects of continuous improvement: (1) progress toward goal attainment, and (2) degree of implementation. The former is equivalent to teachers progress-monitoring with their students; the latter is equivalent to an algebra teacher examining the degree to which students understand quadratic equation formulae, or a world-language teacher monitoring the degree to which students perform verb conjugation in their new language with high levels of automaticity. Both teachers apply equal focus to the protocols or process of learning as they do to the final outcome. Tier 2 data always examines the process of acquiring proficiency in teaching as well as student progress. Exhibit 4.3 provides *Leadership Maps* items that examine the degree to which leaders understand what needs to be done and whether their leadership has resulted in the deep implementation needed for success.

The first items in Exhibit 4.3 pertain to school leaders, but the third item refers to *Leadership Maps* items for central-office, state, provincial, or support-agency leaders.

Tier 3 Indicators

Tier 3 is a narrative description of successes and challenges for the school, district, or educational-support agency (Reeves 2004, page 263). It is the reflective analysis of what caused the results that were achieved. If Tier 1 is the

EXHIBIT 4.3

Leadership Maps Sample Items—Tier 2 Indicators

ITEM	RANGE OF RESPONSES	
Collaborative scoring of student work in my school occurs with:	More than 90 percent of the teachers participating	Less than 10 percent of the teachers participating
I estimate the proportion of teachers at my school who have aligned curriculum, assessments, and instruction to state content standards at:	More than 90 percent of the teachers	Less than 10 percent of the teachers
Each observation and supervision conference narrative for administrators and support personnel references the following:	How leadership performance affects district goals	Observed activities, rather than districtwide goals
Each observation and supervision conference narrative for teachers references the following:	How teaching performance affects school initiatives or goals	Observed activities, rather than schoolwide initiatives or goals

30,000-foot big picture of what needs to be achieved, and Tier 2 is the description of how those needs will be met, then Tier 3 represents the reflective analysis of why the school or district or province achieved the results as reported. Tier 3 is often overlooked, because it represents a thoughtful examination of cause-and-effect variables and a measure of what worked, what didn't work, and why. Exhibit 4.4 describes *Leadership Maps* sample items about Tier 3 leadership.

Both items in Exhibit 4.4 assess leadership in terms of reflection about best practices and of being accountable by responding to current realities. Tier 3 represents the story behind the numbers and provides a structure for educators to analyze their efforts and make adjustments from lessons learned. The architecture of accountability provides a foundation to accountability in action.

Six guiding principles are used as filters to determine the quality of an accountability system.

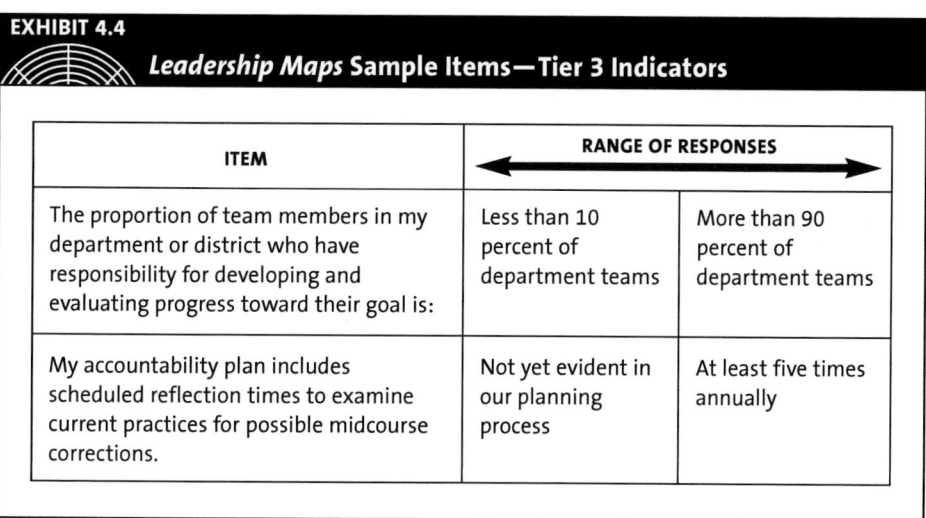

EXHIBIT 4.4

Leadership Maps **Sample Items—Tier 3 Indicators**

ITEM	RANGE OF RESPONSES	
The proportion of team members in my department or district who have responsibility for developing and evaluating progress toward their goal is:	Less than 10 percent of department teams	More than 90 percent of department teams
My accountability plan includes scheduled reflection times to examine current practices for possible midcourse corrections.	Not yet evident in our planning process	At least five times annually

Six Guiding Principles to Determine the Quality of an Accountability System

Congruence

Congruence is the degree to which the accountability system is compatible with the rewards and incentives that are in place within the school or district (Reeves 2004, page 93). Congruence exists when the organization's vision for the future aligns with the behaviors and accomplishments that the current culture rewards, values, and recognizes. Lack of congruence is evident when personnel evaluations for those with the greatest responsibility and authority are those that are most absent of common performance standards or even protocols for observation or documentation of proficiency. This conundrum, which is most acute for administrative evaluations, is symptomatic of loosely coupled systems where accountability is promised for each administrator but where current practice rarely adheres to that standard.

Congruence means that there is thoughtful alignment about both priorities and processes. If teachers are expected to differentiate instruction to meet the needs of all learners, but the district pacing guide is so voluminous and prescriptive to make differentiation difficult, teachers are entitled to view compliance with one directive as incongruent with the other. If the message from the central office to the principals is to provide honest feedback about teaching practices, but the principal is asked to explain his or her actions every time a complaint surfaces at the central office, the message is clear and unmistakably incongruent.

EXHIBIT 4.5

Leadership Maps Sample Items—Congruence in Accountability

ITEM	RANGE OF RESPONSES	
Rewards and incentives are provided to staff and faculty on the basis of achievement in areas for which individuals and teams are accountable.	More than 90 percent of staff and faculty would agree	Less than 10 percent of staff and faculty would agree
The proportion of my direct reports who organize their program of work to address district and department goals is estimated at:	More than 90 percent of my direct reports	Less than 10 percent of my direct reports
I estimate the proportion of teachers at my school who have aligned curriculum, assessments, and instruction to state content standards at:	More than 90 percent of the teachers	Less than 10 percent of the teachers

Congruence requires leaders to deliberately avoid mixed signals by protecting the focus of the accountability structure. Congruence means that each employee has a role to play at every level and within every department, an opportunity to excel, and a responsibility to fulfill that role in supporting the organization's Tier 1 goals. The most successful organizations (Collins 2001, pages 96–103) are made up of normal individuals who are accomplishing extraordinary things simply by defining expectations clearly and providing a forum for employees to meet or exceed those expectations. Leaders make the difference when they convey that message through their actions. Exhibit 4.5 provides a few *Leadership Maps* sample items to illustrate.

All three examples in Exhibit 4.5 refer to accountability in terms of being responsible for results by addressing the importance of congruent expectations, academic content, and rewards and incentives.

Specificity

The second component of accountability in action is specificity. Does your accountability framework describe what needs to be done to achieve your target for improving achievement, building capacity, or engaging the community? Does it clearly describe the path to effectively steward and leverage financial resources, and does the framework lend itself to personal responsibility for staff and

EXHIBIT 4.6

Specificity Example for Accountability

What:	To build capacity in professional learning communities (PLCs) and data teams (DTs) throughout the district.
Why:	To develop and distribute leadership opportunities for staff and faculty, realize the benefit of collaboration, and create a culture of evidence where staff and faculty are sufficiently skilled and proficient in data analysis to make midcourse adjustments that improve student achievement for all students.
How:	Workshops will be differentiated to serve novice, practicing, and expert principals through three workshop-level entrance points: (1) introduction for principals who are new to PLCs or the district, (2) mastery for principals who are familiar with the four-question PLC framework and the five-step DT process, and (3) expert training for principals where PLCs and DTs are active and functioning across grade levels and departments. Mentors will be assigned to all novice principals from participants at the expert-level training, and weekly assignments and indicators will be developed and reviewed jointly by the participating novice and participating expert principal. Both will maintain a log documenting practice, lessons learned, and next steps. Mastery workshop participants will bring examples of best practices observed in their schools by teams that address the four-part PLC questions and five-step DT process below:

PLC Four-Question Framework:	DT Five-Step Process
1. What do we want each student to learn?	1. Treasure hunt for important data.
2. How will we know when each student has learned it?	2. Analyze data to prioritize needs.
3. How will we respond when a student experiences difficulty in learning?	3. Develop SMART goals.
4. How will we respond if students already have achieved proficiency?	4. Identify powerful instructional strategies to meet prioritized needs.
	5. Develop insightful results indicators of student progress toward the SMART goal and teacher progress in terms of fidelity of implementation.

As Measured By:
- Data displays at each campus of PLC/DT work
- Percentage of principals serving as mentors or mentees
- Percentage of PLCs/DTs submitting minutes monthly by June 20, ____
- Percentage of mentor team logs identifying five or more lessons learned
- Number of exemplary practices shared districtwide by May 1, ____
- Changes in student performance by PLC/DT in terms of attendance, grades, discipline referrals, and gains on district quarterly benchmark assessments in reading and math
- Individual workshop satisfaction from +/Delta Summary
- Thirty-day and ninety-day follow-up feedback forms

students? This area is the arena of loosely coupled assumptions, such as quality professional development delivered well will result in nearly universal, quality implementation. Accountability frameworks often document compliance rather than implementation, as in the case where sign-in sheets for attendance at a writing workshop presume improved writing across the curriculum.

Specificity refers to a description of strategies that guide everyone involved with the accountability framework to understand what needs to be done, why, who will be responsible (accountable) for implementing that action, how it will be completed, when, and with what measure. Examine the action step below:

> Continue to provide workshops for principals on building and sustaining professional learning communities.

The action step describes what needs to be done, but it certainly does not include *how* the workshops will be provided, and it communicates even less about how professional learning communities will be built or sustained. It is fair to say that the action step is nonspecific and that several descriptive and prescriptive statements are needed to achieve accountability. Exhibit 4.6 takes this vague and nonspecific statement and translates it into one that meets the accountability standard for specificity.

The benefit of the added specificity in Exhibit 4.6 is not merely greater clarity and direction for implementation. Specificity assists educators in determining the real requirements for implementing initiatives. In this profession, our zeal to serve children often results in trying to do too much too soon—a practice that

---

EXHIBIT 4.7

Leadership Maps **Sample Items for Specificity in Accountability**

ITEM	RANGE OF RESPONSES	
Performance expectations are outlined for assigned tasks in terms of what is expected, why, who is responsible, how the assignment will be completed, and how successful completion will be measured.	More than 90 percent of faculty and staff would identify this practice as standard operating procedures	Less than 10 percent of faculty and staff would identify this practice as standard operating procedures
Setting and posting clear objectives for every lesson are:	Not yet expected of my teachers	Currently expected from all teachers

often leads to initiative fatigue. By insisting on specificity, as we did in Exhibit 4.6, we quickly understand the complexity involved in achieving a single action step and the real work required to be accountable for its completion.

Specificity in accountability helps educators recognize the challenge before them and determine whether they have the ability to influence results. If the accountability framework is sufficiently specific, those involved will perceive not only the challenge but also the opportunity for success and their role in achieving that success. Exhibit 4.7 provides sample *Leadership Maps* items for specificity.

Both items in Exhibit 4.7 address the need for clarity and specificity, and both indicate the degree to which the leader's actions have resulted in deep implementation and accountability for all.

Respect for Diversity

Accountability systems need to be able to differentiate, just as effective teachers differentiate to meet the needs of individual students. Respect for diversity recognizes that one size does not fit all in terms of teaching and learning, and that schools and school organizations must recognize that varied levels of competence and experience introduced into varied learning environments require a differentiated response. The model described earlier provides an opportunity for that differentiation by holding the Tier 1 district-level targets fixed, but providing each school and department the latitude to address those overarching goals in a way that recognizes the context for learning and growth at that level.

Respect for diversity acknowledges the differences that children bring to school in terms of language, culture, race, and religion, as well as the relative advantages provided by income or social standing of families and the need to accommodate those learners. Leaders can leverage their accountability system to promote respect for diversity and individual differences by being selective and focused in their data reporting. It is one thing to report averages that illustrate the different achievement levels by ethnicity or gender, and something entirely different to report the experience of students who outperform their cohort groups. The leader who can identify factors that accelerate learning and close achievement gaps within the school is certainly respecting diversity. Every time a leader reports data that reveals how schools and teachers can be more effective with more students, he or she telegraphs in no uncertain terms the importance of closing achievement gaps and a belief that they can do better.

Respect for diversity is also achieved when multiple measures of achievement are used. Multiple measures include a whole range of student assessments that provide much greater clarity than the annual high-stakes assessment, such as

EXHIBIT 4.8 *Leadership Maps* **Sample Items for Respecting Diversity in Accountability**

ITEM	RANGE OF RESPONSES	
Improvement goal statements are best when they:	Target gains for subgroups needing improvement on specific content standards and strands	Target overall school gains by subject area
The proportion of my faculty that demonstrates a relentless focus on student achievement by displaying student work, graphing progress toward goals, or analyzing data to improve their practice is estimated at:	Less than 10 percent of my faculty	More than 90 percent of my faculty

grades, district-level benchmarks, common formative assessments, and end-of-course assessments. For an accountability framework to result in continuous improvement over time and across a diverse population, schools will need the latitude to focus on a variety of outcome measures and the support to celebrate gains where they find them.

Leaders also communicate a respect for diversity when they defer to evidence (data) over traditions. When current evidence trumps the continuation of the third-grade ice cream social in favor of project-based learning culminating in a science fair, leaders model a standard for making decisions. Whether you are a superintendent, department chair, principal, or literacy coach, deferring to evidence in decision-making is a powerful way to advocate for students. It also promotes learning from our mistakes and missteps and enhances opportunities to celebrate gains (Kouzes and Posner 2002, pages 354–355). Exhibit 4.8 offers two sample *Leadership Maps* items for respecting diversity.

The first item in Exhibit 4.8 respects diversity by asking leaders how they establish goals and whether those goals focus on efforts to close achievement gaps. The second item reflects on the depth of displaying student work and targeting improved classroom practice throughout the school.

Continuous Improvement

Continuous improvement is like the flag or apple pie; everyone is for it. By definition, continuous improvement identifies both current reality and a preferred reality, recognizing that where we are now is not where we want to be. To acknowledge that where we are now is anything less than worthy of praise is a difficult task, especially for school leaders, and even more so for newly appointed school leaders. Evans found that the mere introduction of change initiatives calls into question current levels of competency and even produces a sense of loss for educators (2001, pages 29–34). For improvement to truly become continuous, leaders need to replace the evaluation mindset of ranking and comparing with a view of incremental, steady improvements; take action on the basis of the best available information; value and model corrective feedback; and celebrate incremental gains.

Improvement is not about evaluating or ranking but about changing practice, and leaders need to communicate an appreciation for attempts that do not work as positively as they appreciate attempts that do. By recognizing efforts to improve practice that have yet to demonstrate improved results, leaders communicate confidence in their faculties and an understanding that *improvement is a journey more than an event.* The journey metaphor only underscores the reality that educators have been subject to much talk about improvement but even more to the demonstration of ranking or evaluation.

Taking action requires leaders to persuade staff or faculty that the change proposed will not be the next flavor of the month. Educators at all levels are very familiar with programs and strategies that are here today and gone next year. Many *Leadership Maps* items invite leaders to reflect on the depth of implementation, simply because one of the best indicators of successful leadership is the degree to which that leadership has been extended throughout the school, and whether the practice would be sustained in the leader's absence.

The third role of leaders in advancing continuous improvement for accountability is to value and model corrective feedback. Corrective feedback consists of two distinct observations: (1) what the individual is observed doing well (strength), and (2) a suggested next step or improvement that will enhance performance (stretch). A strength may be acknowledged with a comment like, "That was a terrific use of higher-order questions. Your use of wait time and selection of "how" and "why" questions were carefully integrated into the lesson, and I think that all but one child were fully engaged." A stretch comment might be as simple as, "I observed George delivering the same unit last week, and he added a great closing, hands-on activity where each student discovered a big idea about centrifugal force before the end of the lesson. I think he might be interested in your questioning techniques as well." Note how the stretch merely encourages the teacher to go deeper, while the strength clearly communicates interest, attention to the details of instructional delivery, and knowledge of teaching, regardless of content expertise by the principal.

EXHIBIT 4.9	*Leadership Maps* Sample Items for Continuous Improvement in Accountability	

ITEM	RANGE OF RESPONSES	
Continuous improvement efforts in my school or department include baseline data and progress indicators reviewed at least quarterly.	By less than 10 percent of teacher teams	By more than 90 percent of teacher teams
I provide same-day corrective feedback following brief, informal classroom observations to:	More than 90 percent of classrooms observed	Less than 10 percent of classrooms observed
Visible displays of data and student work throughout the building should provide:	Clear evidence of challenges, growth, and achievement	No comparisons of teachers or students in any way

Research is extensive on the power of feedback within and outside of education (Pfeffer and Sutton 2000, page 10; Marzano 2003, page 37; Kouzes and Posner 2002, page 92). Feedback also provides additional opportunities to celebrate gains, not only in terms of student achievement but also in terms of professional practice. Savvy leaders will even collect data on their own use of corrective feedback to illustrate its impact on performance. Exhibit 4.9 offers *Leadership Maps* sample items for continuous improvement.

The items in Exhibit 4.9 focus primarily on how leadership in continuous improvement is extended and evident throughout the school.

Universality

Universality refers to the level playing field of accountability, where teachers, students, parents, school board members, central-office administrators, and principals participate in the same universal accountability structure to improve school practices, align efforts, and improve student achievement. This factor distinguishes the three-tiered model from most accountability systems where student performance is the primary, if not the only, indicator of success. Universality has several important benefits.

Universality is about fairness in that it holds the superintendent and school board to the same expectations as other internal stakeholders. The three-tiered system allows each department and school to determine the goal targets that align with the systems-level targets. If the achievement target is to increase the level of advanced performance on the state assessment by 13 percent in three years, the school board's action plan might address this target by changing its recruitment policy. Or, it might direct the human resource department to report, by school and the central-office department, any advanced training received by faculty. Perhaps the target for hiring would take the form of retaining teachers by publishing the average tenure within the district and establishing a process for interviewing those who choose to leave the system. The same 13 percent gain target for the high school may take the form of increased emphasis on writing and extensive use of scoring guides, a more focused and aligned course offering, or coordination with the middle school in the implementation of an AVID program. Each school and department would be responsible for results unique to their setting and department.

Transparency and open communication offer good-faith evidence of each school's commitment to its community. Exhibit 4.10 provides *Leadership Maps* sample items for universality.

Universality with transparent reporting and open access to accountability plans is a bedrock principle of accountability for improvement.

EXHIBIT 4.10 *Leadership Maps* **Sample Items for Universality in Accountability**

ITEM	RANGE OF RESPONSES	
At my school, accountability in action is evident by assigned responsibilities for specific interventions and action plans and gains in performance:	By less than 10 percent of teacher teams	By more than 90 percent of teacher teams
At my school, goals and objectives are determined by student achievement needs:	As perceived by faculty and staff	As revealed by data and aligned to district goals
My accountability plan is easily accessible to the public, and results are disseminated to parents, students, teachers, and administrators:	If requested to anyone requesting the results	Annually in written form, language of parents, the press, and the Internet

Reciprocity

Reciprocity invites two-way, candid input and open communication channels within the accountability framework. It encourages public display of data and frequent communication with its stakeholders. Teachers in a holistic accountability framework are encouraged to provide feedback to their principals regarding the effectiveness of the organization. In an accountability framework that displays universality, respect for diversity, commitment to continuous improvement, specificity, and congruence, reciprocity means that stakeholders view the opportunity to provide input as an obligation. An accountability system that advances candor, defers to evidence (data), and welcomes alternative viewpoints and ideas over time impacts the culture of the organization, while focusing efforts to improve performance from day one. Three aspects of reciprocity are recommended to foster a high level of trust and openness: (1) an effective listening system, (2) an extensive public display of data, and (3) candor in evaluating current performance levels.

Candor simply means that stakeholders avoid embellishing successes or exaggerating failures. They defer to the evidence from data available to them and triangulate that data to reveal patterns and trends that would otherwise remain obscured. Reciprocity demonstrates a commitment to all stakeholders that they have a voice, are invited to express it, and have an obligation to support recommended changes with evidence. Candor can be abused and destructive, but by structuring input and feedback mechanisms to resolve issues at the lowest level and rely on evidence and facts rather than hearsay and rumor, candor can be a very powerful element of accountability that distributes responsibility for results.

Public display of data is integral to reciprocity, because it both defers to evidence and is transparent and available to the public. Considerable evidence indicates that merely taking time to examine data in teams and increasing the frequency of assessments improve achievement and even close achievement gaps (Viadero 2004, page 9; Marzano 2007, page 13). Displaying data can have a powerful impact on students and professional practice, perhaps best illustrated by the trophy display. Most schools celebrate athletic championships in their trophy displays, and each trophy holds special meaning, not just for the participants but for the entire school and often for decades after the achievement. What if trophy cases displayed such victories in student achievement or capacity-building or community engagement?

The third component of reciprocity is a comprehensive listening system that gathers information and ideas from all of its stakeholders. Input is gathered in multiple ways, at multiple times, and reciprocates in terms of communication by

EXHIBIT 4.11

Leadership Maps Sample Items for Reciprocity in Accountability

ITEM	RANGE OF RESPONSES	
I encourage input from all stakeholders several times annually through multiple means that are convenient to each group as a means of listening to and responding to concerns.	More than 90 percent of my staff can describe multiple examples across stakeholders	Less than 10 percent of my staff can describe more than one example
The proportion of my faculty who collaboratively score student work from a colleague's classroom is estimated at:	Less than 10 percent of the faculty	More than 90 percent of the faculty
Results of our efforts to improve performance at my school are prominently displayed and periodically updated throughout the year.	Less than 10 percent of staff and faculty agree and can offer specific examples	More than 90 percent of staff and faculty agree and can offer specific examples

publishing results and responding to concerns. Systems that invite input in ways convenient to the stakeholders and respond promptly to their comments promote the level of reciprocal communication necessary for holistic accountability. Exhibit 4.11 depicts *Leadership Maps* sample items for reciprocity.

The items in Exhibit 4.11 examine the depth of implementation regarding the public display of data, reciprocity in terms of candor among staff, and the degree to which holistic listening systems are in place.

Connecting the Dots

The three-tiered accountability framework and six principles of holistic accountability are proven and established best practices for urban, rural, and suburban school systems. Accountability provides districts permission to pursue long-term Tier 1 achievement by paying attention to Tier 2 needs with practical and effective strategies and specific monitoring structures. The utility of these practices is most clearly revealed by the adult science fair, a simple accountability tool long advocated by Dr. Douglas Reeves.

Adult science fairs are recurring events where schools and central-office departments display accountability plans to tell their story of continuous improvement. Many report this simple practice as improving and extending accountability more effectively than any previous sanctions or incentives. Why? The science fair process, coupled with the three-tier system of accountability, is universal, as all schools and departments, including the superintendent and the school board, participate. The science fair is specific, as each unit describes with clarity and precision their goal targets and their action plans to achieve those targets. The science fair respects diversity as it welcomes diverse and creative ideas, documents local needs unique to each school or unit, and defers to evidence and data to draw conclusions and tell the story behind the numbers. The adult science fair focuses on continuous improvement, offering starting-line baseline data and reporting trends over time in terms of results. It expands the feedback loop by identifying successful practices and inviting other schools and departments to replicate them. Year to year, adult science fairs refine their objectives and strategies and continuously improve results by learning from each other. The process celebrates gains, recognizes achievement, and promotes excellence. The adult science fair is reciprocal in that it invites two-way candid discussion across levels and administrative units. It is a public display with which schools everywhere are familiar, and it represents each district's unique listening system where data is gathered from all internal constituencies, from the boardroom to the classroom. What's more, the adult science fair framework is easily adopted, transparent, and fun. It is also a far cry from accountability as "gotcha."

Reflection

Essential Questions

Is the primary purpose of accountability systems to evaluate or improve current performance? Which is the most difficult to implement and why?

Distinguish between the holistic accountability principles of reciprocity and universality. How are they alike and how do they differ?

Describe in your own terms the most important elements of an effective accountability system.

What is the advantage to districts that adopt The Leadership and Learning Center holistic accountability framework? Are there potential disadvantages?

Big Ideas

Accountability is about responsibility for results.

Accountability requires courageous leadership to implement well.

Principles of holistic accountability can be implemented at the school, district, state, regional, or provincial level.

CHAPTER 5

Leading Change

"Change We Can Believe In"
BARACK OBAMA, 2008

Virtually every election in modern democracies is about a change in personnel and a change in policies. This slogan underscores the difficulty any leader faces in effecting and sustaining change, and change in education is never easy, as educational stakeholders are at least as skeptical as the general public about promises for change. This difficulty in leading change has been documented and addressed by thought leaders in a wide variety of contexts (Casciaro and Lobo 2005, pages 92–99; Collins 2001, page 11; Evans 2001, pages 32–38; Heifetz and Linsky 2002, page 146; Kotter 1996; Pfeffer and Sutton 2000, pages 87–106; Quinn 2004, pages 65–67; Reeves 2006, page 99; Sarason 1996, pages 283–286).

In the late 1990s, Governor Roy Romer of Colorado stepped aside from political office and accepted the challenge of running the nation's second largest school system, Los Angeles Unified School District, which serves more than 700,000 students. During the fall of 1999, Governor Romer returned to Colorado and joined his fellow superintendents at a monthly breakfast. At the appropriate moment, Romer rose to his feet to address the intimate fraternity of thirty to forty superintendents from metropolitan Denver and Colorado Springs.

He began:

> I so appreciate your honoring me this morning and I really do count it a privilege to be considered one of your own, and not only as a Coloradan. You know my love for this beautiful state, but you've welcomed me as a school superintendent, something I never expected to be doing, and unlike each of you, something for which I have no formal training. What I've learned in the past six months may surprise you, given the fact that I was on the executive side of the legislative process for so many years, and given the fact that most of my adult life has been spent in public service, elected service, and political service—three terms as your governor, a stint as chairman of the Democratic National Committee, extensive networks with the movers and shakers in both parties from coast

to coast, and, if I can humbly report, even advisor to multiple presidents and the Congress. This morning, however, all of that pales in contrast to the challenges of my current job and yours. You see, I thought I understood politics, but I found out what politics was really all about when I . . .

The audience jumped to its feet, interrupting the governor and providing what seemed to be a thunderous standing ovation of several minutes. It was probably closer to sixty seconds, but Superintendent Romer struck a chord with school leaders that would not soon be forgotten. His brief speech never made the papers, probably to his relief, and to my knowledge, this is the first time that the moment has been recorded in print, with his gracious permission. He finished his sentence, ". . . when I became a school superintendent," and humbly took his seat and finished his eggs as our meeting turned to more tedious topics such as responding to unfunded mandates or lobbying plans for the upcoming school finance budget.

Leading change is intensely political, a term defined so astutely by Patrick Lencioni as silos or ". . . barriers that exist between departments within an organization, causing people who are supposed to be on the same team to work against one another" (2006, page 175). Politics is seldom intentional, but school leaders live with politics and respond to political realities each and every day. School leaders will understand all too well the reaction to Governor Romer's remarks that crisp fall morning, because the job of leading change is so complex and challenging.

This chapter will not attempt to add to the mountain of literature on change or even describe the process of leading change. Instead, it will challenge school leaders to reach deeper and higher to more effectively lead and manage the change in their midst. *Leadership Maps* examines this complex topic from two complimentary world views: (1) change occurs within the context of the day-to-day work of an organization (implementation), and (2) change is all about how decisions are made when the context is novel or the situation is unfamiliar (uncharted waters). Neither of these viewpoints is earthshaking or particularly profound. In fact, leading change in *Leadership Maps* is more about the mundane, day-to-day acts of leadership (Exhibit 1.4) than it is about the qualities of leadership (which will be addressed more thoroughly in Chapter 10). This bias toward action and implementation is based on a solid foundation of leadership research where the context is more important than the pronouncement, the functional culture stronger than the vision statements or strategy (Fullan, Hill, and Crevola 2006, page 91; Kouzes and Posner 2002, pages 181–220; Pfeffer and Sutton 2000, pages 248–263; Rushkoff 2005, pages 78–106; Schmoker 2006).

Leadership Maps items about leading change are filtered through these two lenses: implementation and decisions about uncharted territory. Another politician describes it in a wonderfully roll-your-sleeves-up way.

"Always sweat the small stuff."
RUDY GIULIANI, *Leadership* (2002), page 46

This chapter focuses on six actionable opportunities to lead change more effectively. Each describes actions that leaders can take to "sweat the small stuff" and advance the changes that are most important to the success of their school or department. We begin like the real estate agent who instructs us that there are three important variables in real estate: location, location, location. For leadership, the three variables are: relationships, relationships, relationships.

Relationships and Distributed Leadership

Richard Boyatzis and Anne McKee (2005, pages 141–145) identify mindfulness as the key leadership attribute that allows leaders to know themselves deeply and make smart choices about how they respond to people and situations. To Boyatzis and McKee, this form of emotional intelligence sets the stage for leading change but requires a context built on relationships through the day-to-day work of leading. Others describe a need for authentic application such as Stephen Covey's emotional bank account (1989, pages 188–190). In virtually all conceptual models of leadership, relationships provide the foundation for action and require a deep level of self-awareness that will allow leaders to differentiate responses and empower the individuals whom they are charged with leading. Collins' (2001) oft-quoted reference to getting the right people on the right seats of the bus speaks to the role of leadership in developing others, and John Kotter's eight-stage process for leading change includes stages to create a sense of urgency in others and empower broad-based action (1990, page 21). Relationships are the vehicle for action, and no leaders at any time in history can accomplish everything for which they are accountable without the willing and enthusiastic support and commitment of those who follow them. Leading change can be distilled to distributing opportunities where others can lead, grow, and accomplish great things, and *Leadership Maps* items are designed for that purpose, as illustrated in Exhibit 5.1.

The first item in Exhibit 5.1 elaborates on the residual benefits of distributed leadership, and how stewardship delegation (Covey 1989) actually develops leadership by encouraging calculated risk-taking. The second item asks leaders to

EXHIBIT 5.1

Leadership Maps Items—Distributed Leadership

ITEM	RANGE OF RESPONSES	
Distributed leadership that empowers staff to assume responsibility, exercise authority, and take calculated risks within defined parameters is:	Evident across all key functions in my department or district	Not yet evident in key functions in my department or district
Delegation is important at my school within the following framework:	I reserve final decision-making authority on all teams	Faculty facilitate meetings and exercise leadership on my behalf
The percentage of staff and faculty with the authority to stop obsolete or ineffective practices without consulting me is estimated at:	More than 90 percent of staff and faculty	Less than 10 percent of staff and faculty

reflect on the degree to which they are willing to delegate "deeply," empowering others to represent them in decisions that may need to be made on the spot. The most effective leaders make delegation work for them by building leadership capacity even more than by completing tasks and achieving objectives. The final item speaks to the degree to which building leaders have distributed leadership deeply to all staff and faculty, empowering all who report to that leader with the trust and professional judgment to make important decisions that improve the school or their classroom. Notice how this sample of items reflects strong relationships between the leader and his or her staff, indicates high levels of trust and coaching, and extends real leadership capacity throughout the organization.

Compliance or Commitment

Leaders everywhere wrestle with the challenge to lead work groups to embrace the vision and apply creative energies to exceed expectations, going above and beyond in order to contribute to the school, district, or educational service center. A fair question to ask is, "What produces a compliance mentality?" Kotter views complacency as the culprit, with sources such as too much happy talk, absence of a visible crisis, poor feedback structures, and a punitive climate for candor (1996, page 40). John Maxwell tells us that commitment in others is a function of commitment by the leader, evidenced by a relentless effort to improve practice personally (1999, page 15). Others view commitment as the natural outgrowth of a clearly articulated vision (Boyatzis and McKee 2005, pages 162–164) or a lack of clarity and meaning (Kouzes and Posner 2002, page 177; Pink 2006, page 218).

A particularly insidious challenge regarding the commitment–compliance dichotomy for educators is the reality of having to respond to many masters. Schools are accountable to governmental action at multiple levels, complex funding streams with varying compliance requirements, and public-interest initiatives that may be only remotely associated with teaching and learning. Leaders who recognize the need to limit new initiatives and who go slow in order to go fast in terms of building capacity are, at best, subject to timelines, grant guidelines, and new legislative initiatives that distract from the most important work. Such environments invite compliance and task completion rather than focused collective thinking that improves practice. In addition, the pace of change in terms of educational innovations continually introduces new initiatives before prior initiatives are fully implemented. Teachers and school leaders have become accustomed to being introduced to the newest and best innovation since sliced bread before the ink dries on the previous best idea. We should not be surprised when educators respond with skepticism and a compliance mentality rather than with a commitment to the innovation in a way that exceeds expectations.

What is necessary to lead change in such an environment? Several acts of leadership are required: (1) create a sense of urgency by serving your followers with meaningful data about their work, (2) invite candor by modeling your own vulnerability and rewarding risk-taking that results in learning, (3) clearly describe the intended purpose for each change by identifying the current reality and the preferred reality in terms of benefits to staff as well as to student achievement, and (4) transform compliance to commitment by providing corrective feedback.

Address the sense of urgency by sharing evidence of current challenges, such as the instructional time lost due to office referrals and your willingness to reduce that time by meeting with students briefly outside their classrooms. Charts and tables of data have the same capacity to communicate with adults as nonlinguistic graphic organizers have with students, and school leaders who leverage data to create a sense of urgency can help make the shift from compliance to commitment. This will require closer attention to the data that occurs within your area of influence and operations. It will require that you "sweat the small stuff" and celebrate the small gains and efforts of your staff or faculty.

Candor can be structured in meeting agendas simply by adding an item where team members identify a counterpoint before reaching a decision. Simply by adding that step to the decision-making process, leaders help teams discuss alternate viewpoints. Candor must first be modeled, however, and when leaders can describe a mistake they made and ask for help to avoid repeating that mistake, candor is advanced. A related strategy would be to showcase risk-taking by staff, even when the result was less than desired. Leaders who use local examples, such as a less-than-successful recent bargaining session with the teacher association, or a slightly humorous anecdote from teachers regarding their experience in redirecting students or meeting with parents, model candor just by telling the story. Each and every day, leaders have opportunities to recognize risk-taking and lessons learned, and each time that lesson is communicated, commitment is advanced and compliance thinking is diminished. Candor is willingness to be vulnerable without lowering standards and expectations for high performance, and the decisions and actions of leaders communicate the degree to which candor is valued and whether it is safe for staff to be equally candid. Increase your awareness of the day-to-day opportunities to promote commitment through your own candor and celebration of risk-taking.

Providing the big picture so that all team members understand the purpose of the change can go a long way toward transforming compliance into commitment, and one of the most effective ways is to identify up front the anticipated benefits to justify the time and effort. Sometimes, this requires a clear description of changes that will occur if the desired change is not implemented. In all cases, however, leadership must outline the change sufficiently for team members to see the benefit. For example, if the change is development of common formative assessments by each professional learning community or data team, it would be wise for the leader to describe how the common formative assessments provide a common language for staff to discuss results and share the most effective strategies. The leader may also want to emphasize the obvious benefit of increased opportunity to make informed midcourse adjustments that reduce achievement gaps.

The final suggestion is to engage in corrective feedback where task completion is not quite good enough. Corrective feedback recognizes strengths that are evident but always couples that recognition with a suggestion for improvement. "I really appreciate your attention to detail in completing the safe schools report. Have you considered identifying lessons we learned as part of your summary?" Or, "The process you used to transition from reading to science was extraordinarily effective, losing almost no time at all. Could I call on you to share that process at the next faculty meeting?" Finally, "I loved how you activated prior learning by asking students to use the Pythagorean theorem to solve inscribed angles and intercepted arcs. You might consult with Mrs. Ainsley at the MS, as she has all kinds of strategies to activate prior knowledge in mathematics." All three examples provide positive feedback but also introduce an element to improve the quality of work. Corrective feedback always communicates ideas for improvement, and the message is unmistakable to staff and faculty to get creative to raise the bar and get beyond compliance.

Exhibit 5.2 describes a few *Leadership Maps* items designed to elicit thoughtful reflection about one's own commitment in leadership and to provide an assessment regarding the degree to which commitment characterizes the workplace at school or within the district.

The first sample item in Exhibit 5.2 examines the underlying level of commitment as measured by unsolicited ideas for improvement. Many times,

EXHIBIT 5.2

Leadership Maps Items—Commitment Versus Compliance

ITEM	RANGE OF RESPONSES	
I estimate the percentage of staff who volunteer an idea to improve the organization to me each month at:	More than 90 percent of those whom I supervise	Less than 10 percent of those whom I supervise
It is important that the culture in my school or district be represented by:	Awareness of a collective capacity to accomplish goals	Respect for diverse viewpoints and opportunities for personal growth
Commitment to key schoolwide initiatives or major projects is most effectively encouraged when responsibility is assigned to:	The entire staff or faculty	Individuals who are willing and able to coordinate, communicate, and monitor completion of the initiative
Changes are always described in terms of anticipated benefits to all affected before being introduced.	At least 90 percent of staff would be able to describe a personal example in the past six months	No more than 10 percent of staff would be able to describe a personal example in the past six months

invited commitment represents just another form of compliance, while this item attempts to ascertain the richness of dialogue within the organization. The second item asks leaders to consider a preference for types of commitment, ranging from a collective capacity to opportunities to pursue individual goals. While both represent commitment, the former represents a collective commitment that is deeper and more focused on realizing the vision set forth. The third item refers to the means by which commitment is encouraged, with very different assumptions about commitment. The middle column assumes that commitment is encouraged when everyone shares the same responsibility for completing projects or key initiatives, while the right column assumes that identifying individuals who are passionately engaged around certain projects will demonstrate a deep commitment by the opportunity to facilitate an improvement with some autonomy. Ironically, the assignment of responsibility to individuals is itself a means to distribute leadership (Kouzes and Posner 2002, page 181). These and other items capture the essence of best practices regarding commitment or mere compliance. The final example merely asks participants to assess the degree to which they identify the purpose and benefit of changes prior to their introduction.

Saying "No" to Get to "Yes"

When leaders achieve consensus on key issues, it is something worth celebrating, particularly when faculty or staff members are cognizant of a collective capacity to accomplish goals (see Exhibit 5.2). Such consensus and agreement do not occur automatically or easily, but a schoolwide focus is a powerful predictor of improved achievement and success at leading change. Many refer to such a consensus as "buy-in," a premise valued so strongly that a number of comprehensive school-reform models insist on 80 percent agreement before implementation (e.g., Success for All [Borman and Hewes 2002]). The point in a discussion of leading change is that it is as important as it is difficult to achieve that consensus or tipping point to initiate change effectively. Once it is achieved, it is absolutely critical that the focus be protected and nurtured.

Unfortunately, many valuable and important areas of focus are diluted when other initiatives that may not be as essential to the entire school are introduced. Consider how difficult it is to convene a key meeting when team members have multiple competing priorities and competing meeting schedules. Saying "no" to get to "yes" is a critical skill in leading change, and every time a leader says "no" to an additional initiative, he or she is really saying "yes" to the area of focus.

The problem is most evident in school-improvement efforts, where a

EXHIBIT 5.3

Leadership Maps **Items—Saying "No" to Get to "Yes"**

ITEM	RANGE OF RESPONSES	
A guaranteed and viable curriculum is best represented by:	Agreement by teams about what gets taught, and when	Autonomy and flexibility about what topics to teach, and when
Our improvement plan represents priorities for our organization that can be listed and explained from memory by:	10 percent of faculty or staff	90 percent or more of faculty or staff
Adoption of new initiatives at my school is:	Determined by teacher perceptions of student needs	Made only if ineffective or obsolete practices are also discarded

particular strategy (e.g., questioning strategies for reading) is identified as the focus area for the upcoming year, but in November, a conference introduces a new approach to writing to influential staff members who want to adopt the writing program. When leaders agree to pursue the new program, the initial area of focus is immediately compromised and diluted. Patrick Lencioni put it this way: "If everything is important, nothing is" (2000, page xiii). School improvement or school accountability plans hold great potential for improvement when the focus is protected, but when changes introduced outside of the improvement plan become the area where staff energies and enthusiasm are committed, both the original area of emphasis and the recently adopted one are short-changed. Leaders who respond to extraneous requests with a "no" or "not yet" sustain the focus on what is important and communicate with clarity the school's focus for the year. Leading change requires each leader to carefully weigh decisions in terms of the message communicated about priorities.

Finally, if the written plan represents the most important schoolwide-improvement efforts, then the message will be clear to all stakeholders. If it does not represent what is most important, then even the new writing initiative is vulnerable to the next great suggestion, and there is little chance to build capacity deeply that will be sustained over time. Exhibit 5.3 provides example *Leadership Maps* items.

The first item in Exhibit 5.3 speaks to the importance of a common focus, while the remaining items refer to the degree to which each leader's protection of areas of focus is evident with staff and faculty. Leading change acknowledges the importance of being as strategic in saying "no" to distractions or premature changes as we often are in selecting our top current priorities.

It's All about Them: Leadership Through Collaboration

Leading change requires a fundamental understanding that changes are always implemented by those who follow the leader, rather than by the leader him or herself. In fact, a flawed understanding of leadership assumes that the leader's fingerprints need to be on the change in order for the change to be effective. Superintendents, directors, and principals are constantly tempted with opportunities to associate valued improvements with their name. Real and effective changes will always be associated with the leader anyway, as will real mistakes and failed attempts. Leadership is about empowering others, and servant leadership recognizes that success requires putting those whom you serve first,

---

EXHIBIT 5.4

Leadership Maps Items—Leadership Through Collaboration

ITEM	RANGE OF RESPONSES	
My effectiveness as a leader is most evident by:	The degree to which goals and objectives are completed on time and within budget	The degree to which I influence my staff to successfully realize their potential
My leadership influences the way a team functions by:	Encouraging unguarded debate and passionate exchange of ideas	Promoting unity in an effort to minimize conflict
My staff or faculty report that I invite them to contribute ideas in decisions that affect them.	Less than 10 percent of my faculty or staff would agree at this time	90 percent or more of my faculty or staff would agree at this time

nurturing their potential, and equipping them to do the work well in your absence (Collins 2001, pages 197–198; Boyatzis and Mckee 2005, pages 134–136; Quinn 2004, page 6; Maxwell 2001, pages 17–18; Kouzes and Posner 2002, page 286). The need for leaders to be the lead in public may actually diminish the impact of the change and mitigate against sustaining the desired change. Put simply, *it's not about you. It is all about what you do to create a sense of urgency and meaning for those who are charged with changing practices at the school and classroom levels.* As Dwight D. Eisenhower once said, "Leadership is the art of getting someone else to do something you want done because he wants to do it" (Thinkexist.com, 2009). Exhibit 5.4 presents sample *Leadership Maps* items that address this fundamental aspect of leading change.

The first item in Exhibit 5.4 reveals a leader's viewpoint of success, with the preferred response the one that views success in terms of impacting those whom the leader services. The second item examines team dynamics in terms of promoting a passionate exchange of ideas, while the third item asks leaders to reflect in terms of a reality check about generating ideas.

Leading Is Thinking

One of the most critical elements of high-yield instructional strategies is that the strategy engage students in thinking—an element present in the oft-referenced nine categories of instructional strategies (Marzano, Pickering, and Pollock 2001). Students can complete a Venn diagram by filling in the blanks, or they can compare and contrast concepts, time periods, genres, or species by creating a Venn diagram that illustrates similarities and differences. Filling in the blank using a graphic organizer requires very little thinking, while selecting or creating a graphic organizer requires much higher-level thinking to select the most appropriate nonlinguistic representation. Few educators would argue with the notion that the most effective, most engaging, and most enjoyable learning experience with students occurs when they must think collectively to solve interesting problems and challenges. In leading change, the same principle applies to adults. When we engage adults to collectively apply their best thinking, not only are they engaged, they are also committed; not only are they informed, they are also apt to apply their best energies and expertise to solve common problems.

Peter Senge, in his description of a learning organization, referred to team learning as a critical component (2000, pages 73–77). Stephen Covey defined synergy as the gestalt when the whole becomes more than the sum of its parts (1989, page 263). Covey was referring to the interactions that occur among adults when they work together, and how their collective win–win attitudes and willingness to "seek first to understand, then to be understood" combine to discover real solutions and develop powerful practical innovations. Surowiecki (2004) discovered that teams are essentially smarter than expert individuals, underscoring the need for leadership to leverage the energies, ideas, and expertise of professionals in mindful and meaningful activities. Leading is all about thinking and devoting a considerable slice of time and focus to engender more thinking and smarter thinking among the individuals whom each leader is obligated to lead.

The strategies to lead changes that promote more transformational and smarter team thinking are surprising, because they are so mundane, routine, and day-to-day. Exhibit 1.4 identified ten acts of leadership in which effective and ineffective leaders engage. Some allocate resources carelessly, while others are mindful of the impact of each decision about time, materials, and training. Three of these leadership actions engage the clutch to activate and advance the needed changes, because they facilitate thinking in the workplace in meaningful ways: (1) generating and testing hypotheses, (2) replicating successful practices, and (3) making midcourse corrections. Each action represents opportunities to lead by engaging staff and faculty in reflective thinking and analysis.

Hypothesis Testing

Developing and testing hypotheses in leadership allow leaders to challenge assumptions, root out bias, ask questions that reveal alternate solutions, and insist on evidence to support those solutions or reveal novel breakthrough approaches and opportunities. Leaders who help their staff to step back and question current practices raise the level of professionalism and precision in responding to current needs. They lead change when they respond to suggested courses of action with, "How will that course help us fulfill our mission to close achievement gaps? Do you have any evidence that warrants a change from current practice?" *Challenging assumptions and asking for evidence to support ideas clarify possible alternatives and empower staff to hone their skills, enhance data analysis, and focus efforts to achieve ambitious goals.* Educators who can describe what will be accomplished if certain actions or antecedent structures are put in place foster a culture of evidence where educators examine current practice for correlations with improved achievement. To the degree that hypotheses are generated and reduced to writing, goals are apt to be more precise and action steps to achieve them will be clarified.

Leaders who facilitate the development and testing of hypotheses communicate an expectation for thoughtful design of powerful interventions. They lead change initiatives by equipping others to engage in reflective thinking and analysis. A powerful method to generate questions that lead to powerful hypotheses is to include a process of inquiry in every accountability or improvement plan. Adding a formal inquiry process focuses teams on developing questions about teaching and learning that lend themselves to hypotheses, SMART goals, and explicit, meaningful changes in the action steps and master design of each plan. This area will be developed more fully in Chapter 9, but leaders can advance the quality and quantity of thinking by creating structures.

Replication of Best Practices

The second critical act of leadership that fosters a culture of evidence and powerful thinking is replication of best practices. Here, leaders promote needed changes by being mindful of opportunities created by local successes. This ability to optimize teaching and learning is associated with second-order adaptive levels of change (Marzano, Waters, and McNulty 2005, pages 120–121). Teachers and teaching are treasure chests of innovation and inspiration, but only leadership can create protocols and structures that capture, expand, and apply practices that work the best to as many settings to reach as many students as possible. Leadership alone provides the context for replication. Without the explicit approval of leaders, few teachers feel permitted to advance their strategy with colleagues, regardless of the level of success they enjoy.

In terms of data analysis, replicating good ideas should be the reason we analyze data in the first place, in order to extend what works as quickly and efficiently as possible. Replication is nothing less than the evidence of a dynamic and effective data-management system. If schools fail to replicate best practices or to eliminate ineffective practices, where is the improvement? While schools routinely honor teachers of the year in almost every school district, and virtually all educational organizations recognize success through their associations, few teachers are honored because their most effective practices are replicated. A fair question to ask is, "Why aren't effective practices routinely replicated within schools and across school systems?" One obvious answer is the need for data to provide evidence that such practices are actually occurring. Leaders play powerful roles in generating hypotheses and in gathering and analyzing data to verify those hypotheses. A second, more subtle, barrier to rapid assimilation of best practices and internal replication in schools is reluctance among educators to "toot their own horn." Only leaders can communicate to faculty and staff that it is the obligation of professionals to share effective practices with colleagues.

Consider the polar responses to opportunities in Exhibit 5.5, and assess the

EXHIBIT 5.5

Optimizing Mundane Opportunities for Replication

INCIDENT	LEADER #1	LEADER #2
Teachers identified several instructional approaches as effective across the curriculum, and those that required students to explain reasoning more than three days per week in each class were twice as likely during the first quarter to close achievement gaps; only one-third were as likely to have behavior referrals from their classrooms.	At faculty meeting: "We are observing a pattern in terms of ELL achievement and behavior referrals based on the 'explain your reasoning' strategy we learned in September. Think about increasing the frequency with which you ask your students to explain their reasoning."	At faculty meeting: "I want every PLC to examine the following data I gathered from class-room walk-throughs the past month and draw as many inferences from it as possible. Understand that these distinctions cross content areas, making the results even more com-pelling. Be prepared to report out and plan on devoting your next PLC meeting to applying your best thinking to replicate or extend the successes experienced here."

choices that leaders have in such situations to make replication work for students.

Leader #1 in Exhibit 5.5 missed the opportunity to develop and test a single hypothesis, while leader #2 assigned teams to collect data more consistently, develop the hypothesis, and test it during the coming month. Accountability was established and leadership was distributed with this simple decision. Note how this assignment put in motion the process of replicating what is working; at the same time, it empowered faculty to test the principal's hypothesis based on available data. Leader #2 also used the opportunity to make a midcourse adjustment for each PLC without directing wholesale changes or creating a power struggle. In the day-to-day work of serving as a principal, one leader demonstrated how to lead change, while another missed a key opportunity in the mundane, day-to-day operation of his or her school to improve the quality of teaching. In *Beyond the Numbers* (White 2005), Chapter 9 offers numerous strategies that have since been tested across the country in terms of replication. You may find that resource particularly valuable as you lead change by reflective thinking and empowerment of staff and faculty.

Midcourse Corrections

The final act of leadership that advances a culture of evidence and deep, savvy, smart thinking from staff and faculty is to institutionalize the practice of making midcourse corrections. To lead change effectively, leaders need to create multiple opportunities to review progress toward goals and the degree to which implementation is thorough and at standard. Such reviews present opportunities to adjust instruction, modify curriculum, and refine delivery rather than observe gaps in achievement and practice without agile and powerful interventions.

For schools or district departments, such reviews are not unreasonable every six to eight weeks. For PLCs and DTs at grade or departmental levels, such a process should be a deliberate part of monthly meetings. Reviews promote reflective thinking merely by posing the Dr. Phil question, "How is it going, really?" Teams at all levels need to become fluent in thinking together about the purpose and power of their actions; they also need to be empowered with the authority to alter directions and redefine strategies to reach more students more effectively tomorrow than is being done today. Leaders will lead changes in practice merely by creating these opportunities and welcoming changes

---

EXHIBIT 5.6

Leadership Maps Items—Leadership as Thinking

ITEM	RANGE OF RESPONSES	
I estimate the percentage of staff who volunteer an idea to improve the organization to me each month at:	More than 90 percent of those whom I supervise	Less than 10 percent of those whom I supervise
My staff members expect me to challenge their assumptions and test specific hypotheses for improvement.	At least 90 percent of staff would be able to describe a personal example in the past six months	No more than 10 percent of staff would be able to describe a personal example in the past six months
Midcourse adjustments are not only permitted, but encouraged in my area of responsibility.	No more than 10 percent of staff would be able to describe a personal example in the past six months	At least 90 percent of staff would be able to describe a personal example in the past six months

midstream during a school term, district fiscal year, or program cycle. The process also invites and models an evaluation process at intervals that are frequent enough to advance a culture of evidence. Exhibit 5.6 describes example *Leadership Maps* items around leadership as thinking.

The first item in Exhibit 5.6 addresses the issue of replication, revealing to leaders the degree to which ideas are generated and discussed to improve effectiveness. The second item refers to the degree to which hypotheses are generated and tested at the school or within the department, and the third example asks for evidence about the extent to which midcourse adjustments are made within the organization. These and other items are a critical part of *Leadership Maps* that helps leaders ascertain the degree to which their leadership invites reflective thinking and analysis to lead and sustain change.

Clarity Over Certainty

Change always introduces uncertainty and often a sense of loss and fear (Evans 2001, pages 21–27). During such times, a common language is essential, preferably using familiar structures and terminology. Because changes frequently require new learning and some degree of unlearning, clarity in purpose, promise, and protocol is absolutely essential. Like every aspect of leading change discussed in this chapter, clarity is not guaranteed or even likely without a deliberate, conscious effort by leaders to provide it.

Clarity of purpose connects the change initiative to the vision, to the greater purpose being pursued (e.g., student achievement, closing of achievement gaps, equal opportunity, path to prosperity, informed citizenry). If the change involved is a tactical change, such as a time-saving protocol for purchase orders, leaders should never assume that the purpose is evident; rather, they should take the time to illustrate the degree to which time and resources will be saved and materials and resources delivered more quickly and at lower costs in terms of time and effort. If the change involved is a major one, such as the development of common formative assessments across departments and grade levels, the leader must demonstrate how the change will improve student achievement or staff performance beyond current levels by providing evidence that the practice is an antecedent (predictor) of excellence.

Clarity of promise helps adult learners, reluctant learners, and even resistant learners understand how the change will benefit them in time. Clarity of promise allows us to connect with staff and faculty who are accustomed to the "flavor of the month" change initiative to understand that the change is worth the effort and perhaps the sacrifice of old ideas. Attention to early gains and frequent monitoring helps clarify the benefit by demonstrating improvements in achievement, efficiency, or degree of implementation by staff. If the change requires professional development and an unfamiliar degree of collaboration, the effective leader will lead the change initiative by assuring involved staff of support structures being instituted to bridge between current practice and the desired level of practice (e.g., available coaching, refresher supports, and celebration of early gains). Anything less fails to provide clarity when it is needed most.

Clarity is also critical in terms of protocols, or well-defined procedures. This has the dual benefit of providing each staff or faculty member with a means to replace the previous standard operating behaviors with a process that allows the teacher or staff member to practice changes supported by professional development and coaching. When teachers are given a means to post standards, or when classroom walk-throughs consistently monitor higher-order questioning, protocols allow faculty to begin to practice the changes desired.

EXHIBIT 5.7

Leadership Maps Items—Clarity of Purpose, Promise, and Protocol

ITEM	RANGE OF RESPONSES	
How do you best advance an important change initiative in your department, district, or work unit?	Through the chain of command relying on administration to ensure implementation	Through highly respected, non-administrative personnel who can influence colleagues
Steady, incremental change requires:	Incremental changes in practice	Dramatic, well-defined changes in practice
Introduction of important changes warrants:	Incorporation of existing language and procedures into desired changes	A clean break in language and procedures from past practice
The purpose of major changes introduced at my school/district in the past year can be described by:	At least 90 percent of faculty or staff accurately in their own words	Less than 10 percent of faculty or staff accurately in their own words

To illustrate the power of clarity in protocols, consider the degree of implementation of standards-based instruction if neither of these protocols (for posting standards and for focused classroom walk-throughs) was provided. Clarity in protocols goes beyond what leaders communicate verbally or in writing (clarity of purpose and promise) by providing a means for those implementing the change to embrace it. Exhibit 5.7 describes sample *Leadership Maps* items designed to examine how leaders provide clarity as part of their repertoire in leading change.

The first item in Exhibit 5.7 inquires about the best way to introduce a change, recognizing that change rarely occurs in a linear or hierarchical manner, while the second item describes the need for clarity of protocols in advancing any change initiative. The most successful changes are explicit and provide a well-defined bridge from current practice to the desired change in practice. The final items examine the degree to which leadership has equipped staff and faculty to understand the purpose of the proposed change.

These final items estimate the depth of clarity across the organization and delineate the process used by leaders to activate prior knowledge and learning so that they can establish and institutionalize the change.

Becoming the Change You Desire

Leading change is much more challenging than identifying what needs to change or even developing a meaningful, practical vision of a preferred future. To lead change, leaders must be able to discern where to go and why, and they must be vigilant and ready to respond to unforeseen events and unintended consequences. To lead requires a deep understanding of yourself (Hallmarks of Excellence® 2007), the maturity to balance personal and professional demands, and the discipline to ensure execution with deep and quality implementation. Chapters 9 and 10 will go into greater depth in these areas, but this chapter described six opportunities for leadership to be demonstrated in the day-to-day operations of schools and district departments.

The lesson of relationships and distributed leadership is simply that relationships are best developed through a process that empowers followers to become leaders themselves. Strategic efforts to distribute leadership by identifying champions of projects, and even champions of tasks within projects, distribute and expand leadership capacity by placing those individuals most skilled and most passionate about practices in positions to see them implemented well.

To lead change, a compliance mentality must be replaced by increasing levels of commitment, a process that is advanced when leaders acknowledge quality work and effort to date but consistently suggest next steps and collaborative networks. *Leadership Maps* addresses issues of feedback, candor, and well-defined expectations to lead change.

Saying "no" to get to "yes" protects focus. When leaders recognize that deep implementation in one area almost always bleeds over into improved practice in another, they realize the power of doing one thing very well.

The fourth area recognizes that leadership is less about the leader and more about the ability of followers to embrace the vision and employ their own creativity and passion to see the vision realized. The most effective leaders introduce changes with as little fanfare as possible, using familiar structures and language to launch needed changes. To make any meaningful change a reality worth sustaining, the emphasis must help others see the change as their own.

Leading change requires challenging work that stimulates intellectual curiosity and encourages collective creativity and wisdom. Leadership in action means that reflective thinking, reliance on evidence, and the development of hypotheses for improvement become routine at all levels. Leadership celebrates and advances thinking.

Leading change requires clarity in the face of uncertainty, where leaders describe the purpose of proposed changes, the promise of more effective practices to students and teachers, and clarity in protocols to implement the change. Effective leaders overcome resistance to needed changes by communicating why they are needed, who they benefit, and how the changes will become a reality.

Acts of leadership determine the degree to which changes bring improvements that can be sustained. *Leadership Maps* challenges leaders to take advantage of those opportunities every day by assisting them to be mindful of the impact that their decisions, attitudes, and questions have on others.

Reflection

Big Idea

Leading change requires mundane acts of leadership.

Why are the acts of leadership (Exhibit 1.4) referred to in this chapter as mundane, requiring one to roll up one's sleeves and sweat the small stuff?

Which acts of leadership support transformational changes that can be sustained? Why?

Big Idea

Relationships are developed through distributed leadership.

Why might this be true?

To what degree are both of these big ideas related?

Big Idea

Leadership is thinking.

How might development and testing of hypotheses improve the quality and quantity of reflective dialogue within an educational unit or school?

Why is active, collective team thinking critical to leading change?

Big Idea

It doesn't matter who receives credit for changes as long as the change is an improvement over current practice.

Describe at least three actions you will take to create a sense of urgency for faculty and staff that will advance needed changes within your organization.

CHAPTER 6

Creating Your Own Leadership Maps

"Where am I?
Do you want to know where I am at this very
moment? And how to get from here to
absolutely anywhere? I'll tell you with the help
of a few maps."

HARVEY WEISS 1995, page 6

Weiss's book for children illustrates so clearly the purpose of maps everywhere, and *Leadership Maps* is no exception. Professionals who use *Leadership Maps* will have access to thirty validated, reliable, discrete maps that are closely aligned with current research across the eight domains reviewed in this volume. Each map, whether twenty-five items or one hundred, has been calibrated to assist leaders to better understand practices that have predictive value for improved achievement (antecedents of excellence). Each map will also help leaders to assess, with precision, the degree to which that understanding has translated into application and action for deep implementation. When antecedents of excellence are both understood and applied, the likelihood of sustaining success and instituting these professional practices into a culture of schools is greatly enhanced.

Leadership Maps elaborates on the theory of action depicted in Exhibit 1.1. Do you want to know where you are at this very moment? That guiding question is what Chapter 6 is designed to answer. It will provide strategies to access *Leadership Maps'* thirty maps and offer some tools to design your own *Leadership Maps* in areas that are unique to the local context and that reflect the challenges faced by each leader. Realtors routinely tell us that the value of real estate is all about location, location, and location, providing an axiom that is applicable to educational leadership, which is all about local context, local context, and local context. Hence, this chapter will equip you to advance your own understanding of what works and why, using your own antecedent variables and performance measures in the process. Mapping leadership is primarily a process of self-assessment, and your participation is key to your success. For that reason, this interactive chapter has been placed in the center of the discussion regarding the eight domains of *Leadership Maps*. The scoring process described in Chapter 1 relies on reflective, accurate, and candid responses from you as a leader regarding your understanding of best practices, professional disciplines, and estimates of depth of implementation with staff and faculty.

Leadership Maps is a self-assessment of practice, values, and vision. The next section offers fifteen practical ways to access and utilize the thirty maps that serve as the foundation of this growing body of research around leadership.

How to Use *Leadership Maps*

Leadership Maps is organized around the framework in Exhibit 6.1.

In the hypothetical example of Exhibit 6.1, scores vary from 30 percent for understanding and application of high-yield leadership and instructional

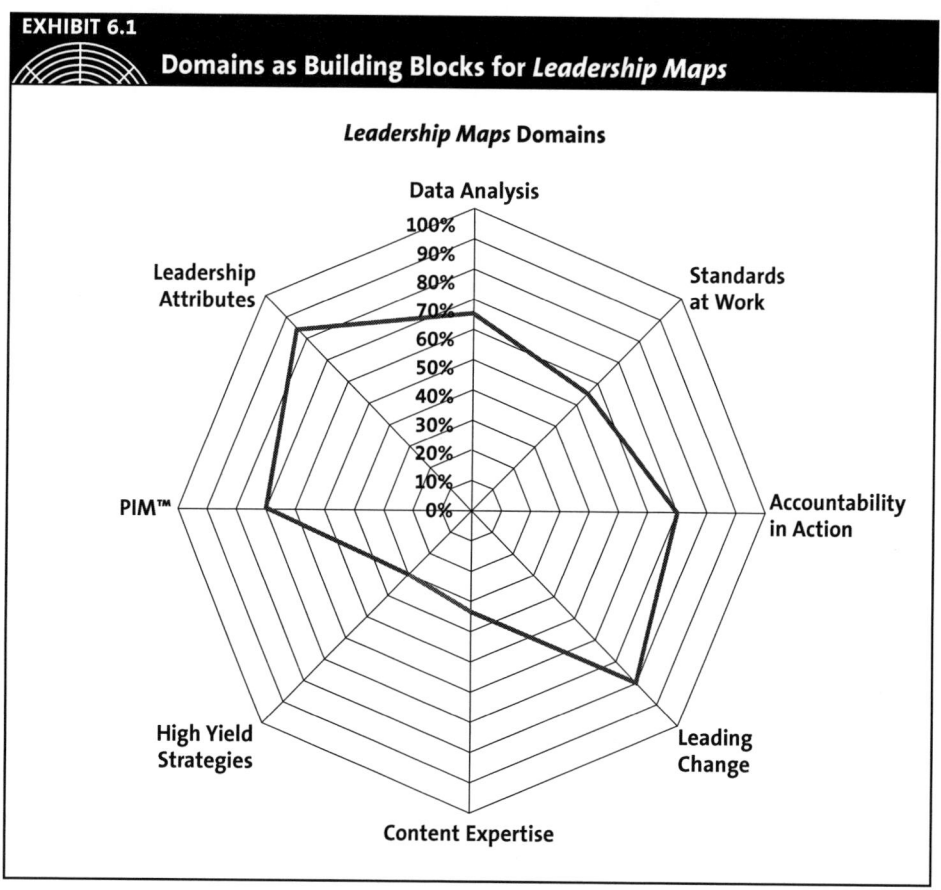

EXHIBIT 6.1

Domains as Building Blocks for *Leadership Maps*

Leadership Maps Domains

strategies, and a limited expertise in academic content (35 percent) to 85 percent in terms of leadership attributes and 80 percent for leading change. Leaders clearly possess the qualities of courage, discipline, commitment, vulnerability, and resilience needed to lead successfully, and they understand the difficulties and challenges in leading change, but their knowledge base in terms of effective strategies and content will limit their effectiveness.

Seven maps assess the interaction of these domains for leaders at the campus level (principals and assistant principals), and seven maps assess the same interaction for central-office administrators and superintendents. They vary from the comprehensive, 100-item assessment that requires approximately forty-five to sixty minutes to complete on-line to a series of twenty-five- and fifty-item assessments that can be completed in fifteen minutes and thirty minutes, respectively. The purpose of these maps is to assess individual leaders, leadership teams, and supervisors in identifying strengths, determining the professional development needed to improve practice, and examining the interaction of each domain variable. Each assessment provides a balanced number of items in each domain so that participants can have confidence that the map result they receive for shorter item assessments reflects their leadership as clearly as the extensive, 100-item assessment.

Sixteen additional twenty-five-item maps represent the eight domains of *Leadership Maps*, with two maps per domain. These maps provide additional depth to leaders who seek to improve their understanding and practice in specific domains. Together, twenty-three maps are available to individuals, and thirty maps are available to districts (central-office and building-level principal assessments) to review performance within and between domains. This section suggests eight ways to utilize the annual subscription period most effectively.

Using *Leadership Maps* As Formative Assessments of Leadership

Participants begin with a 100-item map self-assessment introduced at either one of The Leadership and Learning Center's institutes (Leaders in Transition; Senior Leaders), followed by twenty-five- and fifty-item assessments throughout the remainder of the subscription year. This process enables schools and districts to monitor changes in practice and understanding. In addition, it offers a forum for discussion and reflection that is separate from a review of student achievement and is focused exclusively on leadership. Exhibit 6.2 illustrates a suggested sequence based on The Leadership and Learning Center's Leaders in Transition and Senior Leaders institutes mentioned above. Because many participants take *Leadership Maps* as part of these institutes, sequences have starting points in both June (Leaders in Transition) and November (Senior Leaders). Participants may

EXHIBIT 6.2

Suggested Sequence—Comprehensive *Leadership Maps* by Length

	Jan	Feb	Mar	Apr	May	June	July	Aug	Sep	Oct	Nov	Dec
Leaders in Transition (June–May)		25		25	50	100		25		25		50
Senior Leaders (November–October)	25		25		50	25		25		50	100	

design their own schedule, but the sequence is offered as a viable way to form leadership understanding and apply antecedents for improved performance.

For leaders who do not attend either institute, a simple calendar-year sequence is offered with the same six- to eight-week intervals. Exhibit 6.3 illustrates this sequence.

EXHIBIT 6.3 **Comprehensive *Leadership Maps* Sequence for Calendar Subscriptions**

	Jan	Feb	Mar	Apr	May	June	July	Aug	Sep	Oct	Nov	Dec
January–December	100		25		25	50		25		25		50
July–June		25		25		50	100		25		25	50

For comprehensive *Leadership Maps* that examine all eight domains, the 100-item assessment provides a baseline to monitor the formative changes that follow.

Leadership Maps by Domain

Leadership Maps offers sixteen domain-specific maps to build capacity in strengths and areas of challenge. Exhibit 6.4 suggests a sequence for the hypothetical leader whose profile was referenced in Exhibit 6.1, assuming a calendar-year sequence. It will provide leaders with a sequence for assessing the interaction between domains with the seven comprehensive *Leadership Maps*.

EXHIBIT 6.4 Comprehensive *Leadership Maps*— Strengths and Challenges Scenario

	Jan	Feb	Mar	Apr	May	June	July	Aug	Sep	Oct	Nov	Dec
Strengths— Leading Change (LC) and Leadership Attributes (LA)	100	LC		LA		50		LC		LA		50
Challenges— Content Expertise (CE) and High-Yield Strengths (HYS)			CE		HYS				CE		HYS	

Note how, in Exhibit 6.4, the strengths and challenge domains are assessed twice and repeated, while the assessment strategy continues to access the comprehensive maps three times annually. Also, by staggering strengths and challenges, leaders can examine their leadership from multiple perspectives throughout the year (eleven months of formative leadership assessment).

Let's consider a scenario where the leader has a balanced profile with little variation between any of the eight domains. In that case, the leader may want to examine the degree of implementation and understanding across all eight domains.

Exhibit 6.5 depicts a schedule that probes all eight domains, but continues to anchor the assessments with comprehensive probes into leadership in practice.

EXHIBIT 6.5 Comprehensive *Leadership Maps*— Sequence for Domain Assessment

	Jan	Feb	Mar	Apr	May	June	July	Aug	Sep	Oct	Nov	Dec
Domains Data Analysis, Making Standards Work, Accountability in Action, Leading Change, Content Expertise, High-Yield Strategies, PIM™, Leadership Attributes	100	Data Analysis	Making Standards Work	Accountability in Action	Leading Change	50		Content Expertise	High-Yield Strategies	PIM™	Leadership Attributes	50

EXHIBIT 6.6

Leadership Maps for Coaching Purposes

	Jan	Feb	Mar	Apr	May	June	July	Aug	Sep	Oct	Nov	Dec
Strengths	100	1st	2nd	3rd		50	4th	5th	6th			50
Challenges			1st	2nd	3rd			4th	5th	6th		

Two other scenarios reveal the flexibility provided to leaders through *Leadership Maps,* as two coaching situations are depicted in Exhibit 6.6. The first presumes that the focus of reflection for the year is to deepen areas of strength, while the second presumes reflection throughout the year on areas of challenge.

The situation depicted in Exhibit 6.6 allows leaders to probe for improved performance and understanding through six formative assessments in a selected strength area and six formative assessments in an area of weakness—again, anchored by probes across domains. Conceivably, participant leaders and teams could access all thirty maps without limit by spacing assessments monthly and varying the domains assessed to provide optimal benefit. The specific months recommended are merely based on entry points with entry points for each subscriber. The self-assessment and reflective benefits of *Leadership Maps* will not be fully realized unless leaders have the ability to create their own maps by comparing performance levels with self-selected antecedent practices and conditions for learning. The following section describes how leaders can develop their own *Leadership Maps* easily and as frequently as they like.

How to Create *Leadership Maps*

Creating *Leadership Maps* is simply the process of determining the relationship between student achievement and adult actions to improve achievement. When we discover strong, positive relationships between what educators do and successful gains in achievement, their actions become predictors of improvement or antecedents. It matters not whether the action was adopting a particular program, implementing a high-yield strategy, establishing a new protocol, or providing time and opportunity in a structured way. We know from the research, for example, that the added focus provided by posting standards for each lesson is an antecedent condition that is predictive of improved student achievement. We also know that increased use of nonfiction reading and writing is a predictor of improved achievement, as is frequent data analysis, explicit feedback, collaborative scoring of student work, use of metaphors across the curriculum, and the macro-strategy—reciprocal teaching (Reeves 2002b, pages 92–96); Marzano 2007, pages 34–35). We begin by determining the scale for the vertical Y axis (student achievement) and the horizontal X axis (degree to which antecedents are implemented with fidelity).

Scaling for Emphasis and Clarity

The L^2 Matrix described in Exhibit 1.1 plotted performance from a negative -1.0 to a positive +1.0 to represent the most-desired performance in the upper right quadrant, and the least-desired performance in the lower left quadrant. The simplest *Leadership Maps* can simply be plotted by cross-tabbing results from a specific student-achievement assessment (Y axis) with a single antecedent practice or condition.

Let's examine the intersection of scores on a quarterly performance assessment for high school English teachers who reference metaphors and analogies in daily lesson plans and who are observed eliciting them from students every week. For the Y axis, teachers may agree that 100 percent of students meeting the standard on the quarterly assessment would represent 1.0; 0 percent would represent -1.0 on the scale; and -0- would represent the dividing line between the standard for proficiency and those falling below that point through the designation -0-. In this way, practitioners can specify different performance levels based on their own standards. In fact, *Leadership Maps* participants are encouraged to assign their own standard of achievement, selecting achievement targets of 50 percent, 60 percent, 70 percent, 80 percent, and 90 percent as the performance level they would accept to distinguish leading and lucky from learning and losing ground. For Exhibit 6.7, let us assume that the assistant superintendent for Instruction set the midpoint standard at 70 percent for student achievement. Zero on this scale represents a threshold, as he or she expects schools to score above the line and views any achievement below 70 percent as problematic.

For the X axis, the antecedent measure for our example is simply the number and percentage of teachers who formally utilized a metaphor or analogy in daily written work for the past two weeks. For the X axis antecedent scale, the assistant superintendent of instruction set the midpoint at 72 percent, or five of the seven teachers. Hence, our example has a reasonably high standard for both achievement and implementation during the initial quarter of the school year. Now, estimate the results that are found in Exhibit 6.7 for three hypothetical high school English departments.

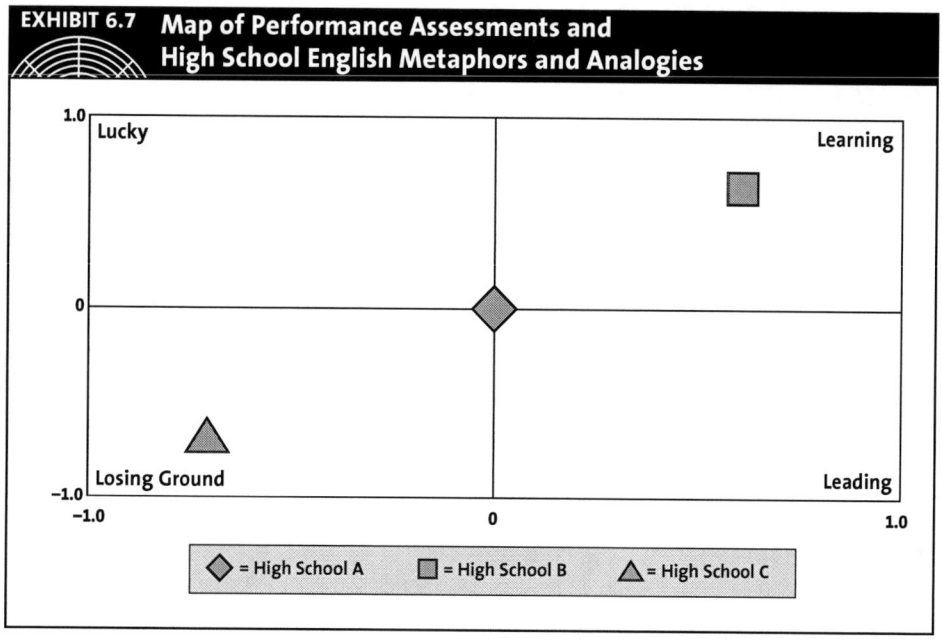

EXHIBIT 6.7 **Map of Performance Assessments and High School English Metaphors and Analogies**

◇ = High School A   ◻ = High School B   △ = High School C

Did your calculation from Exhibit 6.7 agree with the following?

Degree of Implementation		Proficient on Quarterly Assessment
High School A	5 Teachers (72%)	**70 percent** of Students
High School B	6 Teachers (87%)	**85 percent** of Students
High School C	3 Teachers (43%)	**52 percent** of Students

Note that if you examine one antecedent and one assessment result, the *Leadership Map* is instructive regarding current practice. In addition, it reveals practices that should be continued, expanded, replicated, or discarded. In our hypothetical *Leadership Map*, the assistant superintendent would see a very clear correlation between student achievement based on the use of metaphors and analogies in high schools. Consider what practices you want to map against which assessments of learning and performance.

Scaling need not adhere to the -1.0 to 1.0 framework, as a simple percentage scale would have worked in our example. However, many leaders will benefit from examining performance data in terms of gains in scores from year to year and in multiple-year trends. In this case, a continuum that offers both positive and negative gain scores is particularly helpful in discerning what is working and what is not. The antecedent scale for the example presented above has been calculated by the number of teachers or by the proportion of classrooms where the antecedent was practiced. At each school of seven teachers, the total possible number of antecedent possibilities is thirty-five, and the dividing line between proficient and not proficient at twenty-five classes would represent the same proportion as the 72 percent level described. Several different measures are possible for both the Y and X axes, and the level of precision is contingent only on the degree to which antecedents are defined, measurable, and monitored to gather and analyze results.

How do you plot multiple and apparently unrelated measures, such as schools with after-school tutoring or credit recovery (yes–no dichotomies), or numbers of students passing AP exams where enrollment and pass rates are more important than percentages or averages? In these cases, a common scale is needed, such as the leadership–learning -1.0 to 1.0 continuum, or values from 0 to 10. The essential element is that the continuum defines excellence, proficiency, and insufficient evidence adequately, and that the continuum weights the component parts fairly.

The Y Axis: Achievement and Performance

The vertical or Y axis represents the achievement and performance outcomes (effects) that are valued by leaders and the educational communities they serve. Three kinds of performance outcomes will be described: (1) assessment outcomes, (2) leading indicators of student achievement, and (3) lagging indicators of student achievement. Each category and the individual performance data identified within these categories are possible effects that leaders may select for their tailored and individualized *Leadership Map*. Let's begin by examining student achievement assessments, the most common form of data and the data most commonly accepted as evidence of success (Exhibit 6.8).

How to Establish a Scale of Measurement

The wagon wheel icon from *Beyond the Numbers* (2005, pages 114–120) is included in Exhibits 6.8, 6.11, 6.12, 6.14, 6.15, and 6.16 because it offers a consistent means to chart assessment findings on the vertical Y axis even though selected assessments frequently use differing scales. For example, state or provincial assessments may be reported in percentile scores or percent proficient or above, while performance assessments are more apt to use four- to six-point rubric delineations. Comparisons of assessments on discrete content strands, such as Dynamic Interventions for Basic Early Literacy Skills (DIBELS) reading fluency, offers three levels. Northwest Educational Assessments use RIT scores at a completely different scale, and grades present another scale of performance on

---

EXHIBIT 6.8   **Range of Possible Student Assessments for Tailored *Leadership Maps***

Assessments	

• High-stakes state/provincial annual assessments
• Common formative assessments
• Quarterly district benchmarks
• Commercial diagnostic and standardized assessments (ITBS/ITED, NWEA, DIBELS, DRA, ITBS)
• Grades
• Gain scores (+/−) on any of the assessments above to reveal trends and patterns
• Performance assessments (career and tech ed, fine and visual arts, performing arts, etc.)
• Content-specific assessments by strand:
    • Reading, vocabulary, comprehension, phonemic awareness
    • Writing by trait, process, genres
    • Math by number sense, algebra, measurement, problem-solving
    • Science by concepts, inquiry, labs
    • Social studies by concepts, time periods, movements
• PLC/DT intervention, pre–post assessment data
• Achievement gains by student subgroup
• Action research findings
	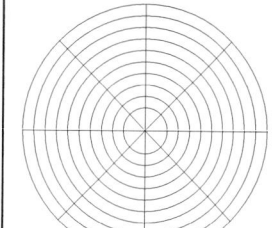

---

assessments. Appendix B provides explicit directions to create "wagon wheels" for divergent types of data.

Exhibits 6.9 and 6.10 provide illustrations. Exhibit 6.9 shows a simple 1:1 cross-tab between state assessment results in reading and adherence to five dimensions of reading: (1) instruction based on ongoing assessment, (2) phonological and linguistic skills through five discrete instructional strategies, (3) reading comprehension, (4) oral and written language, and (5) explicit use of model content standards for literacy instruction. This exhibit has a single point where achievement on the state assessment intersects in terms of student achievement results where teachers apply the selected reading model. The Y axis represents achievement for those students on overall reading on the state assessment in participating classrooms, and the X axis represents the percentage of teachers observed implementing all five components in lesson plans every week. Exhibit 6.10 represents the same classrooms but includes achievement on the state assessment by reading domain, performance by students on common formative assessments, grades, and performance in science and social studies—disciplines requiring students to apply their reading skills with increasing precision and clarity.

Exhibit 6.9 provides some insights into the effectiveness of the selected reading approach, while Exhibit 6.10 reveals how students participating in the program performed on a whole range of assessments. Exhibit 6.9 reveals some correlation between reading achievement and success on the state assessment, and Exhibit 6.10 reveals a wide variation in student achievement for classrooms participating in the reading program on differing assessments and on differing components of reading. The *Leadership Map* in Figure 10 offers the school or district insights into the degree to which assessments were aligned; raises questions about the delivery of instruction; and may help explain what practices warrant replication and what practices require additional monitoring, practice, refinement, or even abandonment. The power of the *Leadership Map* is evident in this example, as a wide array of distinctions in student achievement can be evaluated in terms of this single antecedent (implementation of the selected reading model). For content areas in which success is highly correlated, the practice should not only be continued but probably extended. If there is limited success associated with a particular professional practice, the *Leadership Map* provides the same level of insight in terms of lessons learned. The remedy is to discontinue or scale back rather than continue or extend. Leaders who are able to cast a wider net in terms of assessments will discern with greater precision what is working and what is not. The process of examining multiple antecedents across multiple performance indicators will be described later in this chapter.

Leading Indicators of Student Achievement

Student achievement is the basis for all Y axis data in a *Leadership Map*, but creating maps that look beyond the numbers to identify indicators that provide early warnings or early celebrations of success can be very instructive. The Y axis examines results or effects rather than antecedent causes, and some of the best results indicators are identified by simply identifying "look-fors" that represent observed strengths or obstacles faced by staff and students. The DT process structures PLCs around the work of examining and responding to actual work samples, and student data has as Step 2 in its five-step process the analysis and prioritizing of data by describing strengths and obstacles observed within classrooms.

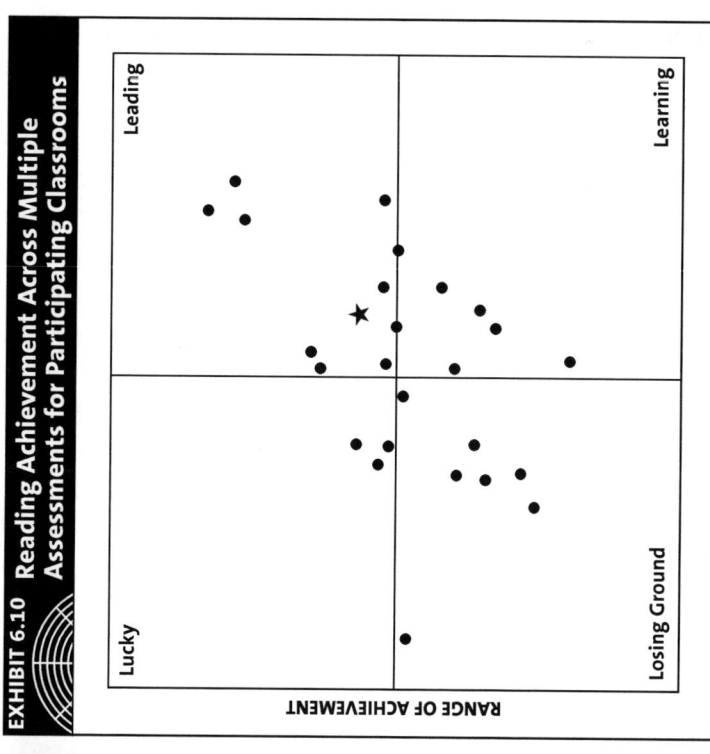

EXHIBIT 6.10 Reading Achievement Across Multiple Assessments for Participating Classrooms

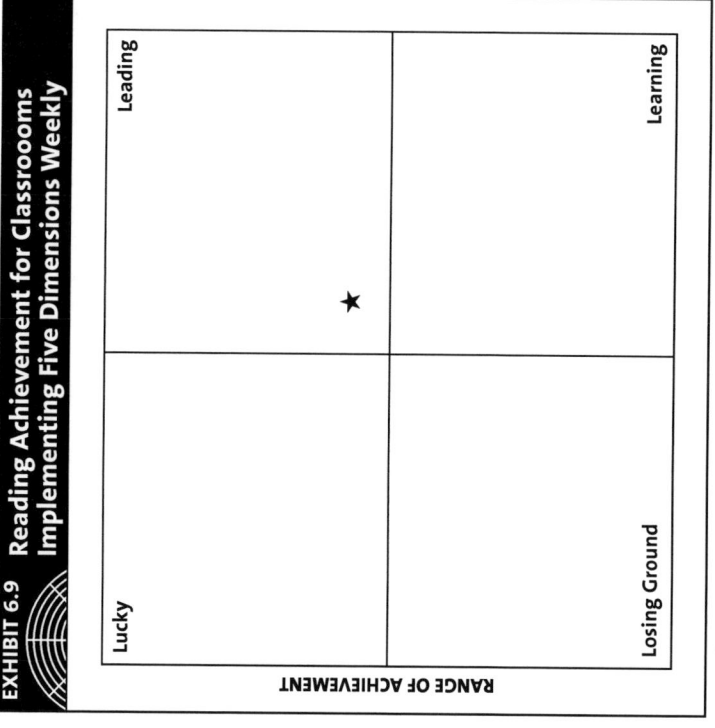

EXHIBIT 6.9 Reading Achievement for Classroooms Implementing Five Dimensions Weekly

Although teams initially struggle with this step, the ability to precisely identify observed strengths, such as "students ask insightful questions about connections to prior learning," or observed obstacles to learning, such as "students are dependent on teacher or peer directives to complete multiple-step activities," offers real insights into teaching and learning. Teams can then develop very effective methods to make high-yield strategies work for their students in the context of those strengths and obstacles that inhibit or promote advancing to the next level. Exhibit 6.11 describes a set of common leading indicators from which to select in order to populate the Y axis of a probing *Leadership Map* with examples for teachers, school principals, and central-office administrators. The locations for analysis are in parentheses.

All of the indicators in Exhibit 6.11 examine results or effects within the

EXHIBIT 6.11

Potential Leading Indicators for Y Axis *Leadership Map* Results

Leading Indicators of Performance

- Safe-harbor expectations for student subgroups will exceed current performance levels for all but Asian students in the coming year based on five-year trends (central office to principal)
- Proportion of students who initiate tasks and complete multiple-step lessons without requiring assistance from a classroom teacher (teacher DTs/PLCs)
- English language learners (ELLs) are increasing 31 percent annually, with no current full-time ELL staff at school (principal to central office)
- Changes in bus driver applicants versus miles per driver (central office)
- Percentage of administrators who can retire in the next five years (central office)
- Participation in student activities for the past three years, all levels (central office)
- Percentage of substitutes who are licensed teachers up 41 percent in three years (central office to principal)
- Teacher attendance for combined reasons declined 2.4 percent in last twelve months (principal to central office)
- Action research findings (DTs/PLCs to principal to central office)
- Percentage of students who come prepared to all classes (DTs/PLCs to principal)

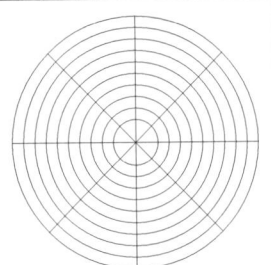

school community; some are very positive, while others are warnings to take action now. The range of possible leading indicators includes information about student strengths and obstacles to their learning, measures of capacity-building for teaching, support personnel indicators of effectiveness, demographic trends, and readiness in terms of administration. All of these data points, however, represent results data—effects rather than causes (antecedents)—and all of them invite action that is proactive.

Lagging Indicators of Student Achievement

Lagging results indicators also help school leaders determine the degree to which schools and districts are on track to improve student achievement. Exhibit 6.12 offers a set of indicators that are often the result of dramatic changes in practice that illustrate a healthy, improving school system. As in Exhibit 6.11, the locations for analysis in Exhibit 6.12 are in parentheses.

Whereas leading indicators tend to be similar to the canary's warning in the coal mine, lagging indicators are reflections of capacity-building and culture. Leaders are encouraged to identify both to get beyond the numbers as *Leadership Maps* are created to address local needs, concerns, and successes with depth and thorough analysis. Note that none of the indicators represent actions of adult educators; rather, they seek to understand the impact of the antecedent actions. Changing grading patterns may be an initiative of the district or school, but the measure of success belongs on the Y axis as an effect of that initiative. In the same way, trends portending that state or federal accountability expectations are outpacing growth rates by student groups are equally powerful indicators of current results—information that is worth paying attention to through tailored, locally developed *Leadership Maps*.

The X Axis: What We Know and Do

The Y axis examines the effects or results of our efforts, but the horizontal X axis examines the adult actions that impact those results. Our ability to identify with some certainty the degree to which our efforts and actions are predictive of improved performance is essential to any serious effort to improve and sustain achievement. The thirty maps that represent the foundation for *Leadership Maps* provide hundreds of items that invite leaders to reflect on antecedent actions and leadership decisions to improve achievement, but this section is designed to elicit the rich and unique practices at local levels. *Leadership Maps* is careful to revise and update its maps to reflect the best of current knowledge about teaching and learning, but nothing can substitute for on-the-ground, current practices to

EXHIBIT 6.12

Potential Lagging Indicators for Y Axis *Leadership Maps* Results

Lagging Indicators of Performance

- Frequency of school improvement goals over time (central office to principals)
- Time lines to establish responses to intervention that reduce achievement gaps (principal to DTs/PLCs)
- Changes in grading patterns from year to year by departments (principal to DTs/PLCs and central office)
- Percentage of students scoring advanced on state assessments (DTs/PLCs to principal to central office)
- English language learners (ELLs) are increasing 31 percent annually, with no current full-time ELL staff at school (twenty-four to thirty-one last year) (central office)
- Staff retention and length of tenure (central office to principal)
- Distributed leadership in terms of faculty and staff serving in leadership roles that extend beyond job responsibilities (principal to central office)
- Number of grant awards aligned to district- and school-improvement goals (central office to principal)
- External publications and policy initiatives impacting the larger school community (county, state, nation) annually (central office to principal)
- Student attendance, absence, and tardiness rates (principal to central office)
- Ratio of As/Bs to Ds/Fs (DTs/PLCs to principal)
- Action research findings (DTs/PLCs to principal to central office)

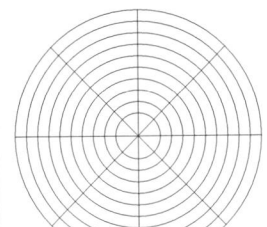

guide the profession in identifying and replicating best practices. This section will discuss types of antecedents and examine the selection of antecedents from the perspective of teaching practice and actions of leaders across both leading and lagging indicators.

Antecedent Identification

Antecedents or predictors are the causes or factors that are correlated to improved student achievement. They are the adult actions and decisions made by educators to make the learning experience for all students as successful as possible. The identification of antecedent routines, strategies, and administrative structures requires a specificity that allows leaders to distinguish types of antecedents, target data collection, and conduct more precise analysis of the factors that influence student achievement. Exhibit 6.13 depicts three major types of antecedents for that purpose: (1) teacher behaviors and routines, (2) instructional strategies, and (3) structures and conditions for learning. For administrators, these three types of antecedents would be represented by leadership behaviors and routines, leadership strategies, and structures and conditions for learning.

Teacher behaviors and routines are often described as instructional strategies, perhaps because so many teacher routines and classroom practices have an immediate and direct impact on student engagement and classroom management. An upstate New York classroom teacher recently reported how she had changed the way she collected student work in class. Rather than the traditional in-basket, where students leave their desks, turn in assignments, and return to their seats to transition to the next task, this savvy teacher had students place completed work on their desk in the upper right corner with a pencil on the top to indicate completed work, proceed to the next content or assignment, and wait for the teacher to come by, examine the work, and score it based on a rubric. The teacher took advantage of the opportunity by also recording grades on her Palm Pilot as she moved about the room. How simple! She saved time on task,

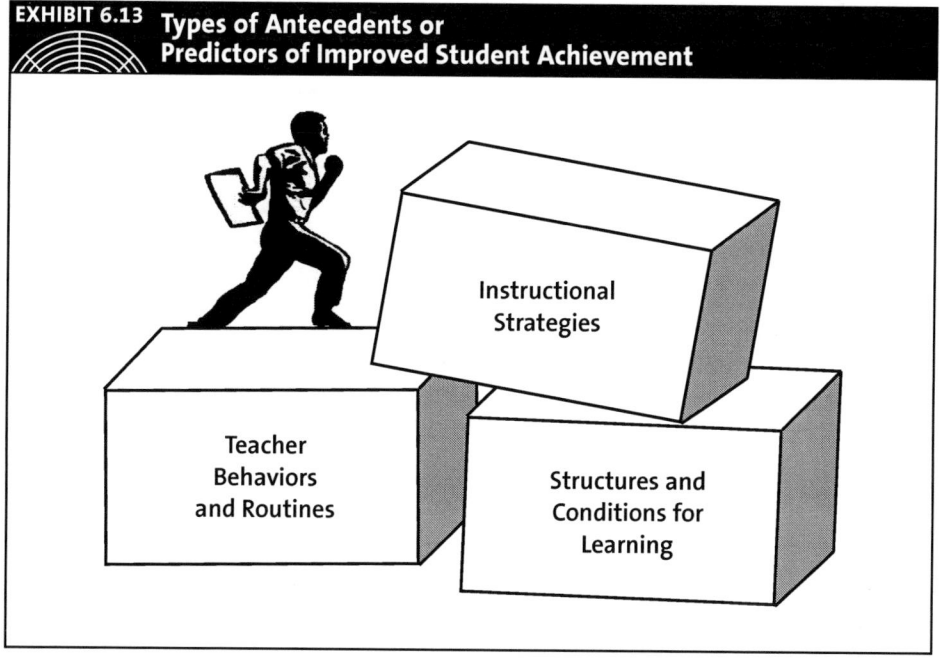

EXHIBIT 6.13 Types of Antecedents or Predictors of Improved Student Achievement

Instructional Strategies

Teacher Behaviors and Routines

Structures and Conditions for Learning

EXHIBIT 6.14

Classroom Routines That May Be Antecedents of Excellence

Classroom Routines as Antecedents

- Redirection techniques
- Homework guidelines
- Closing lesson activities
- Greeting students
- Classroom jobs
- Posting anchor papers
- Use of visuals
- Hands-on activities
- Arrangement of room
- Rework policies
- Classroom rules
- Bell-to-bell teaching
- Teacher-directed and student-directed time allocation
- Ticket-out-the-door

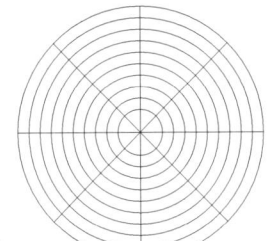

reduced distractions, and actually increased the frequency and immediacy of feedback to students, one to one. Students didn't have to think about it and no special training was necessary, but this teacher behavior was clearly a factor that may contribute to improvements in student achievement. Identifying and monitoring these antecedents may have just as much impact on closing achievement gaps as any highly touted, high-yield instructional strategies that require training, practice, and feedback to master and that engage students to think.

Exhibit 6.14 describes several potential teacher routines to monitor, as each could be the most important change in classroom practice that a teacher or a school could make to improve student achievement. You only need to gather the data and cross-tab that evidence against selected student achievement measures in a tailor-made *Leadership Map* of your choosing.

The list in Exhibit 6.14 is hardly exhaustive, but each bullet represents a practice to help determine whether a relationship is strong enough to warrant replication by others. Data from selected teacher behaviors and routines allows us to populate the X axis data against selected effects measures, such as common formative assessments, classroom grades, or performance on a district benchmark.

Instructional Strategies

Instructional strategies differ from the two other antecedent types in five distinct ways:

1. Instructional strategies are face-to-face teacher–student interactions.

2. Instructional strategies engage students in thinking.

3. Instructional strategies require professional development to acquire proficiency.

4. Instructional strategies require practice and feedback to develop mastery.

5. Instructional strategies are defined by established protocols or parameters.

The research basis is deep and wide that describes high-yield instructional strategies that are predictive antecedents of excellence (Reeves 2008; Marzano 2007; Ainsworth and Viegut 2006; Hill and Flynn 2006; Zemelman, Daniels, and Hyde 2005; Heacox 2002). How to determine the degree of implementation of instructional strategies, however, has had far less attention in the literature. Analyzing that data and making meaning of it are key processes of leadership, and ones that *Leadership Maps* has been created to address.

The five attributes that define an instructional strategy provide a structure to isolate strategies for analysis, and to ensure that data can be reliably gathered on the use or non-use of that strategy. If the instructional strategy is defined too broadly, as in differentiated instruction or inclusion without referring to defined characteristics, every teacher and principal in every classroom could report that instruction was differentiated, and any attempt to measure with precision would be compromised.

Referencing critical elements of instructional strategies assists school leaders in designing a practical monitoring system that measures development and implementation of selected strategies at a standard that all can apply, that is reliable across settings, and that is valid on its face because the strategy has a defined protocol, level of proficiency, and sequence for delivery. When this occurs, broad interpretations of strategies, such as differentiated instruction, are defined with precision. Examples include the seven elements of flexible grouping (Heacox 2002, page 87) or jigsaw strategies with expert and home base sharing to define and monitor differentiation (Gregory and Chapman 2002, pages 100–103).

Teaching and learning are extremely complex endeavors (Darling–Hammond 1997, page 69) and defining the attributes of instructional strategies recognizes that complexity by including detailed, embedded professional development

EXHIBIT 6.15

High-Yield Instructional Strategies as Antecedents of Excellence

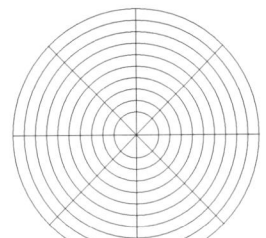

High-Yield Instructional Strategies as Antecedents

- Reciprocal teaching
- Use of missing information as a stimulus for engagement
- Use of three-dimensional, nonlinguistic representation
- Cooperative learning by multiple intelligence strengths
- Five-step writing process
- Madeline Hunter's seven elements of lesson design
- Advanced organizers and questioning techniques
- Cross-curricular nonfiction writing
- *5 Easy Steps to a Balanced Math Program*
- Helping students identify errors in thinking
- Discrete instructional design to ensure student-centered learning; democratic, collaborative process; and cognitive experience
- Generating and testing hypotheses
- Reinforcing effort

applied in practice and refined with feedback. Exhibit 6.15 describes a wide range of powerful high-yield instructional strategies that leaders may choose to populate X axis variables as they develop their *Leadership Map*.

The strategies listed in Exhibit 6.15 range from macro-strategies applicable to any content at any level (reciprocal teaching), to precise targeted strategies (use of missing information or the five-step writing process), to a framework for effective strategies that is student-centered, democratic, and collaborative and that builds on cognitive experience. This list is also far from exhaustive, but it offers leaders multiple opportunities to select practices that have been shown to be antecedents in other applications. The use of Madeline Hunter's (1985) seven-step lesson design grew out of her research on actual practices of highly effective teachers whom she observed. As more and more local school leaders design *Leadership Maps*, it is anticipated that the antecedents that are established as strong predictors of improved achievement will eventually become widely disseminated instructional models. One very clear benefit of using *Leadership Maps* is the framework it provides to discover new antecedent practices with powerful predictive capacity. *Leadership Maps* both anticipate and discover action research opportunities.

EXHIBIT 6.16 Administrative Structures and Conditions for Learning as Antecedents

Administrative Structures and Conditions for Learning

- Percentage and number of scoring guides used by department or grade by quarter
- Dual-block algebra enrollment by semester
- Ratio of number of common planning periods to common plans implemented
- Rubric on expectations for lesson planning posted in each classroom
- Midcourse improvement plan review three times annually
- Schoolwide improvement goal to generate and test hypotheses in every content area
- Reporting requirement that all teachers describe ideas borrowed and ideas given away each week
- Expenditure percentage that directly supports school-improvement goals
- Number of students per semester participating in credit-recovery tutoring (required for students below 2.0 GPA)
- Number of faculty coordinating specific action steps for the school improvement plan

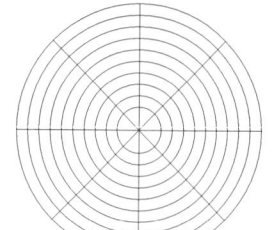

The third type of antecedent is the least likely to be quantified and measured but represents the support system for the preceding two. Examination of administrative structures and conditions for learning is rarely reduced to the data level necessary to indicate whether a practice is working, not working, or in need of some adjustment. In Chapter 1, a conceptual framework of ten acts of leadership (Exhibit 1.4, page 11) was introduced. This framework neatly offers ten routine and common acts of leadership that occur every day in every school and district. Exhibit 6.16 draws measurable actions from each category to populate the list of administrative structures and conditions for learning.

The list in Exhibit 6.16 is also not meant to be exhaustive, as each suggested data point represents a key act of leadership. From lesson plan expectations to midcourse corrections, each example offers a potential antecedent or predictor of improved achievement that is quantifiable and easily accessible to school leaders.

Translating X Axis Data to Create Leadership Maps

Two examples describe ways to examine the impact that instructional strategies have on achievement. Exhibit 6.17 provides a simple 1:1 cross-tab between 5 *Easy Steps to a Balanced Math Program* (Ainsworth and Christianson 2006) as the antecedent and gain scores (+/-) for state assessments of reading and mathematics. A single antecedent data point intersects a combined average for these assessment results where teachers utilized *5 Easy Steps to a Balanced Math Program* in lesson plans every week.

Exhibit 6.18 represents the same classrooms and includes the same assessments (reading and math), but this time the illustration distinguishes implementation across four antecedent practices listed in Exhibits 6.14 through 6.16: (1) classrooms implementing all components of *5 Easy Steps to a Balanced Math Program,* (2) classrooms posting anchor papers that are updated monthly (teacher behaviors and routines), (3) classrooms reporting cooperative learning groupings by multiple intelligence strengths (instructional strategies), and (4) schools requiring that teachers describe ideas borrowed and ideas given away each week to promote replication. The first map (Exhibit 6.17) presents achievement by *5 Easy Steps* districtwide, while the second (Exhibit 6.18) illustrates the varied achievement levels based on degree of implementation of the four antecedents.

Exhibits 6.17 and 6.18 provide examples of *Leadership Maps* developed from the same antecedent (*5 Easy Steps to a Balanced Math Program*). Exhibit 6.17 reveals only that implementation is essentially at the level of chance, as the district implementation is midway to the desired implementation level (full districtwide implementation). The achievement levels suggest that gains are positive but modest. From this data alone, school leaders can infer that the *5 Steps* initiative is producing some gains even though implementation is not as deep as the district prefers.

Exhibit 6.18 takes the analysis deeper by distinguishing results from several antecedent practices. We find that the practice of displaying anchor papers has produced a mixed bag, with some schools implementing fully with virtually no gain in student achievement on the district benchmarks, while others are implementing fully and show dramatic gains. Displaying anchor papers results in scores within each quadrant, and at this point, there is no locally determined relationship between this antecedent and achievement despite the research basis that describes it as a powerful best practice. It may be that our measurement for full implementation lacks rigor, or simply that the practice, separate from other best practices, just does not yield the expected gains. A similar result occurs in terms of cooperative learning from a multiple-intelligence perspective, as schools are found in all four quadrants, and there appears to be no significant relationship between the

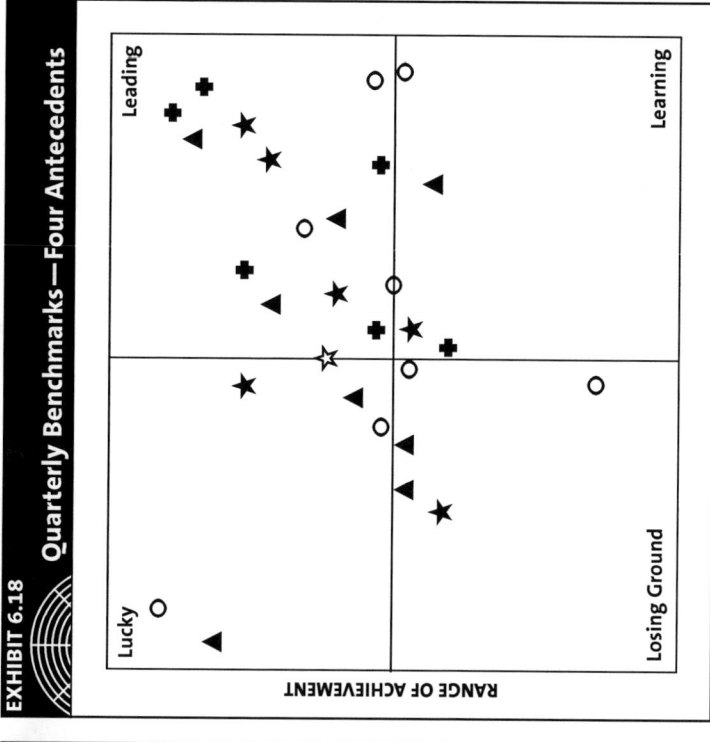

EXHIBIT 6.18 Quarterly Benchmarks—Four Antecedents

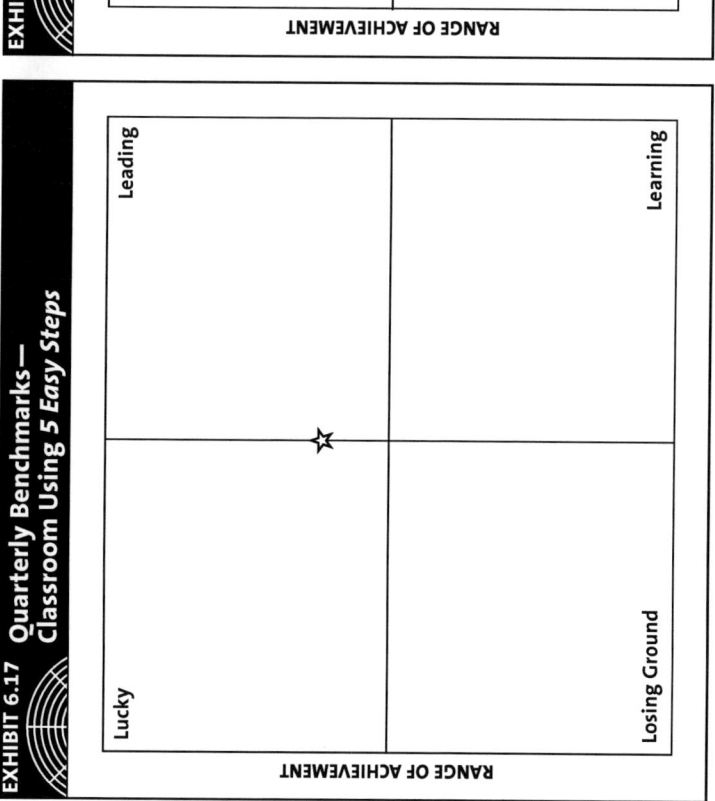

EXHIBIT 6.17 Quarterly Benchmarks—Classroom Using *5 Easy Steps*

LEGEND

☆ *5 Easy Steps to a Balanced Math Program*—all levels

★ *5 Easy Steps to a Balanced Math Program*—grades 3, 4, 5, 6, 8, 10

○ Anchor papers posted in classrooms—grades 3, 4, 5, 6, 7, 8, 9, 10, 11

◄ Cooperative learning and multiple intelligence—grades 3, 4, 5, 6, 7, 8, 9, 10

✚ Ideas borrowed and ideas given away—grades 3, 4, 5, 6, 7, 8

practice and achievement gains. We are able to infer that these component practices are not yet producing the anticipated gain.

Exhibit 6.18, however, reveals a very strong relationship between the *5 Easy Steps to a Balanced Math Program* antecedent and student achievement, as 75 percent of the tested grade levels fall within the leading or learning quadrants. The greater the fidelity of implementation, the more likely there will be gains in student achievement on district benchmarks. This pattern is repeated even more convincingly in terms of the administrative structure to report sharing of ideas to promote replication. The *Leadership Map* reveals that all but one grade level fall within the leading quadrant and that most grade levels show gains that are very close to the desired level. Hence, leaders in this system can glean from this *Leadership Map* that two practices are having a dramatic impact, while two others are not having the anticipated impact locally, even though all four practices are heralded in the field as high-yield strategies. This does not mean that any of the four practices should be discarded, but it does mean that, in this case, posting anchor papers and sharing ideas systematically have had the greatest impact and should be extended systematically.

The Places You'll Go and *Leadership Maps*

Maps like that in Exhibit 6.17 provide some insight (gains are being made and implementation is uneven), but maps like that in Exhibit 6.18 provide clarity in identifying the most powerful elements of a powerful initiative. The potential for creating *Leadership Maps* is limited only by the degree to which leaders are able to define and distinguish strategies, structures, and practices. This is uniquely dependent on your ability to measure the occurrence, frequency, and quality of local professional practices. By cross-tabbing those measures with select achievement measures, the relationships between them become evident, and like the example above, the insights can be highly instructive.

Without such a structure to analyze both results in student achievement and the professional practices that influence those results, our profession will not be able to answer the fundamental question: "What do we do that really makes a difference in our community with our students?" The inability to answer that question has plagued the profession long enough, with the predictable but unintended consequence of single, high-stakes assessments as a single, crude, and incomplete measure of effectiveness. As we describe the four remaining domains of *Leadership Maps,* you are encouraged to begin the process of creating maps that are tailored to the unique leadership challenges faced by your school and district.

Reflection

Big Idea

Leading indicators are the educator's "canary in the schoolhouse."

What actions do leading indicators invite for school leaders? Why is it important to measure results (effects) data other than student achievement?

Big Idea

Gain scores on the vertical Y axis reveal trends and patterns.

We often scale achievement in terms of the percentage of students proficient. Discuss the benefit with colleagues of scaling your leadership maps in terms of +/- gain scores.

To what degree are both of these big ideas related?

Big Idea

Mapping is its own treasure hunt.

Given a preponderance of research advocating for best practices, why is it important to verify such practices locally within your school or school system?

Big Idea

Fidelity of implementation is its own antecedent of excellence.

To what degree do you agree with this statement? Why?

CHAPTER 7

Content Expertise

"It is, after all, the responsibility of the expert to operate the familiar and that of the leader to transcend it."

HENRY KISSINGER 1982

Carol's first teacher observation as a high school principal was an eye-opener. She was transferred midyear after six years at the largest elementary school in the district, and when her superintendent asked her to fill the shoes of an esteemed veteran who had to take early retirement due to a terminal illness, not only did she feel a moral obligation, she also was honored by his confidence in her. School was well underway that November morning, and because Carol had four very competent assistants and probably the brightest secretary she had ever met, her calendar, her contacts, and just about everything went very smoothly. What set her back was her initial teacher observation of the local band director, a legend in the community. Eighty-seven students warming up was followed by a comment from the director about last week's performance at the football game, after which independent practice was continued by most of the eighty-seven students. One student took attendance, a few others in the horn section practiced as a team, and the others enjoyed the social opportunity to visit with friends or line up to speak privately to the band director, who, by now, had retired to his office to receive students one-on-one. Carol sat with her clipboard, awkwardly maneuvered around the room, unaware of the students around her, and the bell rang without opportunity for her to confer with the band director, who had exited through an alternate door. The lesson was over.

Carol knew that the band director was loved in the community and apparently by his students, but the observation was a formal one of two for his three-year evaluation, and nothing at the elementary level had prepared her for this. As a former sixth-grade teacher, then a literacy specialist, then a principal, every lesson observation as a teacher, coach, and principal had been characterized by a clear learning path, explicit feedback, and extensive data-gathering to inform the post-observation conference. Today's experience left her with a pit in her stomach and a sense that something was dramatically wrong.

Carol's experience is not so unusual. In fact, how is it possible to supervise, coach, or evaluate teachers whose content expertise is so different from one's own? Carol attempted to match the expertise of her assistants with their own content experience, but when two of her assistants themselves came from the elementary level—one was a former physical education teacher, and one taught math at the middle school—the effort hardly addressed the problem. For the band director, the drill had been anything but helpful, and this exercise to satisfy the paper requirements for human resources had been a classic example of someone wasting his time for years.

Reeves (2008) found that teachers, as well as administrators, value the opinions and feedback of peers above books or articles, coursework, or even feedback from supervisors. This fact advocates for routine, face-to-face collaboration for teacher teams, and the explosive growth of PLCs, DTs, and whole-faculty study groups attests to a recognition of the power of collaboration. In fact, the most effective leaders work very hard to establish collaborative teacher teams, increase trust levels, model vulnerability, and encourage risk-taking to create a more reflective and professional environment (DuFour, Eaker, and DuFour 2005, pages 23–26; Lencioni 2002, pages 188–190).

The band director would certainly be better served if colleagues who shared his expertise had the opportunity to provide feedback and interact as part of a band director's data team. The problem is, with whom will he collaborate and what peers will review his work? Collaboration with peers is essential for developing expertise, but if you are the only technical education teacher in the district's middle school, or sole band director for the community, or lone art teacher for the elementary school, it may only occur electronically with infrequent face-to-face contact.

Administrators like Carol need to be able to support and supervise the band director. Both pedagogy and content expertise are important, and it is the legitimate, expected, and appropriate role of leadership to provide it. There is plenty to suggest that the role of instructional leadership in coaching, supervision, and evaluation has been less than stellar (Little, Gearhart, Curry *et al.* 2003, page 187; Reeves 2004, pages 1–9; Schmoker 2006, pages 137–139). Keller (2008, page 9) found that, in five short years, the cost of teacher disciplinary action accelerated almost $50,000 per case, and the proportion of cases for teacher discipline or dismissal that resulted in a financial settlement increased almost 50 percent. What content expertise is needed for school leaders to support their faculties across content areas, and what content expertise should central administrators bring to their role as coach, colleague, supervisor, or evaluator of building administrators?

To answer these questions, content expertise is included as one of eight major domains of *Leadership Maps.* This chapter is divided into three sections that examine the notion of expertise, review best practice by content, and identify antecedent structures and conditions for learning related to subject content for diverse learners.

Expertise Defined, Recognized, and Encouraged

The challenge to leaders is to recognize expertise within discrete content areas, encourage its extension within and across disciplines, and offer resources and structures to sustain it over time. Berliner studied expertise across professions (1994, Chapter 7) and identified three ways in which experts differ from novices:

1. Experts bring knowledge to bear more effectively on problems than do novices.

2. Experts solve problems more efficiently and do more in less time than do novices.

3. Experts are more likely to arrive at novel and appropriate solutions to problems than are novices.

Berliner's definition of expertise identifies insights, knowledge, and efficiency as measures of expertise in each content area. The challenge to leadership is to develop a process that elicits information that helps recognize expertise and then to encourage its growth and expansion. For our purposes, we will define expertise as:

> Expertise is the ability to apply knowledge for greater effectiveness with a greater proportion of students (or staff) in the shortest time frame.

Experts do the same work but more efficiently and more effectively than others. They achieve their objectives faster, because they understand their craft deeply and know how to apply that knowledge with greater precision, achieve greater influence on the behavior of students or staff, and demonstrate more consistent implementation of planned improvements.

This definition guides the school leader to engage faculty across content areas to improve their practice simply by providing reflective questions about how teachers address the challenges they face every day. We will now apply this principle of questioning the way teachers apply content knowledge to be more effective, to solve problems, and to create novel applications by returning to Carol's post-observation conference with her band director, Bill.

Carol:	I noticed a high degree of independence for almost all band students this morning, ranging from the horn section's group practice to independent work to your one-on-one conferences with students. Could you describe what you have done to create that level of personal responsibility and initiative?
Director	Students know my expectations for in-class work, field practice, and performance. They also understand what it takes to become first chair and what I expect from those positions (**efficient problem-solving**).
Carol	How do you communicate that and how do you sustain it?
Director	I work with middle school music teachers to prepare kids for our band with written and oral instructions that are fixed. By the time students arrive here, I've met each one personally, and students and parents know the level of dedication and practice necessary to succeed. The first day of class, veteran band members describe my standards, and the benefit of my methods, and every day I recognize students playing to standard and point out students who are playing below standard. I mince no words, and I address each instrumental section every day. In this way, everyone sees excellence and everyone sees an example of not yet at standard. Students know that they will be called out for quality, and they also know that they may be called out for poor quality (**novel and appropriate solutions**).
Carol	That sounds a little harsh. Have you ever lost students or invited a parent complaint by being so direct?
Director	A couple of times early on I saw tears, but I am careful to point out shortcomings with humor, often using the flaw in their play quality to develop an elaborate and ridiculous illustration that

nonetheless makes my point. I point out the impact it has on our next performance, then on the election, or global warming, or the price of cheese—that kind of thing. If a student takes it hard, I ask first-chair students to speak with him or her, and if I need to, I will. I like to stay away from a counseling role, however, because I want every band student to know that I am relentless about excellence (**bring knowledge to bear**).

Carol

I know you just had your second-to-last football game performance. When can I come back when you are doing whole-group instruction?

Director

Thursday would be a good day for you to come in. I am introducing a new piece and you will see how we start and where we end up.

Carol

Sort of like a pre- and post-test within the same lesson, right?

Director

I guess so, but I am very deliberate and adjust when and to what group I give feedback based on the piece (**novel and appropriate solutions**).

Carol

That is fascinating. Could we visit beforehand about that sequence, or would you rather e-mail me with your plan?

Director

Let's do both. My prep is first hour, and we could meet fifteen minutes before class; I'll e-mail you the pattern I will be using later today.

Carol

Thanks, Bill. Given the sixteen disciplines at our high school, I think I can learn a lot from you about differentiating instruction.

Director

I have to tell you that I am pleasantly surprised. Nobody has ever really asked me what I do. They just tell me how wonderful it is, and I knew that already!

Carol's treasure hunt for expertise was able to identify discrete strategies that Bill was utilizing to make his classroom and program very successful: his considerable skill at coordinating very diverse instructional elements; and his creative methods for providing feedback, setting expectations, and reinforcing effort. The classroom that appeared unstructured and chaotic was, in fact, focused, student-centered, and highly differentiated. By helping teachers describe

EXHIBIT 7.1

Leadership Maps Items—Expertise

ITEM	RANGE OF RESPONSES	
I can describe a discrete instructional challenge faced by each subject area at my school.	True of me for all content areas at my school	Not yet true of me with the exception of my own content area
I can describe a discrete leadership challenge unique to administrator assignments (elementary, middle, high school, district departments).	Not yet true of me with the exception of my prior experi- ence level	True of me for all administration levels and depart- ments in my district
I identify and promote expertise with my faculty and staff by:	Creating oppor- tunities for professional development for all	Systematically inviting teachers to describe how they transform challenges into successful practice

how they apply content knowledge to the classroom, leaders engage faculty at the heart of their particular discipline and reveal the three characteristics of expertise: (1) insight, (2) efficient problem-solving, and (3) application of knowledge to novel solutions. Exhibit 7.1 offers a few sample *Leadership Maps* items designed to address content expertise in general.

The first item in Exhibit 7.1 merely asks the site administrator to reflect on the degree to which he or she is cognizant of any instructional challenges associated with a particular discipline. Respondents should be able to identify the challenge of distributing leadership for the marching band, or how to select the right instructional strategy to facilitate learning in the selected physical-activity setting for physical education teachers. The second item causes the central-office administrator to reflect on his or her understanding of the unique challenges of various administrative assignments, such as managing student behavior for bus drivers or the challenge of incorporating core academic applications in exploratory content classes for middle school principals. In item three of Exhibit 7.1, the ability of leaders to identify that expertise and assist faculty or staff to refine it more succinctly, as Carol did in our example, illustrates how leaders can engage their faculties across content areas.

Best Practice by Content

Expertise is inseparable from content, as the skill of leveraging that knowledge most effectively requires a deep understanding of the content. Our example provided a starting point for Carol, where she was able to probe for expertise in a way that both engaged the teacher and informed her about the nuances of teaching band. The core of content expertise, however, is a general understanding of each content area, and it is critical that leaders be familiar with the factors that distinguish reading from mathematics or science from the arts.

Appendix D provides a list of advocacy organizations in academic content standards in reading, writing, mathematics, science, social studies, the arts, health and physical education, career and technical education, special education, and instructional technology for that purpose. Exhibit 7.2 depicts sample *Leadership Maps* items that address content-area knowledge and their application within schools.

Items one and two in Exhibit 7.2 require an assessment of the degree to which knowledge of best practices in writing, science, and math are currently

---

EXHIBIT 7.2

Leadership Maps **Sample Items—Content Expertise**

ITEM	RANGE OF RESPONSES	
The percentage of my reading teachers who are fluent with guided reading, mini-lessons, and at least one writing-trait protocol (e.g., 6+ traits, simple six) is estimated at:	More than 90 percent of my reading teachers	Less than 10 percent of my reading teachers
The percentage of my faculty who integrate science and math by applying the scientific method with graphs, charts, and tables in a major written project at least quarterly is estimated at:	More than 90 percent of the faculty	Less than 10 percent of the faculty
As a leader, my skill and knowledge regarding specific teaching protocols for English language learners (ELLs) are characterized by fluency in at least one strategy and use of a formal protocol for classroom observations.	ELL methods are well-established at my school	I am not yet familiar with methods for ELL students

EXHIBIT 7.3

Leadership Maps Sample Items—Central-Office Content Expertise

ITEM	RANGE OF RESPONSES	
I estimate the percentage of staff who employ a defined protocol or process to complete a routine job task at standard at:	Less than 10 percent of my staff	More than 90 percent of my staff
I estimate the percentage of staff in my work unit or department who implement at least one project requiring cross-training quarterly at:	More than 90 percent of my staff	Less than 10 percent of my staff
I am familiar with industry standards for best practices for my department, and I apply and communicate those leadership practices:	I do not currently monitor process or results	To monitor adherence to standards for processes and results

operational in classrooms, while item three is a reflection of the principal's current skill level with ELLs.

Exhibit 7.3 delineates a similar set of sample items for central-office administrators. Here, the emphasis is more on how central-office administrators apply their knowledge of their departments and work teams so that they will be as effective and efficient as possible.

The items in Exhibit 7.3 for central-office administrators describe a variety of effective practices designed to improve efficiency and effectiveness and develop expertise for staff at all levels. Defined protocols help ensure uniform practices to a prescribed standard and focus efforts as a result. Cross-training builds capacity for planned and unforeseen transitions, and the last item invites administrators to reflect on their current level of fluency with industry standards. For academic-affairs administrators, this refers not only to the academic content standards, but also to administrator standards, such as the Interstate School Leaders Licensure Consortium (ISLLC) standards used widely in both administrative review and leadership preparation (Council of Chief State School Officers 2008).

Exhibit 7.4 describes a range of *Leadership Maps* items that represent best practice for six very distinct content areas for site administrators.

The series in Exhibit 7.4 examines the degree to which content is aligned, how leaders identify the most salient and effective writing practices (Schmoker

EXHIBIT 7.4

Leadership Maps Sample Items—Content Area Best Practice

ITEM	RANGE OF RESPONSES	
At my school, the percentage of art classes that incorporate academic content and assessment in writing, reading, mathematics, science, or social studies is estimated at:	Less than 10 percent of art classes	More than 90 percent of art classes
Teachers at my school report that their supervising administrator understands the power standards for their academic content area:	More than 90 percent of teachers	Less than 10 percent of teachers
At my school, writing is best characterized by:	Use of a common rubric with routine writing assignments in all content areas	Lessons that include continuous explanation, examples, practice, and feedback
Which statement most accurately describes daily mathematics instruction at your school?	Use of consistent fact strategies across math teachers	Making connections to move from concrete to abstract representations
Which statement most accurately describes daily science instruction at your school?	Elaborate explanations in light of plausible scientific alternatives	Curriculum pacing to ensure annual coverage of an ever-expanding science curriculum
Effective instruction in the visual arts is best promoted through:	Frequent display of select student art pieces based on clear criteria	Daily instruction that includes modeling, guided practice, and independent practice

2006, pages 95–96), and the degree to which faculty report that their leader understands the most essential standards in their curriculum. All six items illustrate a very high standard of content expertise and, like all *Leadership Maps* items, provide leaders with a potential measure of the degree to which their leadership has reached and influenced those whom they serve. The middle items refer to principles for best practice for teachers, while the first and last items contrast an effective, cross-curricular teaching process with a traditional approach to visual arts education.

Consider developing a safe, brief measure of the second item about power standards to examine the impact of your current leadership by creating a simple written response or anonymous three- or four-item survey that you administer several times a year. The data will provide a very clear indication of the success of your efforts to understand teaching content by discipline while also communicating your intention and interest in supporting your faculty. Central-office administrators may choose items from Exhibit 7.3 to accomplish the same purpose.

We now turn to the antecedent structures and conditions for learning that are predictive of improved student achievement.

Antecedent Structures and Conditions for Learning

Leadership Maps also addresses structures and conditions that represent best practices, regardless of the subject content. A framework developed by Charlotte Danielson (1996, pages 3–4) identified best professional practices across four simple domains represented by twenty-two distinct component rubrics. Danielson's *Enhancing Professional Practice: A Framework for Teaching* has been widely adopted for teacher supervision and evaluation across North America and used as the basis for multiple negotiated agreements. It also has provided leaders with a viable description of professional practice. The four domains include: (1) planning and preparation, (2) the classroom environment, (3) instruction, and (4) professional responsibilities. Her framework offers leaders the opportunity to quantify a wide range of measures, including the opportunity to integrate unit and lesson planning to more effectively or more consistently engage students and improve achievement. Danielson's work is consistent with the L^2 Matrix of Exhibit 1.1, as it specifies numerous antecedents or predictive practices of improved student achievement.

Zemelman, Daniels, and Hyde (2005, pages 227–265) investigated best practices across content areas to identify a set of seven structures that were evident and recurring throughout the K-12 curriculum:

1. Small-group activities

2. Reading as thinking

3. Representing to learn

4. Classroom workshop

5. Authentic experiences

6. Reflective assessment

7. Integrative units

Representing to learn addresses the value of nonlinguistic representation (Marzano, Pickering, and Pollock 2001, pages 143–155), and reading as thinking recommends the well-known reading strategy KWL (what students **K**now about the topic, what they **W**ant to find out about it, and following reading, what they've **L**earned about the topic). Macro-strategies, such as reciprocal teaching (Rosenshine and Meister 1994, pages 500–511), include some characteristics of representing to learn, and integrative units extend teacher-directed, cross-curricular units to engage students in their design—a process similar to "invitational learning" (Foster 1993, pages 97–100), which is widely adopted in alternative high schools.

The *Framework for 21st Century Learning* (Partnership for 21st Century Skills 2009) examined the demands that today's students will face in an increasingly global and technological society and economy, and school leaders increasingly are aligning school curriculum to it. Kansas, North Carolina, Maine, Massachusetts, South Dakota, West Virginia, and Wisconsin have adopted 21st Century Learning as their primary reform model. The four outcome areas include:

1. Mastery of core subjects and twenty-first-century themes: (a) global awareness; (b) financial, economic, business, and entrepreneurial literacy; (c) civic literacy; and (d) health literacy

2. Learning and innovation skills: (a) creativity and innovation; (b) critical thinking and problem solving; and (c) communication and collaboration

3. Information, media, and technology skills: (a) information literacy; (b) media literacy; and (c) ICT (information, communications, and technology) literacy

4. Life and career skills: (a) flexibility and adaptability; (b) initiative and self-direction; (c) social and cross-cultural skills; (d) productivity and accountability; and (e) leadership and responsibility

A cursory examination of these constructs reveals that the *Framework for 21st Century Learning* integrates best practices by reframing subject-area content into interdisciplinary themes; it supplements that learning with three rigorous process-skill outcome areas. The framework emphasizes the importance of core content—such as English, reading or language arts, world languages, arts,

EXHIBIT 7.5 *Leadership Maps* **Sample Items— Antecedent Structures and Conditions**

ITEM	RANGE OF RESPONSES	
Common formative assessments at my school include specific triggers that initiate midcourse adjustments to instruction:	More than 90 percent of common formative assessments	Less than 10 percent of common formative assessments
High school curriculum is most effective when:	Skill acquisition precedes hypothesis development to create a knowledge base	Hypothesis development precedes skill acquisition to engage students in meaningful learning
Intervention (RTI) model for IEP students:	By monitoring all six components	I am currently unaware of the RTI components for IEP students

mathematics, economics, science, geography, history, government, and civics—but places its emphasis on the application of such skills through effective communication, innovation, and critical life skills.

Leaders who define expertise with precision, establish frameworks to encourage and recognize that expertise, draw from the academic content standards to support teachers as they refine their craft, and identify key "look fors" that represent best practices by content area become instructional leaders without being expected to be an expert themselves in every content area. Exhibit 7.5 provides sample *Leadership Maps* items that challenge leaders to self-assess how their acts of leadership build capacity.

The three items in Exhibit 7.5 help leaders assess whether best practices are evident throughout the school, contrast traditional instruction with the importance of engaging students in thinking, and assess each leader's familiarity with services to IEP students. All three items examine the leader's content expertise and how it is applied at the school level.

Antecedent structures and learning conditions describe most of the actions of leaders on a day-to-day basis, and the means for communicating expectations,

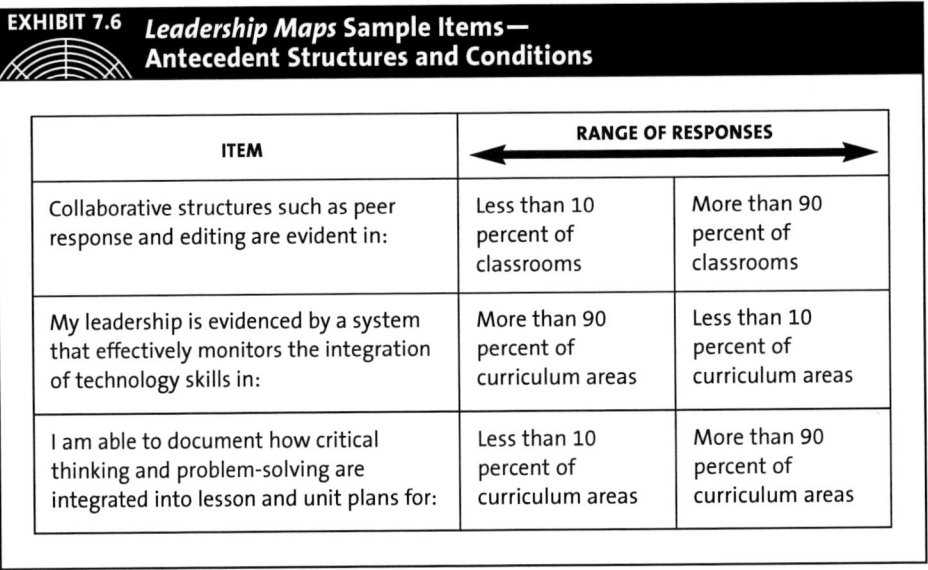

EXHIBIT 7.6 *Leadership Maps* Sample Items— Antecedent Structures and Conditions

ITEM	RANGE OF RESPONSES	
Collaborative structures such as peer response and editing are evident in:	Less than 10 percent of classrooms	More than 90 percent of classrooms
My leadership is evidenced by a system that effectively monitors the integration of technology skills in:	More than 90 percent of curriculum areas	Less than 10 percent of curriculum areas
I am able to document how critical thinking and problem-solving are integrated into lesson and unit plans for:	Less than 10 percent of curriculum areas	More than 90 percent of curriculum areas

committing resources, and scheduling the limited commodity of time all contribute to improved student achievement or improved professional practice when leveraged strategically. Exhibit 7.6 provides additional sample items that represent best practices in terms of antecedent structures and learning conditions.

The items in Exhibit 7.6 address discrete skills, such as collaborative scoring for students, leadership skills regarding monitoring the integration of technology, and critical thinking skills. All three items address the degree to which these practices have been embedded deep within the fabric of the school or the school system.

Content Expertise and Respect

Content expertise for leaders requires both an understanding of expertise and an awareness of content standards for each and every discipline. This chapter examined the notion of expertise and defined it in terms of the ability to apply knowledge for greater effectiveness in the shortest time frame. Three attributes of expertise were identified that need to be both recognized and encouraged, and a very simple process of inquiry about how teachers leverage their content knowledge to anticipate, prevent, and solve challenges in their disciplines was described.

Best practices were examined, referencing the wide array of academic content standards for eleven subject areas and providing numerous examples where leaders, at a minimum, need to be aware of those key power standards. Models of best practices were reviewed, including Danielson's *Framework for Teaching* and the *Framework for 21st Century Learning*, which guides public education reform efforts in a growing number of states.

Finally, we reviewed the antecedent structures and conditions for learning that impact academic content and its delivery with *Leadership Maps* items about special education practices, collaboration, curriculum focus, critical thinking, and monitoring of technology.

Leaders who are prepared to engage their faculty and staff around the work of teaching and learning communicate more than an awareness or knowledge of best practices and efficiency. They communicate respect every time they inquire about the use of inquiry process in science, or growth and development in physical education, or connections in mathematics, or the use of strategies to comprehend or interpret a variety of texts in reading.

Reflection

Big Idea

Expertise is inseparable from knowledge of content.

What is the premise behind this statement? How does it apply personally in your current position?

How did Carol address the issue of expertise in her questions to the band director?

What is needed for you to develop a systematic and recurring treasure hunt for expertise?

Big Idea

Content expertise is directly correlated to respect from each leader's staff or faculty.

Why is it important to be fluent with the power standards or essential learnings for each discipline?

Are there common antecedent structures or learning conditions that are applicable to all content areas?

What strategies have you found to be most effective in keeping leaders abreast of best practices in specific academic content areas?

CHAPTER 8

Powerful Instructional Strategies

"The best strategy in life is diligence."
CHINESE PROVERB

Knowledge of the most powerful instructional strategies is necessary but insufficient to impact student achievement, and the proverb emphasizes the distinction between an awareness of a strategy and mastery of it through practice. The ability to identify the most salient instructional strategy to meet the needs of diverse learners is a function of both the knowledge and application of what works to improve student achievement. Educators can independently attain knowledge of a strategy through many different venues, but *the application of high-yield instructional strategies is almost entirely a function of leadership*. This chapter will describe the leadership necessary to ensure that high-yield instructional strategies are instilled into the culture of schools through the self-assessment lens of sample *Leadership Maps* items.

Powerful Instructional Strategies Defined

In Chapter 6, antecedents were described as the adult actions and decisions that educators make to improve the learning experience for all students. Some antecedents are predictors of improvement, and others are predictive of static growth or even decline, such as punitive grading policies (Reeves 2008, pages 85–87). How teachers open class, collect student work, and manage classroom behavior are all examples of antecedents. When the data demonstrates that certain antecedent practices consistently correlate with improved student achievement to the point that we can predict with some certainty that continuing the practice will yield similar gains, then the practice is recognized as an antecedent of excellence—and a practice worth replicating and sustaining wherever possible. Posting of standards by lesson and using rubrics to guide instruction are examples of practices that are pervasive, because they are accepted as antecedents of excellence, or predictors of improvement gains. How

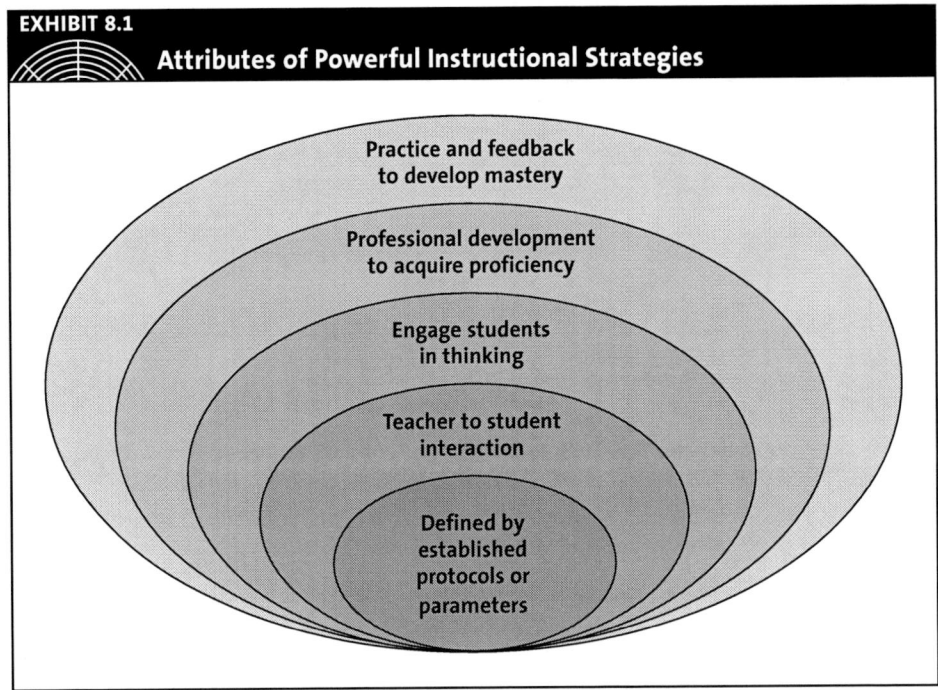

EXHIBIT 8.1
Attributes of Powerful Instructional Strategies

Practice and feedback
to develop mastery

Professional development
to acquire proficiency

Engage students
in thinking

Teacher to student
interaction

Defined by
established
protocols or
parameters

we team, how we make decisions, and even how we display data are all antecedent actions, but they are not instructional strategies.

Instructional strategies were introduced in Chapter 6 as having five attributes that distinguish them from antecedent behaviors and antecedent structures. Those five attributes define instructional strategies and are depicted in Exhibit 8.1.

The stacked Venn diagram in Exhibit 8.1 illustrates the relationship between the five attributes, and the order is intentional. An instructional strategy is first and foremost something that is recognizable as distinct from other practices. Hence, it can be defined by established protocols or limited by precise parameters.

Established Protocols or Parameters

Protocols and parameters define instructional strategies, such as the three distinct characteristics of nonfiction writing assessment: (1) a primary reliance on nonfiction content, (2) use of scoring guides or rubrics that describe degrees of success and proficiency, and (3) an expectation that students or staff will score one another's writing assessments as part of the learning process. The parameters clearly define the strategy, but there is latitude about how the strategy might be delivered. Teachers could score the classroom papers collaboratively for each other's classrooms and benefit from the rich dialogue and calibration of their writing standards and writing instruction. Or, students could score each other's papers collaboratively and benefit from a more precise understanding of quality writing and of the examples and ideas for content and style that they experience from the review. Perhaps the most effective use of nonfiction writing as an instructional strategy is to do both, but *the strategy becomes clear only when it is defined.*

Consider the example of differentiated instruction. Without clearly defined protocols or parameters, such as the expectation that content, process, and product would be differentiated within the same instructional unit (Heacox 2002, pages 10–11), differentiation can be defined as simply grouping students by ability, or providing more homework to higher-achieving students. Consider also the fundamentals of the teaching process: Explain the objective to be learned, demonstrate the objective, provide guided practice where students repeat the process, provide feedback sufficient to allow students to self-evaluate the quality of their work, and reinforce effort until learners independently demonstrate the knowledge or skill inherent in the objective. Such a teaching process, when refined, becomes a powerful although basic instructional strategy, and learners across professions will recognize the teaching process in their own learning. Without the parameters or discrete protocol, the strategy is unclear and open to all sorts of interpretations that may or may not reflect its essential characteristics.

A defined protocol or set of parameters provides the foundation for an instructional strategy, because it helps us understand what it is and what it is not. Note the similarity in this final example with nonfiction writing, as both describe guiding parameters, but educator creativity is not limited by adhering to them. Educators can enrich the selected strategy in countless ways, including adjusting the content or providing a 'hook" to engage students in high-interest, thought-provoking content. They can vary time, integrate the arts into core academic areas, ensure hands-on practice with authentic materials in authentic settings, insist on performance assessments, develop simulations, address learning styles or multiple intelligence, use thematic units, and make literally thousands of modifications that teachers use every day—and still adhere to a common language of what constitutes this foundational element of instructional strategies. An instructional strategy will not be evident unless it can be defined in common language that all can understand. Exhibit 8.2 provides sample

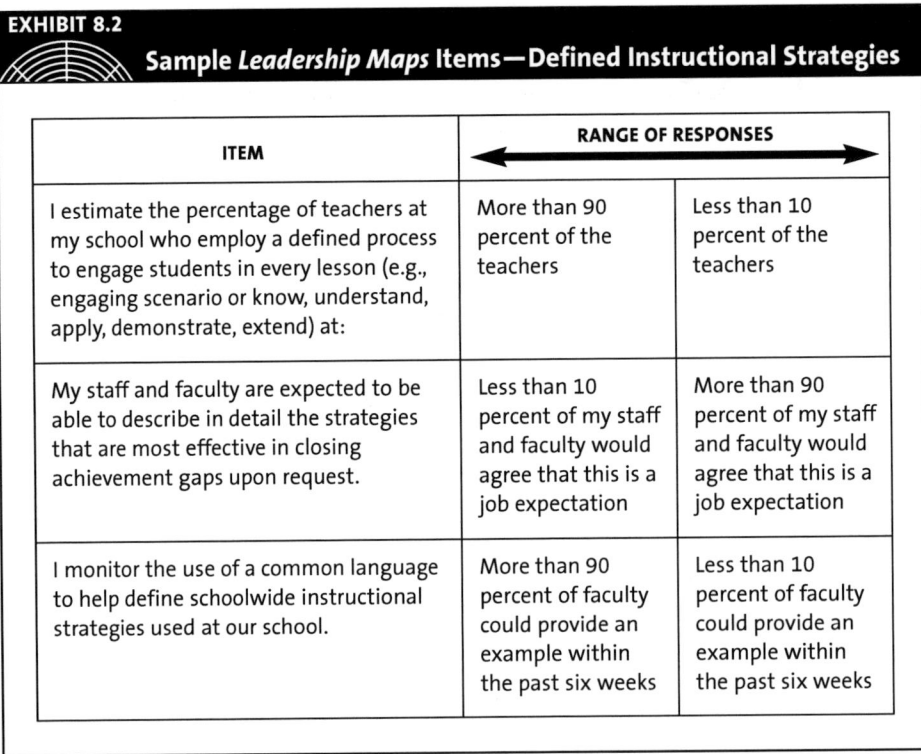

EXHIBIT 8.2

Sample *Leadership Maps* Items—Defined Instructional Strategies

ITEM	RANGE OF RESPONSES	
I estimate the percentage of teachers at my school who employ a defined process to engage students in every lesson (e.g., engaging scenario or know, understand, apply, demonstrate, extend) at:	More than 90 percent of the teachers	Less than 10 percent of the teachers
My staff and faculty are expected to be able to describe in detail the strategies that are most effective in closing achievement gaps upon request.	Less than 10 percent of my staff and faculty would agree that this is a job expectation	More than 90 percent of my staff and faculty would agree that this is a job expectation
I monitor the use of a common language to help define schoolwide instructional strategies used at our school.	More than 90 percent of faculty could provide an example within the past six weeks	Less than 10 percent of faculty could provide an example within the past six weeks

Leadership Maps items that examine the degree to which instructional strategies are clearly understood and implemented by school leaders.

The items in Exhibit 8.2 describe the degree to which teachers actually employ a defined process, the degree to which staff members see knowledge and application of explicit strategies as a job expectation, and the degree to which there is routine monitoring of a common language. All three address the foundational element of powerful instructional strategies for leaders—clearly defined strategies characterized by established protocols or parameters. While these examples are items for school leaders, the need to define key operations in terms of a common language and well-delineated protocols is equally applicable within central-office departments.

Teacher-to-Student Interaction

Instructional strategies are about a direct interaction between students and teachers with face-to-face contact between teachers and their students. This is an important distinction, because as important as time for teacher collaboration or flexibility for teachers or principals in the allocation of resources is to improved achievement, neither practice constitutes an instructional strategy. Powerful instructional strategies occur within the context of instruction, and that means within classrooms. For central-office leaders, powerful instructional strategies also require a face-to-face interaction between staff members and their supervisor. After all, learning is still learning, even for adults, and the most powerful instructional strategies facilitate learning that can be applied successfully in the context of day-to-day challenges.

The research basis is deep and wide that describes how high-yield instructional strategies are predictive antecedents of excellence (Reeves 2008; Marzano 2007; Ainsworth and Viegut 2006; Hill and Flynn 2006; Zemelman, Daniels, and Hyde 2005; Heacox 2002). How to determine the degree of implementation of instructional strategies, however, has had far less attention in the literature. Analyzing that data and making meaning of it is a key process of leadership, and one that *Leadership Maps* has been created to address. Exhibit 8.3 provides sample *Leadership Maps* items that address this key component of powerful instructional strategies.

The items in Exhibit 8.3 examine the degree to which leaders have succeeded at building a culture where discrete and powerful instructional strategies are

EXHIBIT 8.3

Sample *Leadership Maps* Items—Teacher-to-Student Interactions

ITEM	RANGE OF RESPONSES	
At what level are you comfortable teaching improvement strategies to your staff (inviting them into the learning process and preparing them to implement strategies following training and practice)?	I am comfortable teaching my staff improvement strategies	I am not at all comfortable currently
My faculty and staff would agree that their supervisor could identify the most effective instructional strategy used in their classrooms or job assignment.	More than 90 percent of my faculty would agree	Less than 10 percent of my faculty would agree
I provide informal feedback regarding classroom practice and job performance to individual staff and faculty whom I supervise at least:	Every semester	Every week

viewed as an expectation and as an opportunity. The first item addresses the degree to which the leader models the use of powerful instructional strategies; the second references how familiar the leader is with instructional strategies used by faculty and staff; and the third asks leaders to report the degree to which they engage in corrective feedback.

Engage Students in Thinking

The third attribute of an instructional strategy is its ability to engage students in thinking (Marzano 2007, pages 77–79; Hill and Flynn 2006, page 16; White 2005a, page 27). Many classroom routines may be predictive of improved student achievement, but instructional strategies systematically engage students to discover, analyze, relate, connect, and reflect. The quality of questioning, the structures for creating new learning by connecting images and concepts to prior knowledge, and strategies that are applied across multiple content areas promote academic engagement (Marzano 2007, page 100). Fredricks, Blumenfeld, and Paris (2004, pages 62–64) describe several types of engagement, including behavioral, cognitive, emotional, and academic.

Leadership is needed to determine the degree to which lesson plans and selected instructional strategies encourage and facilitate students to apply their best thinking to their schoolwork. Leaders need to understand the full range of

---

EXHIBIT 8.4

Sample *Leadership Maps* Items—Engaging Students in Thinking

ITEM	RANGE OF RESPONSES	
I estimate the percentage of my faculty who employ the use of metaphors, similes, and analogies regularly enough to observe the practice daily in my school as:	Less than 10 percent of my faculty	More than 90 percent of my faculty
The percentage of my faculty who provide evidence in lesson planning of strategies that will generate and test hypotheses across the curriculum is estimated at:	More than 90 percent of my faculty	Less than 10 percent of my faculty
The most effective way to encourage staff to develop hypotheses before submitting proposals for changes is to:	Reduce hypotheses to writing	Discuss anticipated benefits each time ideas are proposed

EXHIBIT 8.5 Sample *Leadership Maps* Items— Professional Development and Proficiency

ITEM	RANGE OF RESPONSES	
Collaborative review of work produced in my department or district occurs at a rate of:	More than 90 percent of staff participating	Less than 10 percent of staff participating
At my school, high-yield strategies are supported with professional development, observed practice, and corrective feedback:	Less than 10 percent of the time	More than 90 percent of the time
Benchmark practices and high-yield strategies are supported with professional development, observed practice, and corrective feedback:	More than 90 percent of the time	Less than 10 percent of the time

best practices in engagement to provide leadership that supports teachers' efforts to more effectively reach all of their students. *Leadership Maps* addresses only a few of the attributes of this critical construct, focusing on the ability of leaders to ensure that instructional strategies engage students cognitively as a foundation. Exhibit 8.4 provides sample *Leadership Maps* items that address the degree to which thinking is emphasized in schools and classrooms by inquiring about levels of implementation of specific instructional strategies.

Items one and two in Exhibit 8.4 ask leaders to reflect on the degree to which powerful strategies that engage students are evident throughout the school, while the last item asks leaders to reflect on their own actions to elicit hypotheses.

Professional Development to Acquire Proficiency

The fourth attribute of an instructional strategy is recognition that teaching and learning are extremely complex endeavors (Darling-Hammond 1997, page 69) and that effective instructional strategies require professional development. Few endeavors, Darling-Hammond asserts, require the same degree of simultaneity, complexity, and multidimensionality. Proficient teachers having a specific instructional strategy means that each teacher must be knowledgeable and cognizant of the purpose and impact of that strategy. Exhibit 8.5 illustrates three sample *Leadership Maps* items regarding professional development.

Far too many change initiatives are proposed without there being an appropriate level of support. Leadership at both the school and district levels creates structures to support each initiative with quality and embedded professional development. If teachers are expected to deliver high-yield instructional strategies, it is ludicrous to expect that to happen without quality professional development that includes feedback, practice, and some level of job-embedded coaching or mentoring.

Practice and Feedback to Develop Mastery

The fifth attribute recognizes that introduction is never mastery and that attendance at a seminar, even an exceptionally well-planned and delivered seminar, does not an expert make. Few of us would select the unpracticed physician to conduct our next surgery, regardless of the pedigree or paper credentials of the particular doctor. We insist on evidence of practice and mastery (e.g., 400 rotator cuff surgeries, all successful), and the same standard must be applied to an instructional strategy. As the "doctors of teaching and learning," those of us who deliver instructional strategies must have sufficient opportunity to refine the practice in order to develop the level of expertise

---

EXHIBIT 8.6

Sample *Leadership Maps* Items—Practice to Develop Mastery

ITEM	RANGE OF RESPONSES	
The percentage of my faculty who understand and apply a powerful and proven standards-based writing strategy daily (6+ traits, Step up to Writing, Simple 6, etc.) is estimated at:	Less than 10 percent of my faculty	More than 90 percent of my faculty
I collect and analyze data about the degree to which instructional strategies are implemented as part of our school-improvement or school-accountability plan.	More than 90 percent of teacher teams submit data about use of instructional strategies	Less than 10 percent of teacher teams submit data about use of instructional strategies
In my department/district, feedback to staff and students is expected, monitored, measured, and analyzed in:	Less than 10 percent of classrooms or work units	More than 90 percent of classrooms or work units

necessary for optimum impact. Exhibit 8.6 provides examples demonstrating *Leadership Maps* items for practice and feedback to develop mastery.

The first two items in Exhibit 8.6 examine practices that are associated with deep implementation and mastery of school-level instructional strategies, while the last item describes the importance of feedback, monitoring, and data analysis at all levels.

Powerful Strategies for Classrooms

Most of the examples in Exhibits 8.2 through 8.6 address proven high-yield instructional strategies that have been well documented in educational research and literature. Each strategy, however, had its birth in a classroom with little fanfare, where a solitary teacher (in most cases) struggled to find novel and improved ways to meet the needs of all students. There is nothing magical about published types of strategies, only a recognition over time that engaging carefully in that strategy should improve student achievement. This section will describe two simple approaches that school leaders can employ to help teachers discover with greater precision what is working and what is not, and why.

Expand the Repertoire of Strategies

Collaborative teacher teams, such as PLCs and DTs, are perfectly designed to expand the range and scope of current instructional strategies as incubators of creative, data-informed improvements in practice. Consider the DT five-step process (Besser *et al.* 2006, page 63) where:

1. A treasure hunt gathers and disaggregates meaningful data about learning and about teaching

2. Teams analyze the data to develop SMART goals by examining the behaviors and characteristics of learning exhibited by successful students in the content area selected, as well as the obstacles experienced by struggling students

3. Teams develop SMART goals that are specific, measurable, achievable, relevant, and timely

4. Instructional strategies are selected to address those obstacles and strengths to achieve the SMART goals

5. Results indicators are created to ensure that progress between the pre-test and post-test assessment is on track in terms of student growth and fidelity of implementation of strategies

The process is straightforward and provides an actionable structure to PLC teams. Step 2, in particular, helps expand the repertoire of instructional strategies by elaborating on the learning characteristics of actual students in actual classrooms. The following example will illustrate.

A fourth-grade DT conducted its treasure hunt and found the area of greatest need in terms of reading comprehension. Team members then brainstormed strengths and obstacles, as depicted in Exhibit 8.7.

The team quickly identified two significant patterns—persistence and foundation. Successful students stayed with tasks, confidently engaging in the learning and following multiple-step instructions independently. A strong foundation was evident as they self-corrected when they read, understood the rules of phonics, and applied multiple reading strategies (such as text-to-text, text-to-self, and text-to-world connections; question-answer relationships; KWL [see page 118]; predicting; clarifying; chunking; and re-reading of sentences).

EXHIBIT 8.7 Sample Fourth-Grade Data Team, Step 2—Strengths and Obstacles

STRENGTHS	OBSTACLES
• Write without needing to be prompted • Self-directed reading for extended periods (ten or more minutes) • **Self-correcting edits are made during reading and in writing** • Very neat work • Readers stretch their own vocabularies by attacking novel words • **Use multiple reading strategies (text-to-text, text-to-student, text-to-world; KWL; predicting; etc.), and select reading material above current comprehension levels** • Multiple-step assignments completed without assistance • Voluntary responses to teacher's questions • Independently ask for help, provide help to others • Rules for phonics recalled with automaticity	• Ideas expressed orally or in writing confused and without apparent organization • **Difficulty describing orally or in writing any reading strategies** • Teacher-dependent to attempt new words • Work begins only when directed • Students rarely volunteer responses to reading selection • Few ask questions of teacher or of text • Students tend to self-select readings below their comprehension ability • **Messy or incomplete work, or both**

Struggling learners lacked the foundation to make meaning of their reading experiences, rarely explained their comprehension, lacked confidence, and were teacher-dependent.

The team decided to explicitly teach all students two of the strengths identified (self-correcting and specific reading strategies) and provide scaffolding to address two obstacles (inability to describe reading strategies and messy, incomplete work). Team members chose to apply two proven, high-yield instructional strategies: (1) setting objectives and providing feedback, and (2) applying a strategic use of questions, cues, and advance organizers. By structuring lessons so that students knew explicitly what would be taught, and providing frequent feedback that was carefully monitored to ensure that all students knew precisely what was expected as the performance standard, the team believed that all students would experience improved reading comprehension. Their hypothesis was that clarity in daily lesson objectives coupled with corrective feedback, would engage struggling learners in terms of explicit comprehension strategies, and that a more consistent delivery of questions, cues, and advanced organizers would stretch and engage successful learners in higher-order thinking while providing the support for struggling learners to establish their own foundation of skills in reading comprehension. They also selected two results indicators (Step 5) to monitor: (1) the degree to

EXHIBIT 8.8 Sample *Leadership Maps* Items— Expanding the Repertoire of Strategies

ITEM	RANGE OF RESPONSES	
As a school leader, I track PLC and DT efforts by analyzing team minutes and routinely displaying data about the effectiveness of specific strategies.	More than 90 percent of DTs submit minutes for each meeting	Less than 10 percent of DTs submit minutes for each meeting
At my school, feedback to staff and students is expected, monitored, measured, and analyzed in:	More than 90 percent of the classrooms	Less than 10 percent of classrooms
As a district leader, I track PLC and DT efforts by school and routinely report data to our stakeholders about the effectiveness of specific strategies.	Less than 10 percent of schools submit summaries of PLC or DT effectiveness	More than 90 percent of schools submit summaries of PLC or DT effectiveness

which students self-corrected and edited their own work, and (2) the proportion of students who completed each in-class assignment according to standards of neatness and grammar. The team expanded the repertoire of instructional strategies by creating its own "hybrid" strategy based on the performance of team members' own students. Most school systems already encourage collaborative teacher teams to meet, but only leadership will ensure that their efforts will result in sustained, continuous improvement.

School leaders who apply the daily discipline to ensure that these team efforts are documented, communicated, celebrated, and extended when they are successful help both their own faculty and the district to improve their practice. District leaders who create systems to capture the lessons learned from teacher teams and school leadership practices not only will help the district—they will also help the profession to improve its practice. Exhibit 8.8 offers a sampling of *Leadership Maps* items about expanding the repertoire of instructional strategies.

Collaborative teacher teams represent one of the most potent structures for sustained improvements in student achievement, and leadership is essential to glean lessons learned from these team efforts. These items address the power of monitoring and feedback to leaders at all levels.

EXHIBIT 8.9 Sample *Leadership Maps* Items— Stay the Course and Keep It Simple

ITEM	RANGE OF RESPONSES	
The percentage of my staff who can describe examples of how I recognize achievement on a regular basis (daily, weekly, monthly, or even by quarter or semester) is estimated at:	Less than 10 percent of my staff	More than 90 percent of my staff
Selection of powerful instructional strategies is best accomplished in school improvement by:	Schoolwide adoption of a particular instructional strategy	Autonomy for teachers to select their own instructional strategy
Accountability and improvement plans within my district are structured to ensure:	A wide range of initiatives and strategies represent the diversity of our schools	A limited number of initiatives and strategies are pursued at any one time

Stay the Course and Keep it Simple

The second approach speaks to the need to avoid "initiative fatigue" for teachers (Reeves 2002, page 83), an acknowledgement that, as fixed resources are divided into a growing number of initiatives, the focus allotted to individual initiatives declines. Initiative fatigue also refers to the collective impact of multiple simultaneous initiatives in terms of stress upon teachers when ambitious school leaders or district officials attempt to do too much too quickly. "Stay the course" is simply an admonishment to leaders to carefully select a few practices, do them well, and do them consistently. We know plenty about effective practices, but the most effective leaders identify the most important area of focus and protect it. Exhibit 8.9 addresses the need for clarity and simplicity through sample *Leadership Maps* items.

By capturing the data around instructional strategies that work, school leaders will be able to identify antecedents of excellence quickly, and by limiting initiatives, school and district leaders will be able to protect their vision and focus efforts to achieve it.

Unlocking Powerful Instructional Strategies in Every Classroom

Powerful instructional strategies have five common elements that distinguish them from routine teacher behaviors or administrative structures that have the capacity to improve student achievement. Instructional strategies have established protocols that define how the strategy is to be applied, and they are interactions between teachers and their students. Instructional strategies always engage students in thinking, and they require professional development to acquire proficiency and extensive practice to master. Leaders determine the degree to which instructional strategies are implemented with quality by the standards they set and the opportunities they provide for faculty to develop and master explicit strategies. The same five elements that define instructional strategies can be used to define operational best practices or strategies, as administrators at all levels learn to apply the L^2 Matrix in Exhibit 1.1.

When teacher teams identify the strengths of successful learners and obstacles struggling learners face (Exhibit 8.7), they provide a context for applying powerful instructional strategies in novel ways, and unlock potential for discovering and defining new strategies to meet the changing needs of students in classrooms everywhere. The result will be smarter, fresher, and more relevant instructional strategies that meet the needs of today's students.

Reflection

Big Idea

Leadership makes instructional strategies powerful.

What is the premise behind this statement? How does it apply personally in your current position?

Which of the five instructional strategy elements is most important in your view? Why?

Big Idea

Collaborative teams are the incubators for instructional strategies.

Why is it important for PLCs and DTs to document strengths of successful learners and obstacles experienced by struggling learners?

To what degree do leaders in your school or district facilitate discovery of new and powerful instructional strategies?

What structures need to be in place to encourage their development?

CHAPTER 9

Planning, Implementation, and Monitoring

*"Action speaks louder than words
but not nearly as often."*

MARK TWAIN

In 1984, the National Governors' Association passed a resolution making school improvement its primary goal (*Education Week,* January 25). In the generation that followed, more than 100,000 schools and approximately 16,000 school systems created annual improvement plans to close achievement gaps and raise the level of student achievement. Many states and provinces in North America required extensive stakeholder participation and input, and the National Education Association (NEA) launched its own comprehensive school improvement model, Keys to Excellence for Your School (KEYS), as early as 1990. Virtually all educators applauded the emerging consensus around school improvement, and a number of reform models articulated in the1980s became the basis for the comprehensive school reform initiatives advanced through No Child Left Behind (NCLB) after 2001. Increased state funding fueled those reform initiatives, and almost all took form through existing structures and planning processes known as school improvement plans.

A generation of well-intentioned planning documents requiring hundreds of labor-hours per plan represents an investment of billions of dollars associated with this reform effort, but the return on that investment is questionable at best. The National Assessment of Educational Progress (NAEP) and Trends in International Mathematics and Science Study (TIMSS) track student achievement across rural, urban, and suburban environments. These studies provide several decades of comparative performance, and despite some encouraging shifts in terms of closing the achievement gaps in recent years, the cumulative efforts of school improvement have produced very minimal gains over time; overall scores are only slightly elevated after almost four decades (Grigg, Lauko, and Brockway 2006, pages 14–21; Gonzales, Gúzman, Partelow, *et al.* 2004).

Schmoker (2006, pages 34–35) refers to "the mirage of school improvement planning." Ruth Mattingley of the Literacy and Numeracy Secretariat of Ontario describes historical school improvement planning efforts as a record of current activities rather than a blueprint of needed changes in practice (2008). Mintrop, MacLellan, and Quintero (2001, page 200) found that plans served largely symbolic purposes, either as rallying points for communication or as public posturing. It is still not unusual to find lengthy, 100-page plans that spend more time describing the history of the school and its facility than planning changes in educational practice. The irony is that the school improvement emphases on collaboration, data-driven decision-making, and implementation of research-based instructional improvements represent timeless best practices across the profession.

This chapter describes school improvement as an overlooked and underutilized improvement cycle that is uniquely positioned to advance needed reforms and quickly impact school cultures. Leaders who leverage the familiar elements of school improvement in a disciplined and coordinated way will protect their focus, celebrate achievement gains, and distribute leadership throughout their organization. The following section examines key elements of school improvement that have the potential to transform documents that are mostly compliant into a process of collaboration and transparency that celebrates teaching and learning every day.

Elements of Effective School Improvement Planning

A number of school improvement models identify the attributes of school improvement that increase student achievement. The most notable model, the seven correlates of effective schools, was recently updated (Lezotte 2008) to reflect the refinements observed during the ensuing time period. The correlates continue to offer a solid and consistent framework for school improvement. Other models, such as Schools that Learn (Senge 2000, pages 5–19), Success for All (Eidi 2001, pages 15–20), and Coalition of Essential Schools (Sizer 2004) have influenced school improvement practices and state and district improvement templates for decades.

A more recent innovation is the PIM™ school improvement process (The Leadership and Learning Center 2005), which identifies planning, implementation, and monitoring as distinct components with fifteen elements and forty-one sub-elements. Each element is supported by a deep research basis in leading change, educational reform, high-yield instructional strategies, data analysis, collaboration, and strategic planning (Boyatzis and McKee 2005; Casciaro and Lobo 2005; DuFour, Eaker, and DuFour 2005; Elmore 2004; Fullan, Hill, and

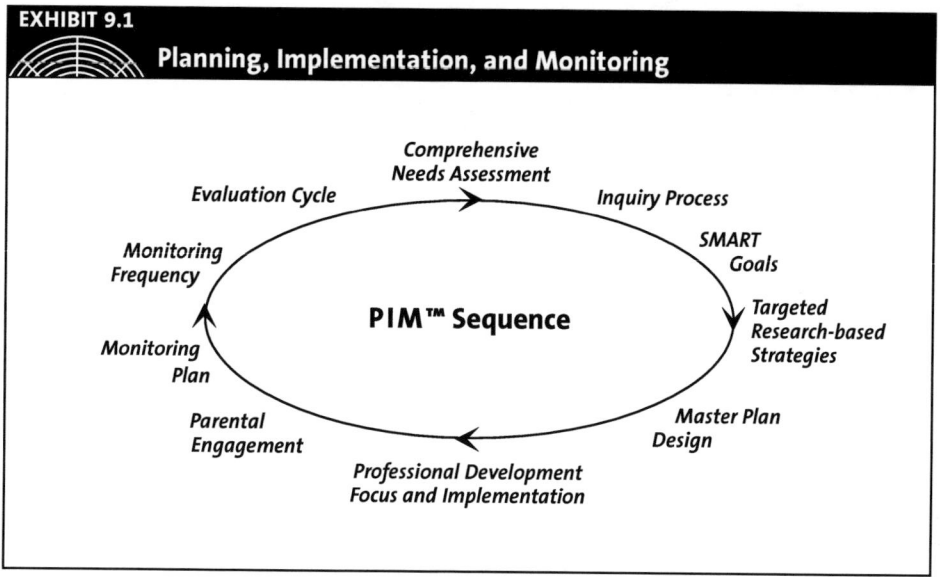

EXHIBIT 9.1

Planning, Implementation, and Monitoring

Comprehensive
Needs Assessment

Evaluation Cycle

Inquiry Process

Monitoring
Frequency

SMART
Goals

PIM™ Sequence

Targeted
Research-based
Strategies

Monitoring
Plan

Parental
Engagement

Master Plan
Design

Professional Development
Focus and Implementation

Crevola 2006; Hernandez 2006; Kouzes and Posner 1995; Lencioni 2002, 2004; Pfeffer and Sutton 2000; Reeves 2004, 2004a, 2006, 2007, 2008; Rushkoff 2005; Schmoker 2006; Surowiecki 2004; Wenglinsky 2002; White 2005, 2006).

The components and elements of PIM™ have been shown to contribute to gains in achievement when compared to schools that omit or inadequately describe the element characteristics (Fernandez 2006). While it is nonprescriptive in terms of school improvement philosophy or program content, PIM™ provides a rigorous audit of school improvement effectiveness by correlating local student achievement gains with each of the fifteen distinct elements. Exhibit 9.1 depicts the PIM™ improvement cycle that is addressed in *Leadership Maps* items.

Quality, comprehensive planning sets the stage for a precise, focused, well-informed implementation strategy that guides leadership teams to design a thorough, insightful monitoring process and powerful evaluation cycle. The PIM™ framework is comprised of fifteen elements within three major components: Planning, Implementation, and Monitoring. Clark County School District (Las Vegas, Nevada) utilized the PIM™ framework; results are provided in Exhibit 9.2.

After completing almost 1,000 school PIM™ audits between 2005 and 2007 (see Exhibit 9.2), significant differences in gain scores emerged for Clark County schools where elements exceeded the PIM™ standard compared to schools where PIM™ elements were not yet at the PIM™ standard. Schools with a higher

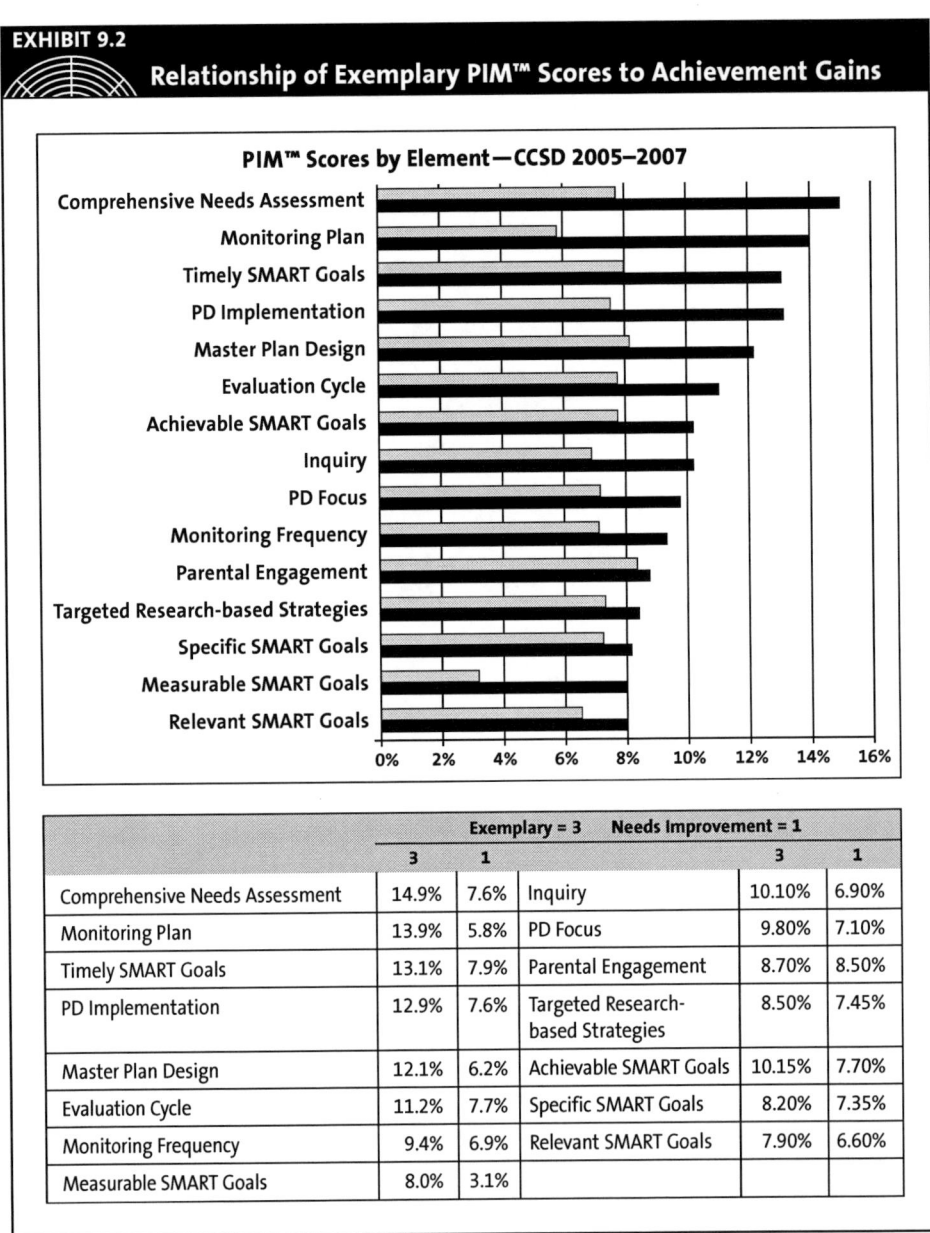

EXHIBIT 9.2

Relationship of Exemplary PIM™ Scores to Achievement Gains

PIM™ Scores by Element—CCSD 2005–2007

	Exemplary = 3	Needs Improvement = 1			
	3	1		3	1
Comprehensive Needs Assessment	14.9%	7.6%	Inquiry	10.10%	6.90%
Monitoring Plan	13.9%	5.8%	PD Focus	9.80%	7.10%
Timely SMART Goals	13.1%	7.9%	Parental Engagement	8.70%	8.50%
PD Implementation	12.9%	7.6%	Targeted Research-based Strategies	8.50%	7.45%
Master Plan Design	12.1%	6.2%	Achievable SMART Goals	10.15%	7.70%
Evaluation Cycle	11.2%	7.7%	Specific SMART Goals	8.20%	7.35%
Monitoring Frequency	9.4%	6.9%	Relevant SMART Goals	7.90%	6.60%
Measurable SMART Goals	8.0%	3.1%			

PIM™ score showed greater achievement gains than schools that needed improvement on each element. In some cases, the distinction was minimal (e.g., parental engagement), but the fact that all fifteen elements were predictive of improved achievement illustrates the benefit of a consistent and thorough approach to planning, implementation, and monitoring.

School and district plans in Clark County that met the criteria for an exemplary designation demonstrated greater gains in achievement than plans that fell short of the PIM™ criteria. In many cases, the differences were dramatic, and in others (e.g., parental engagement), the distinctions were minimal. What was significant about the Clark County experience was that each and every element produced improved achievement gains. Now let's examine the *Leadership Maps* items by its three components and fifteen elements.

Planning

A comprehensive needs assessment is the basis for an effective school or district improvement plan. A quality needs assessment is predictive of almost twice the achievement gains of schools that have an incomplete or narrow assessment of learning and teaching needs. "Comprehensive" means that achievement data includes not only annual state or provincial assessments, but also school-based achievement data such as unit tests, end-of-course finals, or common formative assessments.

For districts, regions, boards of cooperative educational services (BOCES), or state improvement plans, the use of multiple types of achievement data is equally important. For example, if an educational service center services fifteen districts, data about graduation rates disaggregated by district provides a meaningful contrast with the state assessment results, as would ACT or SAT college aptitude examination data. This could be augmented further with data about credits earned, the ratio of AP exams passed to students enrolled, or the degree to which achievement gaps close for struggling student groups over time. Longitudinal cohort tracking using the state assessment provides an additional measure, as would grade point averages by class, by school, or by student groups over time, or a whole host of achievement measures. Many systems administer quarterly or six-week district assessments that allow leaders to triangulate results, recognize patterns and trends, and discover correlations that inform decisions about policy, curriculum, or instruction. As we telescope to the individual school or school cluster level, the range of data options expands to include lessons from performance assessments, end-of-course assessments, or simply grades.

Inclusion of this array (or any array) of assessments beyond the high-stakes annual state or provincial assessment may appear to require inordinate amounts of time and effort, but two factors mitigate against undue complexity: (1) schools and systems are already administering their own array of assessments, and (2) educators are free to self-select from their own existing and available achievement data those that provide the most useful and accessible information. Leadership is needed to limit the range and forms of data collected and to identify those critical few assessments that really do inform practice and decision-making. Each measure added multiplies the possible insights and inferences that may be drawn in terms of student achievement. A quality improvement plan warrants a broad stroke and comprehensive assessment of needs that enables student and staff performance to be analyzed from multiple perspectives.

A second aspect of a comprehensive needs assessment is the presence of data about the degree to which powerful instructional strategies have been implemented with fidelity, or the degree to which antecedent teaching behaviors, administrative structures, or conditions of learning (Chapters 7 and 8) are successful in promoting improved student achievement. A comprehensive needs assessment gathers data about the causal factors that influence student achievement, and any assessment of needs is incomplete without it. PIM™ acknowledges the inclusion of these two data types as proficient, but an exemplary needs assessment would also include data about leadership and about the frequency and process of communication, decision-making, and hypothesis generation. It would also include a wide range of leadership actions, such as those depicted in Exhibit 1.4. Exhibit 9.3 offers a sampling of *Leadership Maps*

EXHIBIT 9.3

Sample *Leadership Maps* Items—Practice and Impact

ITEM	RANGE OF RESPONSES	
I can describe the degree to which key teaching practices at my school/district have been implemented with fidelity.	Precise data is available for multiple teaching strategies	Data is limited to achievement to ensure academic freedom
Analysis of data about leadership is encouraged and welcomed at my school/district.	Less than 10 percent of staff or faculty could provide an example	More than 90 percent of staff or faculty could provide an example
Our comprehensive needs assessment includes data about teaching practices and student achievement for each improvement cycle.	Data about teaching is a requirement of the improvement plan	Data about teaching is rarely gathered and is not required for the improvement plan

items that challenge leaders to examine their practices and the impact of those practices on school improvement.

The items in Exhibit 9.3 address leadership's responsibility to ensure that data is assembled across a wide range of teaching and learning factors, and that leaders can provide evidence about the degree to which best practices are actually being practiced and refined within the organization. There are two basic levels of data analysis: (1) the basic level, where data is gathered and categorized, and where far too many educators stop; and (2) the advanced level, where tools are applied to provide insights that allow educators to make difficult decisions with limited data. It is the advanced level to which we need to aspire, and a comprehensive needs assessment provides sufficient data that is sufficiently categorized, aggregated, and disaggregated across learning, teaching, and leading factors to yield the kinds of insights needed by educators to tackle the most problematic and puzzling challenges. We are now ready for a robust process of inquiry about those practices that serve as causes to the results that our students and staff have achieved.

Inquiry Process

Inquiry is the process of narrowing the focus by winnowing the comprehensive needs assessment data in such a way as to reveal the critical areas that need to be addressed. This occurs by triangulating the comprehensive forms of data, identifying correlations that reveal the strongest practices, forming questions that remain unanswered, and prioritizing those to generate hypotheses. An effective inquiry process will use knowledge about what is working well (strengths) to answer key issues about current performance and plan for future implementation.

The inquiry process should identify correlations between teaching and leading practices and gains in student achievement (learning). By discerning these factors from the data, teams will be able to narrow the focus and prioritize planned actions with the greatest promise of success. The inquiry process then articulates these antecedents of excellence in a few focused hypotheses of action, which then guide the development of SMART goals and precise action steps to achieve them (goals are derived from the THEN statements, and action steps are derived from the IF statements; see Exhibit 9.4). If improvement plans include a proficient inquiry process, educators will have narrowed the focus sufficiently to generate one or more hypotheses that inform possible goal statements and action steps or implementation strategies. Consider how the hypothesis in Exhibit 9.4 serves as a launching pad for a SMART goal and for possible focused action steps or strategies.

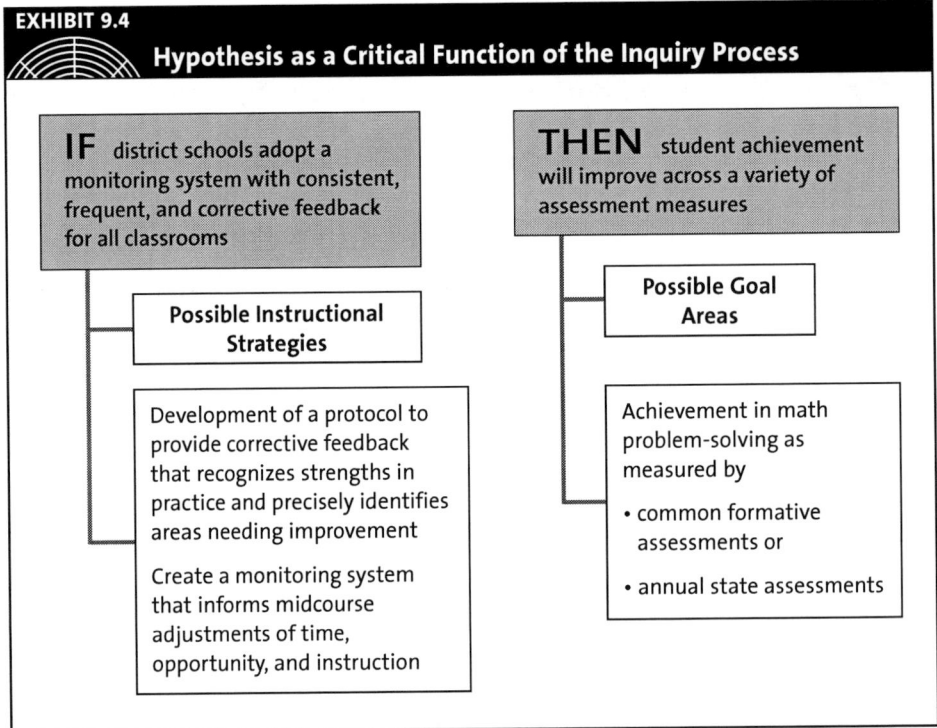

EXHIBIT 9.4

Hypothesis as a Critical Function of the Inquiry Process

IF district schools adopt a monitoring system with consistent, frequent, and corrective feedback for all classrooms

THEN student achievement will improve across a variety of assessment measures

Possible Instructional Strategies

Possible Goal Areas

Development of a protocol to provide corrective feedback that recognizes strengths in practice and precisely identifies areas needing improvement

Create a monitoring system that informs midcourse adjustments of time, opportunity, and instruction

Achievement in math problem-solving as measured by

• common formative assessments or

• annual state assessments

Exhibit 9.4 illustrates how effective planning helps schools increase the level of precision applied to design changes in programs and in practices. The exhibit also illustrates the level of specificity that is possible not only for grade-level DTs or school improvement teams, but also for entire districts or central-office departments. Exhibit 9.5 presents a sampling of *Leadership Maps* items to measure the degree to which inquiry is established in practice.

The inquiry process will be short-circuited when school improvement teams hastily jump to popular current practices or favorite programs as solutions to identified needs. If, however, teams take time to reflect on causal factors and define priorities clearly, improvement plans become aligned and focused, and SMART goals and informed, powerful strategies for action become realities. These sample items describe the depth to which the inquiry process is practiced and is evident, indicators that will emerge only when leadership insists on thoughtful reflection and a deep understanding of best practices.

Specific SMART Goals

The acronym "SMART" is widely recognized in education, government, and private industry as the components of an effective goal statement, with varying

EXHIBIT 9.5

Sample *Leadership Maps* Items—Inquiry Process

ITEM	RANGE OF RESPONSES	
The process of data analysis at my school/district includes identification of adult practices as causal factors for the results we experience.	Less than 10 percent of faculty can describe causal factors for current results when requested	More than 90 percent of faculty can describe causal factors for current results when requested
The number of initiatives in my department or district is limited:	To two or three initiatives per major goal area	Only by the creativity and energy of my teachers and staff
Each improvement cycle includes a formal process of reflection and collaboration that:	Narrows the focus of our improve-ment plan to a few hypotheses for action	Broadens the focus of our improve-ment plan to all identified need areas

levels of clarity. Is a goal to improve reading specific? Does "specific" mean specific content area or specific student group? SMART goals always utilize explicit criteria to minimize interpretation and establish a common understanding of terms. "Improving reading" tells us the general goal, but "improved reading comprehension" provides a greater level of clarity and understanding. "Improved skills in drawing inferences from text" and "making connections between the text and one's life experience" are even more instructive about the areas of need.

To classroom teachers, the goal "to improve reading" communicates a message that working on reading is the focus. Since I work on reading every day, I will do my best to continue to provide reading instruction to the best of my ability. When the specificity increases to reading comprehension, the message is to emphasize reading comprehension and use the other elements of reading (vocabulary, phonemic awareness, word choice, decoding, etc.). The increased specificity increases the level of focus and clarifies expectations.

For that reason, specificity needs to extend to students as well. The conventional wisdom in school improvement is that goals should be for everyone, and that targeting specific learning needs essentially ignores other students. If gaps in achievement (e.g., math problem-solving skills) exist for students receiving free and reduced lunch, should the school ignore this data simply because the goal is for everyone? By addressing skill deficits experienced by a specific targeted group, improved instruction for that area will not only address a schoolwide area of need, it will also refine and enhance instruction for all. Will students who are already at standard on math problem-solving be less so because the improvement plan establishes a problem-solving goal to close the achievement gap? An example of a SMART goal statement is provided in Exhibit 9.6 to illustrate how it is possible to address the need to close achievement gaps for targeted students at both ends of the continuum.

EXHIBIT 9.6

Example SMART Goal Statement

By June 1, 20___, students will independently make connections between information and ideas in nonfiction content areas and their personal experience as measured by improvement from <u>57</u> percent at Levels 3 and 4 on the provincial reading comprehension assessment for all grades to <u>74</u> percent at Levels 3 and 4 and by a decrease in the percentage of Levels 1 and 2 students from <u>50</u> percent to <u>22</u> percent.

Many states and Canadian provinces have annual high-stakes assessments that differentiate student performance in terms of a four- or five-point scale. In Exhibit 9.6, students scoring at the lowest levels (one and two) are targeted for gains, while students at the proficient levels (three and four) are also targeted for improvement. Schools and districts that substitute identified groups by ethnicity, gender, family income, or language can achieve the same level of clarity and focus.

Exhibit 9.7 describes sample *Leadership Maps* items to assist leaders in determining the level of precision and clarity in their goal statements.

The sample items in Exhibit 9.7 ask leaders to consider both the purpose of improvement goals (item 2) and the level of clarity provided in the goal statement. Goals that specify the need area down to the strand level communicate without ambiguity the target for improvement and, in so doing, make it very clear to all stakeholders the area to be addressed in the improvement process.

EXHIBIT 9.7 Sample *Leadership Maps* Items— Specific SMART Goal Statements		
ITEM	**RANGE OF RESPONSES** ← →	
SMART goals at my school/district identify academic targets by:	Content strand area for targeted student groups	Academic content area for all students
School improvement goals should be written:	To close learning gaps for specific subgroups	For the entire school population of students

Measurable SMART Goals

Measurable SMART goals are simply quantified in terms of a beginning baseline level on a selected measure and a goal target for the desired change in performance at a point certain in the future. Many improvement plans miss the opportunity to focus efforts to achieve the selected goal by describing a vague outcome, such as "improve reading performance." Some suggest that goals should be general statements and that objectives should provide the clarity in terms of measurable outcomes, providing sufficient latitude to ensure that educators can explain how goals are being met without being held to a fixed target. This runs counter to an axiom of a standards-based education, where standards (targets and expectations) remain fixed, while time and opportunity to achieve them are varied. The latitude to "spin" regarding generic goal statements is also dissonant with the concept of transparency in communication. Measurable goals, whether they are for states, provinces, districts, schools, classrooms, students, or even nations, should say what they mean in unambiguous terms. Leadership should have the courage to insist on measurable SMART goal statements. Exhibit 9.8 offers three sample *Leadership Maps* items that pinpoint this element of school improvement.

The first item in Exhibit 9.8 reminds us of the importance of both attributes in measurable SMART goals. The following items examine the degree to which goals are measurable, and they include baseline data for school improvement goals and for any common formative assessments that teacher teams have developed.

EXHIBIT 9.8

Sample *Leadership Maps* Items—Measurable SMART Goals

ITEM	RANGE OF RESPONSES	
My leadership is reflected at my school/district by the fact that school improvement goals:	Are developed collaboratively	Include quantifiable baselines and targeted goal measures
Goals developed at my school for student achievement routinely include baseline data and a desired level of achievement for:	More than 90 percent of common formative assessments	Less than 10 percent of common formative assessments
Goals developed at my school for school improvement routinely include baseline data and a desired level of achievement for:	Not yet evident in school improvement goals	More than 90 percent of school improvement goals

Achievable SMART Goals

"Achievable" is often viewed as the point at which educators need to be realistic and set goals that are attainable given current practices. The PIM™ process views this element of SMART goals as more of a question of academic health. If the goal is not sufficiently targeted to close achievement gaps within three to five years, then it is less about achievement and more about maintaining the status quo. The second aspect about achievable SMART goal statements is the expectation that achievement of the goal will actually narrow the achievement gaps by differentiating targets by student subgroup. Our example in Exhibit 9.6 differentiated between the performance levels one through four, with greater gains anticipated for students performing below standard. This is good practice in terms of advocating for students, and it is sound statistically, as students with greater gaps between current achievement and possible achievement should be expected to make greater gains than students who are already achieving at very high levels. Exhibit 9.9 provides *Leadership Maps* items associated with this element.

Relevant SMART Goals

Relevant SMART goals are goals that reflect the most urgent areas of need that emerge from the comprehensive needs assessment, as opposed to pursuit of a popular program or preferred content with which area members of the team are

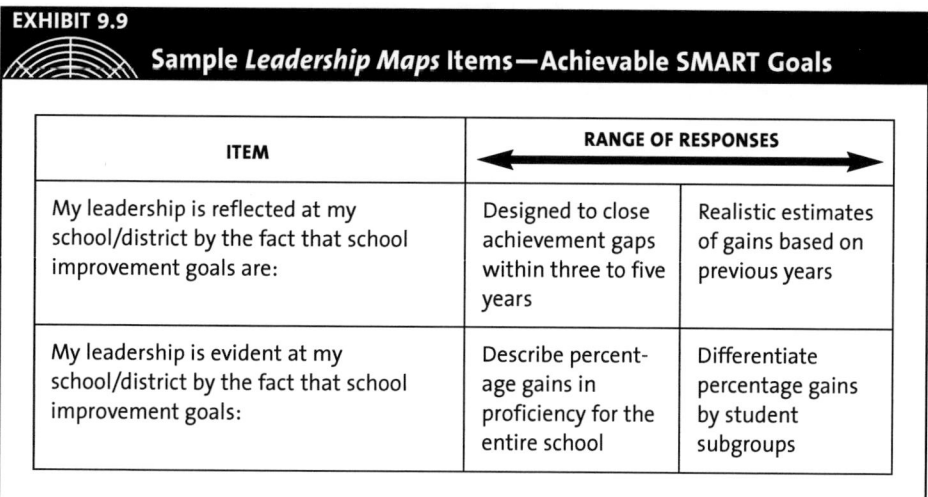

EXHIBIT 9.9

Sample *Leadership Maps* Items—Achievable SMART Goals

ITEM	RANGE OF RESPONSES	
My leadership is reflected at my school/district by the fact that school improvement goals are:	Designed to close achievement gaps within three to five years	Realistic estimates of gains based on previous years
My leadership is evident at my school/district by the fact that school improvement goals:	Describe percentage gains in proficiency for the entire school	Differentiate percentage gains by student subgroups

most familiar. All too often, schools select goals less on the basis of evidence and more on the basis of familiar current practice. Leadership pursues changes in practice to translate best practices into common practices. Exhibit 9.10 offers two sample *Leadership Maps* items.

Timely SMART Goals

Timely SMART goals describe a specific point in time to emphasize to stakeholders the finite opportunity to change practices sufficiently in order to achieve ambitious, relevant, achievable, measurable, and specific SMART goals. The adage that what gets measured gets done is more aptly represented with the

EXHIBIT 9.10

Sample *Leadership Maps* Items—Relevant SMART Goals

ITEM	RANGE OF RESPONSES	
At my school/district, improvement goals represent urgent, critical needs that are evident to staff and faculty.	More than 90 percent of goal statements	Less than 10 percent of goal statements
At my school/district, improvement goals are aligned with clearly established priorities that are evident to staff and faculty.	Less than 10 percent of goal statements	More than 90 percent of goal statements

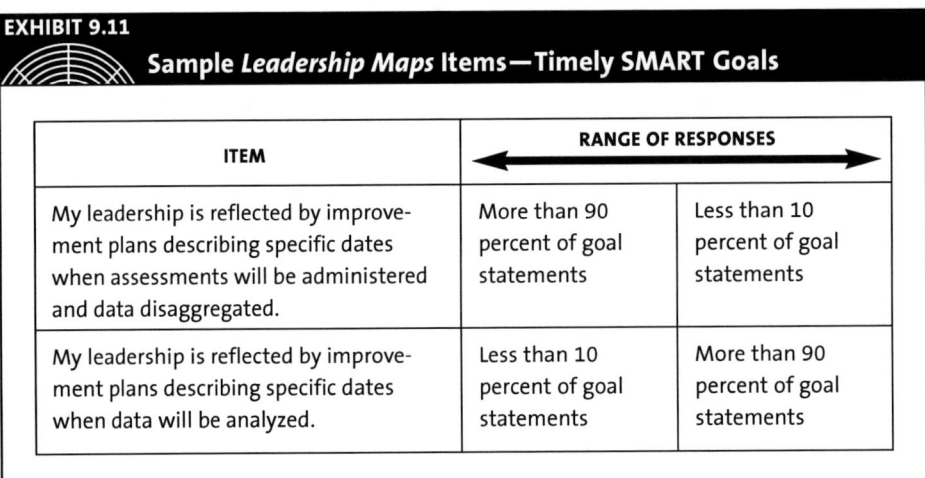

EXHIBIT 9.11

Sample *Leadership Maps* Items—Timely SMART Goals

ITEM	RANGE OF RESPONSES	
My leadership is reflected by improvement plans describing specific dates when assessments will be administered and data disaggregated.	More than 90 percent of goal statements	Less than 10 percent of goal statements
My leadership is reflected by improvement plans describing specific dates when data will be analyzed.	Less than 10 percent of goal statements	More than 90 percent of goal statements

following twist associated with timely SMART goals: What gets scheduled gets done. Timely SMART goals communicate with certainty the point when the school or district will determine whether the goal has been achieved. Exhibit 9.11 depicts *Leadership Maps* items associated with this PIM™ element.

Implementation

The planning component is the building block for quality implementation, which includes the following elements:

- Master plan design
- Targeted research-based strategies
- Professional development focus
- Professional development implementation
- Parental engagement.

These five elements provide leaders guidance to ensure a high degree of fidelity in implementing chosen action steps.

Master Plan Design

Once SMART goals have been established, a school or board should create a master plan design as a series of action steps toward achievement of each SMART goal. A master action plan is supported by four supporting elements: (1) targeted research-based strategies, (2) professional development focus, (3) professional development implementation, and (4) parental involvement strategies. If the inquiry process is thorough enough to allow generation of hypotheses, the master plan design will align with the needs identified in the comprehensive needs assessment and prioritized during the inquiry process. Master plan design, however, has three distinct characteristics that promote a high degree of consistency and implementation. When leadership ensures that the master plan design has these characteristics, the likelihood that schools and school districts achieve their SMART goals is enhanced.

The design of a quality master plan includes action steps that are closely articulated and aligned. Each step will build a foundation for the next step and will equip the school to better achieve its goals and objectives. If the school plans to implement schoolwide nonfiction writing across content areas, the action steps might include some assessment of the degree to which faculty members currently use non-fiction writing and the percentage of teachers who have been trained in a selected writing process. A second, aligned action step may speak to the process that the school is employing to provide and embed professional development in order to ensure that schoolwide instruction occurs in nonfiction writing. A third action step may be to apply that training across content areas, and a fourth action step may address the process for making a midcourse correction or possible modifications based on actual student performance. This example illustrates an improvement plan that is aligned and articulated, where each step better prepares the school or department to achieve its goal.

A second critical characteristic of master plan design is the assignment of an individual or small team to make sure that the action step is fully implemented and carried out as planned. Far too often, plans assume that the changes in practice will simply occur, or that large numbers of persons (e.g., classroom teachers) will all be responsible to carry out the action step. In one sense, everyone involved at the school or within the department should be responsible if the goal is schoolwide or encompasses an entire department. In practice, however, expecting everyone to attend to the details of the action step lacks the clarity needed to ensure the step's completion and full implementation. This occurs because, when everyone is responsible, there is a tendency to assume that someone else will attend to the details of the implementation. Well-intentioned team members may assume that the team leader or department chair will coordinate the action step, or that someone else on the team will communicate about the status of the action step.

The need to assign a champion for each major action step is practical and is a savvy demonstration of leadership. It is practical because it ensures that someone or a small team of individuals will understand *that it is their job* to coordinate and communicate that action step rather than tentatively pursue the implementation as a result of not desiring to overstep their bounds or offend others, especially their principal or department chair. Assigning a champion has a much more important benefit in terms of leadership. It is a quiet acknowledgment that an individual with skills and interest in seeing the step achieved should be invited to coordinate, communicate, and chart the step. This, in turn, communicates a confidence and trust in that individual and demonstrates a level of respect and recognition of ability that is impossible when duties appear to be assigned arbitrarily (Kouzes and Posner 2002, page 181; Lencioni 2007, page 221). Inviting a faculty member to champion an action step is an important demonstration of leadership that in and of itself distributes leadership across staff and faculty.

The third characteristic of a master plan design is a connected timeline that is precise and sequential. Timelines such as "ongoing" or "September to June" leave too much to chance and tend to allow the urgent to trump the important. When time lines are strategically developed, however, to transition from important building-block action steps to full implementation, then they are much more apt to be met, and the action step is more likely to be implemented as designed. Precise time ines also help teams assess precisely the demands being placed on staff to complete the action step in the time allotted, and they limit team members' action steps to those that can be achieved within the given time. Exhibit 9.12 describes sample *Leadership Maps* items for master plan design.

EXHIBIT 9.12

Sample *Leadership Maps* Items—Master Plan Design

ITEM	RANGE OF RESPONSES	
My improvement plan aligns comprehensive needs assessment to reflective inquiry (cause and effect) in order to create goal statements. The master plan design is monitored for quality implementation and a thorough evaluation cycle.	I have not yet aligned my plan to this degree	My plan represents this level of alignment
Implementing specific action steps in the improvement plan at our school or district is the primary responsibility of:	All staff directly impacted or participating in the planned change in practice	Assigned individuals who will coordinate, communicate, and chart progress

Targeted Research-Based Strategies

Most educators routinely select research-based strategies as key action steps in any improvement plan, but often there is a mixed message about the degree to which those strategies should be targeted to specific groups of learners. In fact, a common assumption is that all goal statements should be written for the entire student population, particularly since school or district improvement plans are designed to improve performance for the entire school or district.

The most obvious flaw in this approach is the fact that some school communities might be able to achieve their goal without addressing the student group that is the most in need of assistance. An example is if a school currently has a performance goal of a 3 percent gain—from 69.6 percent to 72.6 percent of

EXHIBIT 9.13

Potential Gains Without Closing Key Achievement Gaps

Student Group	M	F	Enrollment	%	2008 Proficient	2009 Proficient
African-American	✔		16	1.01	49%	45.0%
African-American		✔	19	1.2	61%	68.0%
Asian	✔		42	2.6	86%	89.0%
Asian		✔	59	3.7	82%	90.0%
Caucasian	✔		645	40.5	73%	75.0%
Caucasian		✔	687	43.2	77%	79.0%
English as a Second Language	✔		51	3.2	73%	78.0%
English as a Second Language		✔	61	3.8	69%	78.0%
Hispanic	✔		47	2.9	51%	51.0%
Hispanic		✔	62	3.9	66%	70.0%
Native American	✔		5	0.31	34%	29.0%
Native American		✔	9	0.57	63%	77.0%
Free and Reduced Lunch	✔		81	5.1	50%	48.0%
Free and Reduced Lunch		✔	61	3.8	51%	57.0%
Special Education (IEP)	✔		51	3.2	20%	24.0%
Special Education (IEP)		✔	32	2.01	38%	35.0%
Totals (some in multiple groups)			1,591		69.6%	72.8%

EXHIBIT 9.14 Sample *Leadership Maps* Items— Targeted Research-Based Strategies

ITEM	RANGE OF RESPONSES	
Strategies are selected to match the learning needs of students in developing action steps for improvement plans at my school, department, or district.	More than 90 percent of staff or faculty can provide at least one example	Less than 10 percent of staff or faculty can provide an example
Action step strategies selected for my improvement plan are targeted to address specific needs of students or staff.	Required for ALL action step strategies at my school or department	Not yet expected for action step strategies

students scoring proficient or advanced at the end of the year in terms of a specific content standard and strand (e.g., reading comprehension, as per Exhibit 9.6). Exhibit 9.13 describes a not-so-uncommon scenario where only student subgroups with a baseline over 50 percent proficient demonstrated gains of **any kind**, while subgroups with significant achievement gaps either showed no gains or actually declined.

The scenario depicted in Exhibit 9.13 for this small school district illustrates how average scores on assessments in communities and schools that are largely homogeneous mask pernicious achievement gaps, even though goals may be achieved without addressing the most urgent need. This element of the PIM™ framework is very much related to a specific and relevant SMART goal statement. If our comprehensive needs assessment yields clear enough data to develop a precise and focused SMART goal, it is critical that the implementation plan describes targeted and research-based strategies. Leadership will determine the degree to which these connections are recognized and protected, and Exhibit 9.14 describes sample *Leadership Maps* items associated with targeted research-based instructional strategies.

Both of the items in Exhibit 9.14 ask leaders to reflect on the degree to which their action steps are targeted to needs identified through the planning process in order to ensure that implementation aligns with planning.

Professional Development Focus

If the master plan design describes quality targeted research-based strategies in the action steps, it is critical that such changes (improvements) be supported by professional development in order for capacity and sustainable innovation to be built. Professional development initiatives need to be focused, limited in number, and directly aligned with the change initiative content. Schools, districts, and departments that attempt to accomplish more than time will allow risk dilution of priorities to such an extent that the intended benefit of the training is not realized. Often, unintended consequences result from attempting to do too much, resulting in confusion, frustration, and initiative overload.

Change is difficult enough when plans are well implemented and planned for sufficient oversight, opportunity for collaboration, and replacement of existing practices with the preferred improvements. However, when multiple initiatives are thrust at educators in terms of underestimated time demands and complexity, it is a recipe for failure. If the professional development is important enough to be included in the schoolwide improvement plan, and important enough to invest time and money for the entire team or faculty to acquire the skills and knowledge associated with it, then the application of such knowledge and skills needs to be supported with supervision and follow-up. Leaders demonstrate that focus with reminders, suggestions, and recognition of teacher efforts, and they document such efforts through the supervision process, commenting in observation and evaluation narratives. Failure to do so is paramount to indifference and communicates that other things are of equal or greater importance.

EXHIBIT 9.15	Sample *Leadership Maps* Items— Professional Development Focus		
ITEM	**RANGE OF RESPONSES**		
Professional development at my school is referenced in the supervision process:	Only when necessary		Consistently in each evaluation narrative
Professional development initiatives are limited to those that can be implemented deeply in the time available.	More than 90 percent of faculty would describe my leadership in this way		Less than 10 percent of faculty would describe my leadership in this way

Exhibit 9.15 offers sample *Leadership Maps* items designed to challenge leaders to both limit the number of initiatives and to link the prioritized professional development to the supervision.

Professional Development Implementation

Providing a limited number of professional development initiatives and ensuring that teachers (and principals) are supported and recognized for applying that training to their leadership or classroom practice are necessary but insufficient in maximizing the degree to which the improvement initiative is translated and sustained in practice. The innovation anticipated by the professional development needs to be sustained well after the innovation has been introduced in order to be effective. A common request that I make of educators across North America is to estimate the number of initiatives at their school that are still being practiced a mere two years after their introduction. While some may be able to identify one or two initiatives that have been sustained, the number of professional development initiatives that have been discarded almost always dwarfs the number that have been sustained after the bloom is gone.

To sustain important training and professional development, the PIM™ framework looks for evidence that a system of modeling, mentoring, and coaching is in place. A second element of professional development implementation is the capacity of the school or department to differentiate training in order to meet people where they are on the learning continuum. Differentiated professional development recognizes that adults, like students, require varying levels of support, time, and practice to acquire and master new

**EXHIBIT 9.16 Sample *Leadership Maps* Items—
Professional Development Implementation**

ITEM	RANGE OF RESPONSES	
Professional development in my school is differentiated by modality, readiness, and the match between student needs and staff competency.	More than 90 percent of professional development initiatives	Less than 10 percent of professional development initiatives
I estimate the percentage of teachers at my school who participate in mentoring, modeling, and coaching associated with professional development efforts at:	Less than 10 percent of the teachers	More than 90 percent of the teachers

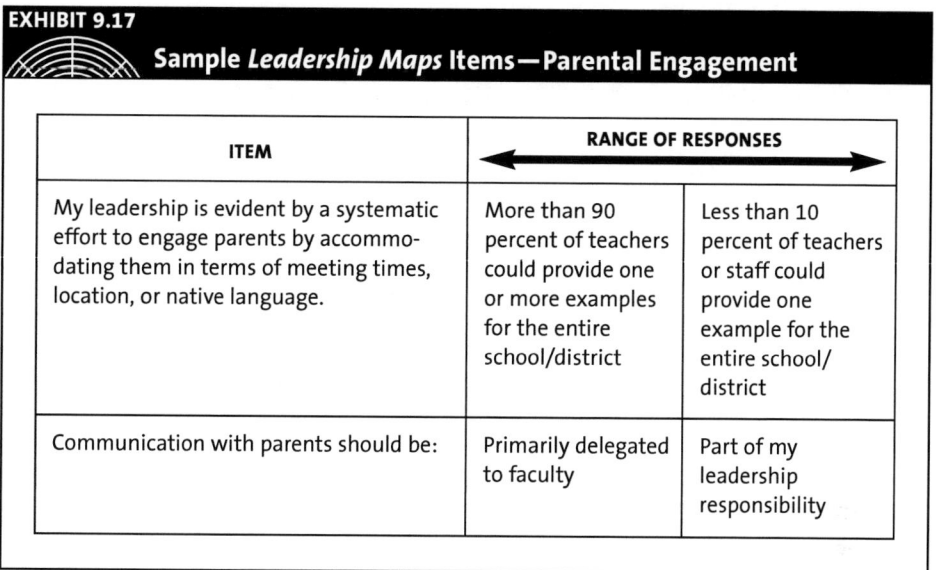

EXHIBIT 9.17

Sample *Leadership Maps* Items—Parental Engagement

ITEM	RANGE OF RESPONSES	
My leadership is evident by a systematic effort to engage parents by accommodating them in terms of meeting times, location, or native language.	More than 90 percent of teachers could provide one or more examples for the entire school/district	Less than 10 percent of teachers or staff could provide one example for the entire school/district
Communication with parents should be:	Primarily delegated to faculty	Part of my leadership responsibility

knowledge and skills. Exhibit 9.16 describes sample *Leadership Maps* items associated with deep implementation of professional development.

The items in Exhibit 9.16 address the need to differentiate professional development and the level of support provided to ensure that the learning is embedded—two critical aspects of professional development implementation.

Parental Engagement

Parental involvement has long been recognized as an antecedent condition for improved student achievement (Epstein and Sheldon, 2002 page 308; Lezotte 2008). Rather than focusing on attendance at school events as the lone indicator of effective parental engagement, the PIM™ process reviews the degree to which parents are given instruction and support regarding academic content and how teachers intend to deliver it to their children. A proficient plan not only provides information to parents, it also provides for training opportunities and consistent communication of student progress and school progress in ways that are appropriate to and accessible by parents (e.g., in their native language, at times convenient to their work schedules). There is a growing awareness that access, education, and transparency in reporting achievement results to parents, for their own children and for the school, are much more accurate indicators of parental engagement than participation on school committees, fund-raising, or attendance at school events. Schools' plans are particularly effective in this component, as they communicate a high degree of respect for parents and community members as partners in the educational process. Exhibit 9.17 describes sample *Leadership Maps* items in this area.

Parents are often referred to as the first teachers of every student, and the evidence is overwhelming that their support is necessary for students to approach their potential as learners. The most effective leaders commit to providing access, being proactive in providing educational opportunities, and communicating the progress in a transparent way—not only regarding individual students, but progress or lack of it for the school and/or district as well.

Monitoring

The final component of the PIM™ framework is monitoring, an area of school improvement planning that addresses the need for a thoughtful system of feedback and midcourse adjustments. Like good teaching, good school improvement requires agility in responding to unanticipated events or changes in the progression toward mastery. Monitoring consists of three elements: (1) a deliberate and thoughtful monitoring plan, (2) the frequency and method of monitoring, and (3) an evaluation cycle.

The monitoring plan describes explicit data to be monitored, when it will be monitored, and who will be responsible for reporting progress toward school

EXHIBIT 9.18

Sample *Leadership Maps* Items—Monitoring Plan

ITEM	RANGE OF RESPONSES	
Monitoring is carefully designed to address both student achievement progress toward goals and progress in terms of implementation of practices by staff or faculty.	Action steps for each goal include monitoring both learning and professional practice	Action steps may monitor learning or professional practice, but not both
The improvement plan at my school, department, or district includes a review schedule to examine progress and make necessary adjustments and midcourse corrections.	Action steps describe at least one midcourse review to examine progress for each goal	Action steps do not currently describe midcourse review of progress

improvement goals. A continuous improvement cycle should be evident in the monitoring plan, as it describes opportunities to alter the school improvement plan (SIP) and make midcourse adjustments. The monitoring plan should articulate the type of data to be collected and analyzed; at least two levels of monitoring are recommended as a minimum: (1) student progress toward the goal, and (2) the degree of implementation or capacity-building for staff and faculty. The first is simply a probe or indicator that the strategy employed is impacting student learning, while the second probes for changes in professional practice. A quality monitoring plan is incomplete without both indicators. The student learning data informs the team of possible needed changes based on student performance, while probing for consistent professional practice reveals the need to modify and support teachers in delivering the action-step strategy. School board plans will monitor both progress in student achievement and progress toward building capacity among staff. Exhibit 9.18 provides sample *Leadership Maps* items for this important element of the PIM™ framework.

The items in Exhibit 9.18 challenge leaders to examine the degree to which the monitoring plan keeps track of student and staff progress and of the presence of structures to ensure a system of midcourse adjustments or corrections.

Monitoring Frequency

An effective monitoring plan ensures that monitoring occurs frequently enough to make necessary changes to achieve or exceed each goal. In fact, the frequency with which teachers assess student progress is directly correlated with student achievement gains (Marzano 2007, page 13). At the school level, the same pattern exists in terms of monitoring frequency (Exhibit 9.2), a finding supported by PIM™ findings in Norfolk, Houston, and the province of Ontario, where schools that monitored student achievement and professional practices five to ten times annually yielded consistently higher achievement gains than schools that monitored less frequently. Monitoring schedules also assist leaders to review student performance, teaching practices, and even leadership practices. Frequent improvement monitoring is similar to common formative assessments in that both practices provide opportunities to refine and revise current practices.

Two elements of the master-plan design—explicit time lines and assigned "champions" for action steps—strengthen each monitoring plan. Both of these elements ensure a rapid, agile, and precise response based on evidence. Exhibit 9.19 offers sample *Leadership Maps* items associated with monitoring frequency.

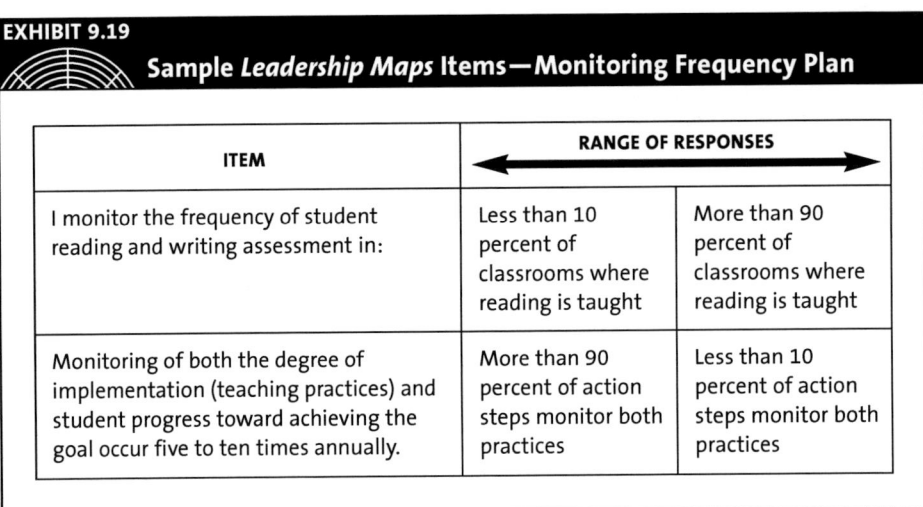

EXHIBIT 9.19

Sample *Leadership Maps* Items—Monitoring Frequency Plan

ITEM	RANGE OF RESPONSES	
I monitor the frequency of student reading and writing assessment in:	Less than 10 percent of classrooms where reading is taught	More than 90 percent of classrooms where reading is taught
Monitoring of both the degree of implementation (teaching practices) and student progress toward achieving the goal occur five to ten times annually.	More than 90 percent of action steps monitor both practices	Less than 10 percent of action steps monitor both practices

Evaluation Cycle

An evaluation plan allows the school to compare planned with achieved outcomes. Specifically, plans should describe how compared results (both positive and negative) are communicated to primary stakeholders (families, educators, staff, patrons, partners, and the public) and how lessons learned will be applied to future school improvement planning, implementation, and monitoring cycles. The evaluation portion of the plan is the final stage of an effective cycle of continuous improvement, where thoughtful reflection is given to examine the evidence, ponder its implications, identify lessons learned, and commit to apply them as next steps. As in every area of school improvement, the lever is a question of leadership that responds to the analysis informed by best practices and research. The most effective leaders will use the evaluation process to inform the subsequent cycle's comprehensive needs assessment, populating it with insights and data about teaching, learning, and leading. Exhibit 9.20 offers sample *Leadership Maps* items to challenge leaders to drill deeper for solutions that make a difference.

The three PIM™ components and the fifteen elements reviewed in this section are predictors of improved achievement over time, in large measure because they reflect research about teaching and learning at every level. Leaders who are willing to attend to the qualitative distinctions presented in *Leadership Maps* items will find that the increased personal attention to the details of daily routines will help them move from good to great (Collins 2001), distribute leadership, and move toward a greater reliance on evidence. Benefits of a

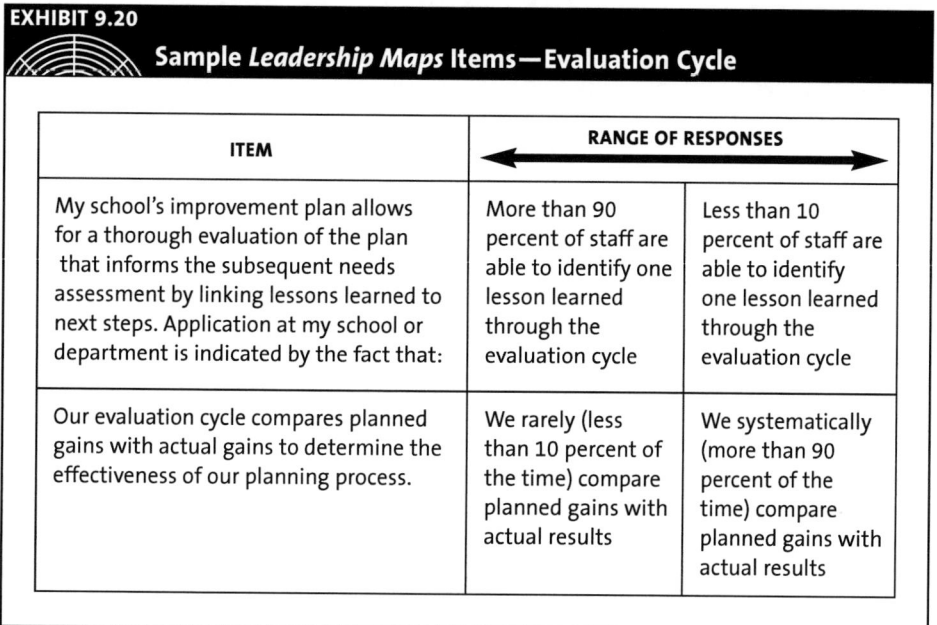

EXHIBIT 9.20

Sample *Leadership Maps* Items—Evaluation Cycle

ITEM	RANGE OF RESPONSES	
My school's improvement plan allows for a thorough evaluation of the plan that informs the subsequent needs assessment by linking lessons learned to next steps. Application at my school or department is indicated by the fact that:	More than 90 percent of staff are able to identify one lesson learned through the evaluation cycle	Less than 10 percent of staff are able to identify one lesson learned through the evaluation cycle
Our evaluation cycle compares planned gains with actual gains to determine the effectiveness of our planning process.	We rarely (less than 10 percent of the time) compare planned gains with actual results	We systematically (more than 90 percent of the time) compare planned gains with actual results

renewed look at school improvement (or district improvement practices) are described below.

Opportunities for Leadership

The school improvement process offers a unique opportunity to advance the profession. Negotiated agreements between teachers and school boards almost universally celebrate the shared decision-making and collaboration that school improvement offers, as contracts often describe minimum criteria to ensure that stakeholders are both represented and involved in the improvement process.

One purpose of accountability and improvement plans is to make needed changes informed by data. While the first generation of school improvement plans struggled with implementation, leaders can ensure that a second generation changes professional practice by incorporating structures that are necessary to achieve SMART goals and sustain them over time. The profession is advanced every time a teacher passionately assumes responsibility for coordinating, communicating, and charting progress on an important action-step strategy, particularly when invited by a school leader whom he or she respects. It is advanced every time a carefully coordinated time line is established and monitored, and it is advanced when incremental gains are charted and celebrated as part of the improvement process. Leaders advance the profession every time they provide a forum where the collective wisdom of practitioners is allowed to guide decisions to improve student achievement.

Leadership That Transforms Culture

Leadership in school improvement has even greater potential to transform culture, as a detailed improvement process that focuses the efforts of an entire staff changes school climate from a series of individuals completing a job to a team of professionals who have a goal bigger than themselves. Culture, or the practices of an organization that occur independent of written policies, procedures, or oversight, shifts from isolation to collaboration, from appearance to substance, and from compliance to commitment when leadership creates opportunities for growth that are safe, empowering, and meaningful (Boyatzis and McKee 2005, pages 138–141). The three universal characteristics of school improvement include:

1. Collaboration, as plans are created by leadership teams and action steps implemented schoolwide

2. Data-driven decision-making, as plans are framed and designed to respond to data about learning to inform instructional practice

3. Research-based instructional improvements, as plans anticipate innovations that will change current practices to yield increasingly higher levels of achievement for a greater proportion of students

Not only are these universally accepted values for educational practice, there also is a compelling basis in research that advocates for their systematic application in schools (Hargreaves and Goodson 2006, pages 33–35; Elmore 2000, pages 1–9; Reeves 2007; DuFour, Eaker, and DuFour 2005; Fullan, Hill, and Crevola 2006). School improvement protocols provide opportunity to distribute leadership with each action step, and the schoolwide, focused improvements translated into changes in practice will promote collaboration. School improvement helps transform culture when decisions are based on evidence provided through a comprehensive needs assessment. When research-based instructional strategies are targeted to address the needs of specific groups of students, a culture of innovation that responds with precision is advanced.

Potential

School improvement has become a ubiquitous fixture for schools everywhere. Unfortunately, as a profession, we are just now discovering its true potential in transforming schools and establishing a more professional, personal, and precise culture of learning. The PIM™ process provides a granular examination of the critical details and disciplines of improvement to help educators translate their goals into reality. However, it will require leaders with the courage to recognize and respond to the opportunities for improvement that are presented to them each and every day to transform schools and make the kinds of gains necessary to prepare students for a very uncertain future. Collaboration—decisions driven by data and research-based improvements in strategies for the classroom, school, and district—becomes a reality when leaders engage in daily disciplines to make a difference. School improvement continues in this generation to hold the promise for such transformation, and the decisions of leaders will determine whether that promise is fulfilled.

Reflection

Big Idea

Improvement means change in practice.

What is the premise behind this statement? How does it apply to the improvement plans generated by your school or district?

Big Idea

Success is best sustained when goals are few.

Why might that be the case? What advantage do schools and districts with few goals have over schools and districts with many goals?

Describe possible indicators you might use to determine whether your plan has too many or too few goals or action steps.

Big Idea

A leader's daily discipline determines successful implementation.

How does leadership at your school/district currently impact the degree to which plans are fully implemented? What changes might you make in your daily routines to promote better implementation of your plan?

Big Idea

Distributed leadership in school improvement changes culture.

What advantage is there in assigning individuals to "champion" key action steps or strategies? How do you intend to more explicitly distribute leadership at your school or district?

CHAPTER 10

Leadership Attributes

*"Every day, in every facet of our lives,
opportunities to lead call out to us. At work
and at home, in our local communities and in
the global village, the chance to make a
difference beckons. Yet often, we hesitate. For
all its passion and promise, for all its
excitement and rewards, leading is risky,
dangerous work."*

RONALD A. HEIFETZ and MARTY LINSKY,
Leadership on the Line (2002, cover)

Heifetz and Linsky are referring to the attributes of leadership from which leaders draw when faced with the conundrums, unexpected challenges, and historical baggage that come from engaging in the complex business of teaching and learning. Courage is most definitely such an attribute, as is resilience, transparency, mindfulness, compassion, and stewardship. This chapter examines the final domain of *Leadership Maps* by drawing on the scholarship of a number of thought leaders in education, government, and private industry to challenge school leaders to "be the change they wish to see" (Boyatzis and McKee 2005, page 201; Parsley and Galvin 2008, pages 4–6; Lencioni 2007; Pink 2006; Schmoker 2006; Marzano, Waters, and McNulty 2005; Fullan 2005; Reeves 2004; Kouzes and Posner 2002; Maxwell 1999). Leadership attributes are the values and dispositions from which leaders draw in order to respond to the challenges they face. We will examine several attributes of effective leaders that are addressed in *Leadership Maps*: decision-making, resilience, servant leadership, leadership development, communication, politics and courage, achievement, and renewal.

Decision-Making

Decision-making is not only a process of prioritization informed by evidence, but also a process of experimentation, risk, failure, and success in a climate of safety and relative transparency. Safety is the corollary to candor, and without a sufficient and even passionate debate of ideas, decisions have the potential of gaining less than enthusiastic support by the very leaders who have been charged with implementing those decisions. Candor was addressed extensively in Chapter 5 as a vehicle to engage leaders and promote safe, open, and thorough dialogue around difficult issues, and it is equally important as a leadership attribute in terms of decision-making. Four recommendations are offered to promote and establish candor in the decision-making process:

- Diversity of ideas: Don't meet without them
- Hunches: Don't leave meetings without one
- Explicit and fun team roles (at least initially) to enhance dialogue
- Homework: Come prepared

The first recommendation suggests that each team meeting include a step where no decisions are reached until an alternative viewpoint is at least voiced. When leaders communicate clearly that they desire a certain outcome, it is awkward at best for their direct reports to challenge that desired action. As a result, the very input that a leader desires from his or her subordinates in leadership meetings is inhibited as a result of the leader's enthusiasm for a course of action. Followers may implement the change in practice, but unless they have been fully heard and the alternative viewpoint has been fully explored, enthusiasm or high levels of engagement are not assured. This can be addressed easily in a few moments by including an item that requires diverse thinking prior to decision-making in meeting templates.

The second recommendation calls for the best thinking of team members by insisting that someone provide a reflective summation of each meeting's discussion via his or her insights as to what transpired and what was learned. Even if the summary represents the viewpoint of the assigned individual rather than the majority viewpoint, the mere inclusion of that voice in the meeting format communicates volumes about the desire to learn together. In most cases, closing the meeting with a brief summation may help determine the degree of consensus that has been reached and whether action is warranted now or whether further deliberation is necessary. The final benefit of having a "hunch" or hypothesis presented is that it advances the likelihood that action will be taken immediately as a result of the decision made. Consider rotating the role of offering one's best "hunch" or hypothesis so that all team members are engaged, and they understand the need for their best thinking every time you meet.

The third recommendation will be necessary only with newly formed team units or units who are unaccustomed to challenging one another. Often, school

EXHIBIT 10.1 Sample *Leadership Maps* Items— Leadership Attributes and Decision-Making

ITEM	RANGE OF RESPONSES ← →	
My leadership team members recognize that I use a defined decision-making protocol that invites their candid and varied perspectives.	More than 90 percent of my leadership team would be able to provide an example	Less than 10 percent of my leadership team would be able to provide an example
Leadership meetings embrace passionate exchanges of ideas to formulate well-informed and innovative solutions to challenges.	Less than 10 percent of my leadership team would be able to provide an example	More than 90 percent of my leadership team would be able to provide an example
I have evidence to support my staff's decision-making and leadership style as:	Compliant	Committed

leaders inherit cultures steeped in years of practice where candor was rarely evident and where decisions were infrequently challenged. Roles such as the skeptic about the ideas presented, or a champion of that idea, can be particularly helpful, especially among teacher teams where harmony so often trumps candor (Schmoker 2006, page 14).

The final recommendation is as much about efficiency as it is about candor, as it refers to a simple professional discipline to complete required readings or draft planning tools prior to the meeting as planned. Decision-making as an attribute of leadership can be advanced with these suggestions.

Sometimes, leadership must engage in decision-making on a "need to know" basis (e.g., personnel issues), but for leadership teams at all levels, the need for transparency and clarity is essential to invite the best thinking from all participants. Leaders create decision-making protocols that drive decisions with evidence and translate decisions into actions that can later be evaluated and improved. Exhibit 10.1 describes three sample *Leadership Maps* items to challenge leaders in their thinking about this important attribute of leadership.

The final item in Exhibit 10.1 examines the degree to which subordinates mirror decision-making that is transparent, focused, and candid.

Resilience

The second leadership attribute, resilience, refers to the ability to respond to adversity and disappointment in such a way that leaders demonstrate a positive, focused belief and commitment to achieve their mission and realize their vision. Reeves (2008) describes a comprehensive framework for leadership assessment where resilience represents a leader's ability to bounce back, turn lemons into lemonade, and convey a sense of purpose and optimism to all those around him or her. Resilience is all about learning from our mistakes, taking stock without taking offense, and focusing on success for the organization rather than personal gain.

The attribute is represented in the optimizer leadership responsibility necessary for second-order, transformational change (Marzano, Waters, and McNulty 2005, page 42). It is a key element of effective leadership in terms of leadership assessment (Reeves 2004a, page 41), and it is a key attribute of team-building (Lencioni 2004, page 188). Exhibit 10.2 provides a few samples of *Leadership Maps* items that challenge leaders to evaluate the degree to which their behaviors reflect resilience.

Resilience is not so much a perception of strength or invincibility, or even of

EXHIBIT 10.2

Sample *Leadership Maps* Items—Resilience

ITEM	RANGE OF RESPONSES	
Previous evaluations of my performance are explicitly reflected in projects, tasks, and priorities at my school, department, or district.	True of my leadership for all major projects and priorities	No connection to previous evaluations evident in major projects or priorities
Resilience in school leadership means that:	I am viewed as a strong leader who gets the job don	I openly accept responsibility for my failures and mistakes
I constructively handle dissent by using it to inform final decisions, improve the quality of decision-making, and broaden support for final decisions.	More than 90 percent of my staff or faculty could provide multiple examples	Less than 10 percent of my staff or faculty could provide multiple examples

exceptional steadiness. Rather, it describes a level of authenticity that means you own your mistakes and model learning from them.

Servant Leadership

"The greatest among you must be servant of all."
MATTHEW 23:11,
New King James Version

The biblical injunction reveals that servant leadership is hardly a new concept, but it is one that, in recent years, has captured the imagination of leaders with a fresh perspective and understanding (Maxwell 1999; Evans 2001, cited by Elstad 2008; Schmoker 2006; Reeves 2008). This attribute enables leaders to more effectively engage colleagues, teams, and followers to pursue a purpose larger than themselves (Kouzes and Posner 2002, page 77; Boyatzis and McKee 2005, pages 120–123). Exhibit 10.3 presents sample *Leadership Maps* items related to servant leadership.

EXHIBIT 10.3

Sample *Leadership Maps* Items—Servant Leadership

ITEM	RANGE OF RESPONSES	
Commitments I make verbally:	Have the same weight as written commitments	Are always reduced to writing before anyone should take action
I am willing to complete any task I ask my staff to accomplish as an example of my commitment to our school or district.	Less than 10 percent of my staff or faculty can provide at least one example	More than 90 percent of my staff or faculty can provide at least one example
My staff and faculty recognize that I value serving others both personally and professionally.	More than 90 percent of my staff or faculty can provide at least one example	Less than 10 percent of my staff or faculty can provide at least one example

Servant leadership is a commitment to providing dedicated service and personal excellence for the benefit of others (Hallmarks of Excellence® 2007, page 55). Quinn refers to this attribute as the "fundamental state of leadership" (2004, page 22), where the process of engaging with one's professional responsibilities is characterized by appreciative inquiry, and where enjoyment of others and support for their welfare and happiness at work are as important as managing any project or completing it on time within budget.

Leadership Development

Leadership development refers to transition planning, stewardship of the public trust, delegation, and distributed leadership. Transition planning provides emerging leaders with the support, mentoring, and opportunities necessary for them to assume greater leadership roles and responsibilities over time. Transition planning should always build capacity in such a way that unforeseen tragedies do not derail the mission or stop progress toward realizing the vision for the school or district.

Leaders are challenged in *Leadership Maps* to determine the degree to which a systematic process is in place to identify potential leaders, provide opportunity for them to take on increasing levels of responsibility, and receive mentoring and coaching that build capacity along the way. Effective leaders also distribute leadership in such a way that hierarchies are less evident and teacher leadership is encouraged (Reeves 2008; Elmore 2000, pages 1–9). Do schools have a process to identify or nurture leadership? How are potential and aspiring leaders identified or brought into the process? Many systems have formal induction processes, while others offer summer school administrative opportunities to test potential leaders who are pursuing a career in school leadership. In Chapter 9, we discussed the power of assigning responsibilities to champions to coordinate, communicate, and champion critical action steps in each improvement plan to better and more fully implement that plan. A second benefit to the school or district of that act of leadership is that it distributes leadership, regardless of title, and does so with little fanfare or formal preparation.

Providing professionals with the opportunity to champion tasks associated with their passion is a powerful antidote to negative influences in the workplace. Leaders who distribute leadership effectively will also find staff looking forward to coming to work, as the likelihood that professionals will experience a sense of irrelevance or anonymity or lack evidence of their talents being appreciated or utilized will be diminished (Lencioni 2007, page 222). Exhibit 10.4 offers examples of *Leadership Maps* items associated with leadership development.

EXHIBIT 10.4

Sample *Leadership Maps* Items—Leadership Development

ITEM	RANGE OF RESPONSES	
Delegation is important at my school within the following framework:	I reserve final decision-making authority on all teams	Faculty facilitate meetings and exercise leadership on my behalf
My management of time and tasks reflects attention to the organization's priorities, and daily tasks and activities directly relate to and influence those priorities.	Not yet evident in my leadership practice	Consistently true of my leadership practice now
When I distribute leadership, I take the time to describe unambiguous expectations about the purpose, process, and desired result.	Less than 10 percent of my staff characterize my leadership style in this way	More than 90 percent of my staff characterize my leadership style in this way

Communication

Communication is its own antidote to almost all organizational ills, and leaders who take care to model a high level of transparency and invite input and feedback systematically are more apt to successfully achieve ambitious goals for their school or district. In *School Leadership That Works* (Marzano, Waters, and McNulty 2005, pages 42–43), no fewer than seven of the twenty-one leadership responsibilities identified through a meta-analysis spanning three decades involved direct communication. Affirmation, communication, ideals/beliefs, input, intellectual stimulation, outreach, and visibility all serve as antecedents of excellence in student achievement over time, and all seven involve strategic forms of communication as leadership responsibilities.

How leaders use the daily interactions with staff, students, and the public to host the conversation around needed changes and invite others to generate and test hypotheses about teaching and learning has a tremendous impact on the results they achieve. Exhibit 10.5 presents a few *Leadership Maps* items associated with this critical attribute of leadership.

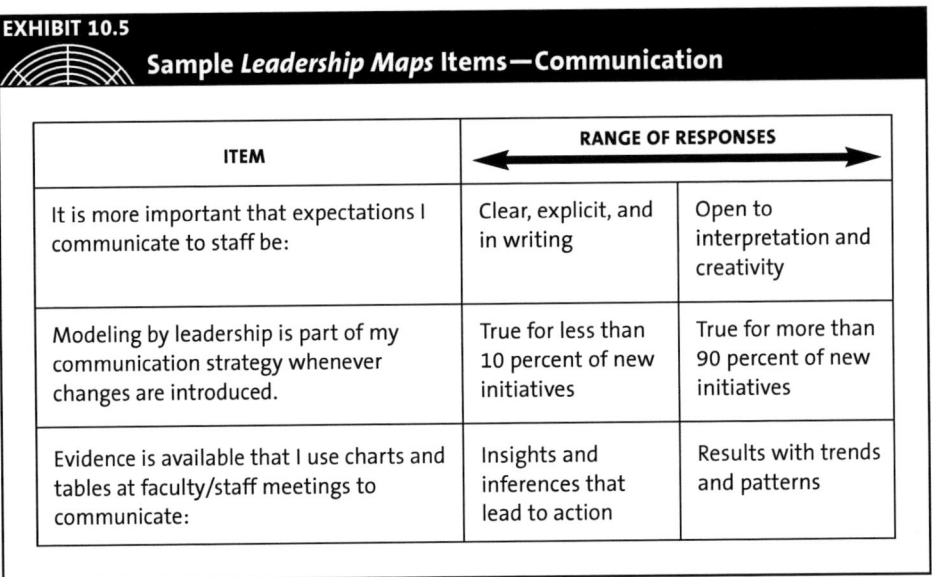

EXHIBIT 10.5

Sample *Leadership Maps* Items—Communication

ITEM	RANGE OF RESPONSES	
It is more important that expectations I communicate to staff be:	Clear, explicit, and in writing	Open to interpretation and creativity
Modeling by leadership is part of my communication strategy whenever changes are introduced.	True for less than 10 percent of new initiatives	True for more than 90 percent of new initiatives
Evidence is available that I use charts and tables at faculty/staff meetings to communicate:	Insights and inferences that lead to action	Results with trends and patterns

The second item in Exhibit 10.5 examines the degree to which communication occurs as part of the leader's role as an instructional leader. Communication occurs in every teaching interaction, and the most effective teachers are careful to model desired changes in practice.

Politics and Courage

Politics, or decision-making on the basis of how the decision will affect your standing with others, is an undesirable but unavoidable element of leadership that can only be mitigated by courageous leadership. When leaders are willing to take ethical and calculated risks, such as reassigning teachers based on student needs, monitoring the application of professional development initiatives, or redirecting budgets away from popular but ineffective or obsolete practices, leaders demonstrate courage. A number of *Leadership Maps* items associated with this dichotomy are peppered throughout each map, as illustrated in Exhibit 10.6.

Achievement

Leadership is often separated from student achievement simply because leaders do not routinely engage large numbers of students directly in the teaching-learning process. However, schools will not realize their achievement goals unless leaders establish clear goals and keep those goals in the forefront of the attention of staff, faculty, and students. It is the leader's responsibility to protect the focus

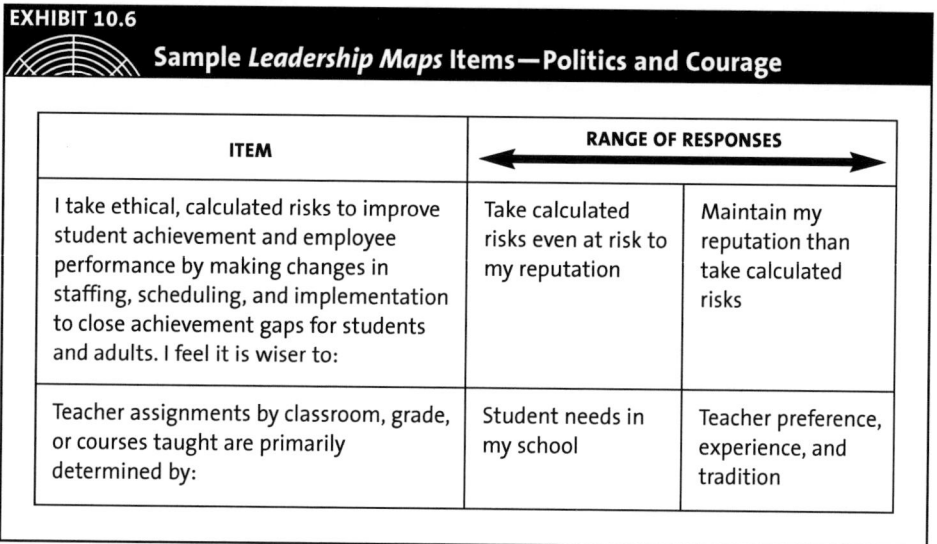

EXHIBIT 10.6

Sample *Leadership Maps* Items—Politics and Courage

ITEM	RANGE OF RESPONSES	
I take ethical, calculated risks to improve student achievement and employee performance by making changes in staffing, scheduling, and implementation to close achievement gaps for students and adults. I feel it is wiser to:	Take calculated risks even at risk to my reputation	Maintain my reputation than take calculated risks
Teacher assignments by classroom, grade, or courses taught are primarily determined by:	Student needs in my school	Teacher preference, experience, and tradition

and celebrate incremental gains. Exhibit 10.7 offers *Leadership Maps* items associated with achievement.

Renewal

In *Resonant Leadership* (2005, pages 207–210), Boyatzis and McKee describe a common attribute of leaders whose effectiveness causes them to burn out, stress out, and generally lose effectiveness. Referred to as the "sacrifice syndrome,"

EXHIBIT 10.7

Sample *Leadership Maps* Items—Achievement

ITEM	RANGE OF RESPONSES	
A wide variation in achievement at my school is best described as the result of:	Student readiness and motivation	Variation in teaching practices at my school
Actions of teachers and their impact on student achievement are something I demonstrate and invite discussion about.	More than 90 percent of my teachers are able to provide at least one example	Less than 10 percent of my teachers are able to provide at least one example

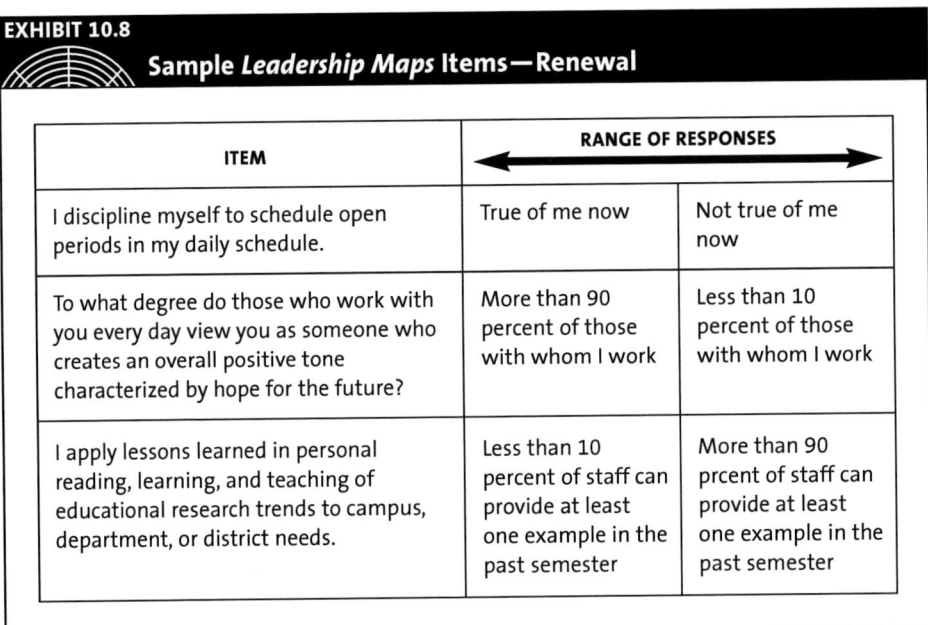

EXHIBIT 10.8

Sample *Leadership Maps* Items—Renewal

ITEM	RANGE OF RESPONSES	
I discipline myself to schedule open periods in my daily schedule.	True of me now	Not true of me now
To what degree do those who work with you every day view you as someone who creates an overall positive tone characterized by hope for the future?	More than 90 percent of those with whom I work	Less than 10 percent of those with whom I work
I apply lessons learned in personal reading, learning, and teaching of educational research trends to campus, department, or district needs.	Less than 10 percent of staff can provide at least one example in the past semester	More than 90 prcent of staff can provide at least one example in the past semester

leaders who give and give and deal with everyone else's stress often ignore or minimize the effect of such a stressful work life on their health and on their performance. Boyatzis and McKee describe a "slip into dissonance." Covey (1989, page 288) calls for a "sharpening of the saw" discipline as an important leadership habit. This discipline involves remaining sharp and current on a professional level but also remaining sharp physically, mentally, emotionally, and spiritually. Exhibit 10.8 provides sample *Leadership Maps* items associated with this important dimension of leadership.

Leadership That Leaves a Legacy

Leadership attributes serve as a compass that directs the actions of leaders. Those who recognize the powerful potential influence they have to shape the culture of their schools through their daily decisions, disciplines, and questions are the leaders who build capacity and make their workplace a desirable place to come every day. More importantly, such leaders maintain and protect the focus on the vision and mission to make a difference for students, staff, and the profession.

Attributes such as decision-making, resilience, servant leadership, leadership development, renewal, communication, and the courage to face the political realities every leader encounters distinguish the most effective leaders from their peers and produce sustained gains in student achievement.

Reflection

Big Idea

Resilience equips leaders for the long term.

What is the premise behind this statement?

How does it apply personally in your current position?

Big Idea

How I communicate *without* words determines the impact of how I communicate *with* words.

What is the premise behind this statement?

How does it apply personally in your current position?

Big Idea

Sharpening the saw applies to my professional, personal, and physical fitness levels.

To what degree of fitness is your level of professional learning?

To what degree do you provide time each day to "smell the roses?"

Reflect on your best next step for renewal.

CHAPTER 11

Leadership Maps for Breakthrough

> *"Education reform is at a stage where many of the components of successful large-scale reform are evident in schools' collective basement. One half of the solution is to seek out and identify the critical elements that need to be in place; the other half is to combine them creatively. This is not simply a job of alignment, but rather one of establishing dynamic connectivity among the core elements."*
>
> MICHAEL FULLAN, PETER HILL, and CARMEL CREVOLA,
> *Breakthrough* (2006, page 15)

Dynamic connectivity requires a reflective, insightful, and informed view of undiscovered possibilities in leadership. It also requires a shift in understanding and application and a new way to communicate new understandings and insights. These efforts will allow leaders to replicate best practices quickly, to make best practices common, and to celebrate the incremental, early wins necessary to build efficacy and shift the conversation. This chapter will discuss how *Leadership Maps* contributes to such changes.

Reflection and Response

Leadership Maps provides school leaders with a tool that allows them to identify areas that need greater precision, more consistent fidelity of implementation, or improved communication prior to the availability of data that will reveal the need for action. This is possible because: (1) *Leadership Maps* challenges leaders to examine values, current practice, and desired levels of implementation across eight very distinct domains of leadership, and (2) *Leadership Maps* invites leaders to examine practices based on emerging research for which they currently have no available data as evidence. *Leadership Maps* is designed to help leaders consider a wide range of possible antecedent measures, then begin to collect data strategically based on the leaders' assessment of their own needs. The level of precision is only heightened when teams of leaders examine their results. Some practical examples (depicted in Exhibits 11.1 through 11.3 and discussed below) illustrate how to maximize the benefit of *Leadership Maps* to each leader as part of a "treasure hunt" for leadership.

Field Experiences

Leadership Maps has the potential to serve educators as a meaningful probe into the effectiveness of their professional practices, both as a granular probe into a specific domain area, and as a more global snapshot of leadership from 30,000 feet. Practitioners have used it as both, as revealed by the experience of leaders across the continent. Superintendent Mark Keene, of Westfield Washington Community Schools Corporation in Indiana, engaged his senior leaders to complete *Leadership Maps* as a team and as individuals. Westfield strategically employed *Leadership Maps* by comparing outcomes and engaging in focused reflection to identify opportunities for learning and opportunities to improve existing practices. Dr. Keene's team elected to:

- Compare responses within domains to identify how to apply areas of strengths to areas needing improvement
- Reflect on the totality of *Leadership Maps* responses as represented in the "wagon wheel" analysis tool (Exhibit 6.1)
- Compare iterations of *Leadership Maps* assessment for insights regarding changes in practice between administrations
- Compare district *Leadership Maps* assessments with assessments from other districts across the nation, with assessments from similar districts, or with assessments from districts that have a similar focus, such as performance excellence (Baldrige) or data teams.

As a result, Westfield was able to determine that their individual and collective performances were balanced across domains and that their self-assessments were consistently higher than the average assessments for both principals and central-office officials across the continent. Westfield used the data from their *Leadership Maps* to focus on distinctions within domains, drawing inferences from hypothetical comparisons, as depicted in Exhibit 11.1.

EXHIBIT 11.1

Sample Within Domain Comparisons—Data Analysis

Survey Questions	Range of Responses		
Analyzed data routinely leads to recommendations, which lead to decisions to take action.	More than 90 percent of the time	9	Less than 10 percent of the time
I triangulate (simultaneously analyze) multiple types of data to inform decision-making about teaching and learning.	I routinely triangulate data to inform decision-making	4	I do not currently triangulate data

When routine data analysis (perceived at a high level) was compared with implementation gaps, such as the use of triangulation analysis, leaders recognized a limited level of depth in current practice and an opportunity to go deeper. Since the district had an established level of examining the data to make decisions, it was also poised to apply that strength to establish a new level of precision by providing training, support, and practice in triangulation using multiple forms of data to better inform decisions.

Steven Achramovitch, superintendent of Greece Public Schools in New York, utilized *Leadership Maps* to reflect on similar distinctions but also chose to use the self-assessment tool to:

- Reflect on the totality of *Leadership Maps* responses as represented in the "wagon wheel" analysis tool (Exhibit 6.1)
- Identify district strengths by item and its relationship to student achievement
- Examine *Leadership Maps* for patterns or trends across levels or between schools and the central office.

Administrators in both districts used the "wagon wheel" to analyze *Leadership Maps* results. Exhibit 11.2 provides an instructive comparison between schools, between iterations over time for the same leadership team, or between school levels.

In Exhibit 11.2, leaders are able to draw inferences from the year-to-year differences as high-yield leadership strategies, PIM™, and leading change showed dramatic improvement, data analysis declined, and all other areas remained relatively stable. Reflective inquiry about the dynamics between these domains

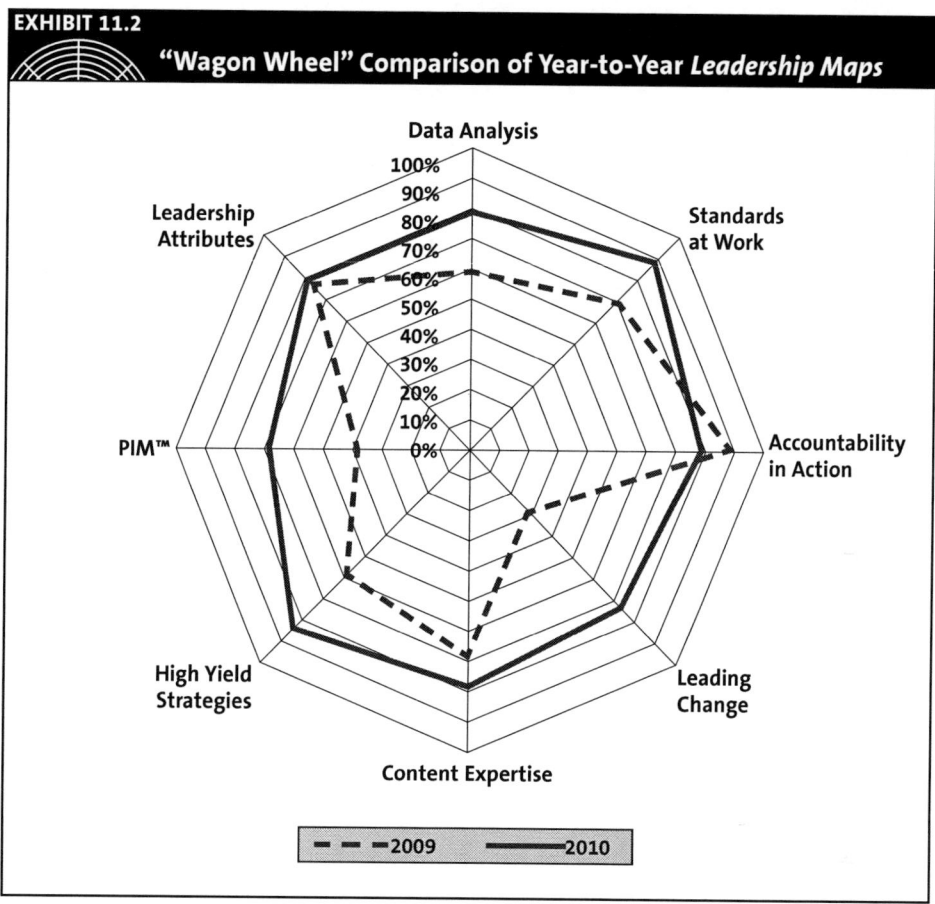

EXHIBIT 11.2

"Wagon Wheel" Comparison of Year-to-Year *Leadership Maps*

Data Analysis

Leadership Attributes

Standards at Work

PIM™

Accountability in Action

High Yield Strategies

Leading Change

Content Expertise

- - - 2009 ———— 2010

assists leaders to discover insights that would otherwise be hidden. One hypothesis could be that the team had a greater awareness of the gaps in their data analysis process because they were more intentional in their PIM™ efforts around school improvement. This, in turn, improved the quality of monitoring and coaching with high-yield strategies. They also may recognize that the reduced number of initiatives and more effective support to teachers through professional development alignment helped lead to needed changes.

The "wagon wheel" in Exhibit 11.2 also reveals that very little change occurred in terms of accountability, content expertise, and leadership attributes. This is an acknowledgment that a strong foundation was in place in 2009 that allowed the leaders to move to much deeper implementation in the subsequent year. These leaders reflect a common observation for those who participate in *Leadership Maps*—that the inquiry process in collaboration is a powerful form of

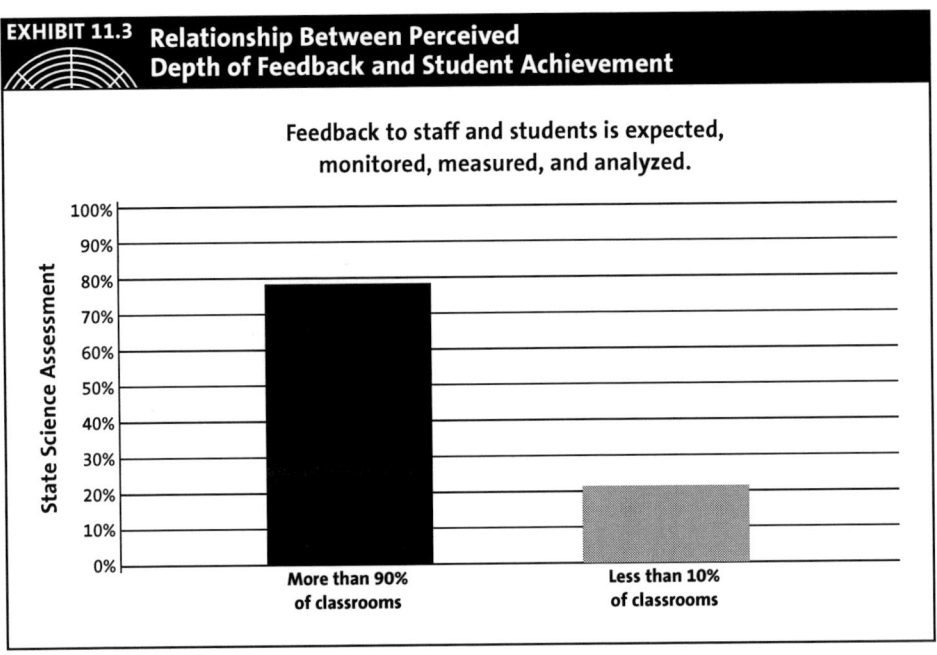

EXHIBIT 11.3 **Relationship Between Perceived Depth of Feedback and Student Achievement**

professional development that protects the focus and vision of the school or district while celebrating successes as they unfold.

Exhibit 11.3 illustrates a deeper examination of data by local districts and school leaders to determine the relationship locally between student achievement and leadership practices. *Leadership Maps* invites leaders to discover relationships across domains.

The districts in Exhibit 11.3 experienced immediate benefits from using *Leadership Maps* as a treasure hunt. The assessment allows leaders to identify areas of need before they become crisis areas and to proactively target areas where they can improve their own knowledge and skills as leaders. The assessment also assists leaders in recognizing the degree to which best practices are implemented with quality and consistently by staff and faculty. *Leadership Maps* helps leaders recognize possibilities and challenges before they become obvious or make it to the "radar screen," equipping leaders to act strategically while hosting conversations about courage and action.

Advancing What Works at All Levels

The assessment errs on the side of deep implementation and evidence of best practices across leadership domains to move schools, districts, and achievement forward. Each of the *Leadership Maps*, however, is designed to elicit daily disciplines of leadership that can transform the mundane operations of schools and districts into opportunities for excellence. Three disciplines in particular—the need to communicate, the need to replicate, and the need to celebrate—illustrate the powerful possibilities that *Leadership Maps* offers to proactively lead rather than follow, despite the complex challenges facing educators today.

The Need to Communicate

In order to realize all of the benefits of powerful instructional and operational strategies available to classrooms, schools, and school systems, leaders need to systematically communicate not only results, but also insights and inferences about those results. To lead educators at any level to display data and rely on evidence to make decisions, leaders must model that practice. Far too many central-office leaders in school systems rely on their principals and assistants to advance their vision, and far too many superintendents rely on their central-office leaders to communicate their message. The best ideas, plans, and practices will realize their potential only when senior leaders themselves model the changes they desire for their organization.

For parents to understand the need to achieve proficiency on challenging academic content standards, principals must communicate the distinction between the application of knowledge as an indicator of success and merely acquiring that knowledge through traditional, select-response assessments. Leadership today requires not only a depth of expertise with the details of instructional strategies and best practices, but also the practice of connecting staff and faculty to the most effective strategies by varied and ongoing communication. A systematic process of communicating the vision will protect the focus if it is routine, relentless, and reliable (predictable).

Leaders have a great opportunity to host the conversation in written and electronic communications, such as school or district Web sites, focus groups, newsletters, e-mail broadcasts, webinars, Web site links with partners, Wiki Web sites, collaborative chat rooms, blogs, and video-conferencing. By the time this book goes to print, additional opportunities will have been created by technology to communicate with any audience at any time leaders choose.

Leaders also have collaborative opportunities at each staff meeting, leadership team event, cabinet meeting, or board meeting to advance key ideas. The *Leadership Maps* items described throughout this volume assume a depth of communication and a reservoir of data to frame the communication. Communication of the value of particular instructional strategies is necessary to lead schools today. *Leadership Maps* provides a thorough examination of the knowledge of those strategies and of the degree to which they have been implemented.

The Need to Replicate

The replication of best practices is perhaps the highest level of leading change, as local, existent practices are identified and extended to serve more students more effectively. The old paradigm of replication (formal experimental-control research studies), where schools participate in validation of an external program rather than identifying local practices that have an immediate impact on teaching and learning, is insufficient for schools today. We need a systematic and agile response system that identifies best practices early and that helps educators at all levels develop skills to implement, monitor, and evaluate such systems in a manner that is practical and user-friendly

Practices that warrant replication can be identified through *Leadership Maps,* such as the need for leaders to be fluent with the standards of academic content across disciplines, or the need to monitor school improvement initiatives frequently regarding capacity-building and student progress toward goal attainment, or the degree to which individual leaders invite staff and faculty to generate and test hypotheses about teaching and learning. In fact, virtually every *Leadership Maps* example item provided throughout this book holds potential for replication because it was developed based on best practices in the field, including data analysis, accountability in action, leading change, and high-yield strategies. Leaders should use this volume to identify replicable practices within their organization, implement them well, and extend them as broadly as possible to reach as many students as possible.

The Need to Celebrate

If leaders communicate extensively and clearly to remove unnecessary ambiguity in language and foster a common understanding of data, evidence, and current reality, and if leaders learn to select the most effective practices in their midst, define them with precision, implement them with fidelity, and replicate them rapidly, students and staff will be poised to launch student achievement and school practices to a new level that creates a "try again" culture of evidence. If the same leaders can add protocols that celebrate incremental, granular gains in student achievement and capacity-building for adults, the potential for growth and excellence will be greatly enhanced. The obvious benefit of data analysis and effective monitoring is to make better-informed decisions, but an even more powerful outcome is an increase in efficacy for both students and staff. Celebrating gains, however incremental, is a reminder to educators that they do make a difference and to students that they can achieve at high standards. By holding a celebration, the message is clear that gains in student achievement are highly valued. Finally, celebrations are fun activities that build personal connections to learning and contribute to creating a culture of evidence.

Early Insights

Leadership Maps offers you an opportunity to stretch yourself to a new level proactively, rather than react or respond to current realities after the fact. It offers you an opportunity to peer into your practice and select a few key measures as indicators of excellence, and to do so in a way that monitors volitional changes in practice as much as it monitors expectations that require compliance. Chapter 6 described a systematic way for leaders to create their own *Leadership Maps* based on the practices that matter in each unique leadership setting.

The eight domains addressed in this volume do not presume to capture all of the nuances and realities of leadership in today's schools. Instead, they focus on the area most neglected (deep implementation) and attempt to stretch leaders to evaluate how their practices are impacting the quality of that implementation. By providing a comprehensive array of measurable indicators of best practices, *Leadership Maps* offers the leaders of tomorrow an important tool to identify, monitor, and replicate practices that are predictive of continuous, sustained, improved student achievement.

By instituting a few simple changes selected on the basis of your own analysis, you and your team will be directing the change to accommodate the realities and context of your own, very real, educational challenges. *Leadership Maps* is a tool that can help leaders identify those granular gains, not only in learning and achievement, but in teaching practices, such as fluency with a particular instructional strategy, consistent application of data teams, or creation of smart, common formative assessments. *Leadership Maps* also speaks to the acts of leadership that establish a safe platform for teacher innovation and risk-taking, explicit monitoring, and thorough, thoughtful, reflective evaluating in cycles. Leaders who routinely help faculties and staff to embrace possibilities in teaching differently, achieving differently, and leading differently will become the change they desire.

Leadership Maps is fundamentally about discovering what works and what doesn't. It invites you, as the reader, to look beyond your intentions to the impact your leadership has on others. In so doing, it is my hope that *Leadership Maps* becomes the road map that empowers you to experience breakthrough, allowing you to make a difference like never before.

APPENDIX A: **Reliability and Validity of** *Leadership Maps*

Both the school administrator and central-office 100-Factor *Leadership Maps* were routinely reviewed in terms of item analysis to determine their effectiveness in assessing leadership actions and implementation by applying the Pearson's *r* coefficient of correlation and the standard error of measurement. The first demonstrates the ability of *Leadership Maps* to yield consistent results across multiple administrations (repeatability), and the second establishes confidence that the items and domains of *Leadership Maps* meet accepted probability levels.

EXHIBIT A.1 **Pearson *r* Domain Correlations— School and Central-Office Administrators**

School Administrator *Leadership Maps* Pearson's *r* Matrix (*n* = 126)								
	DATA Analysis	MSW	AIA	Leading Change	Content Expertise	HYS	PIM™	Leadership Attributes
DATA		0.609	0.666	0.449	0.405	0.548	*0.861*	0.448
MSW	0.609		0.751	0.476	0.663	0.762	*0.867*	0.444
AIA	0.666	0.751		0.544	0.560	0.722	0.763	0.474
Leading Change	0.449	0.476	0.544		0.285	0.497	0.436	0.437
Content Expertise	0.405	0.663	0.560	0.285		0.614	*0.835*	0.471
HYS	0.548	0.762	0.722	0.497	0.614		0.681	0.419
PIM™	0.861	0.867	0.763	0.436	0.835	0.681		0.574
Leadership Attributes	0.448	0.444	0.474	0.437	0.471	**0.419**	0.574	

Central-Office *Leadership Maps* Pearson's *r* Matrix (*n* = 73)								
	DATA Analysis	MSW	AIA	Leading Change	Content Expertise	HYS	PIM™	Leadership Attributes
DATA		*0.886*	*0.895*	0.439	*0.874*	*0.907*	*0.861*	0.576
MSW	*0.886*		0.837	0.476	0.803	0.762	*0.867*	0.460
AIA	*0.895*	0.837		0.407	0.749	0.798	0.835	0.494
Leading Change	0.439	0.476	0.407		0.511	0.497	0.436	0.692
Content Expertise	*0.874*	0.803	0.511	0.511		0.872	0.835	0.681
HYS	*0.907*	0.762	0.798	0.497	0.872		0.789	0.702
PIM™	*0.861*	*0.867*	0.835	0.436	0.835	0.789		0.504
Leadership Attributes	0.576	0.460	0.494	0.692	0.681	0.702	0.504	

Pearson's *r*

Exhibit A.1 examines the correlations across the eight domains of *Leadership Maps*, with the top 10 percent of correlations identified in ***bold italics***, and the lowest 10 percent of correlations identified in boxes. Relationships among the domains for all 100 items ranged from *r* values of .285 to .867—highly significant correlations for the field test sample size ($n = 126$) and for central-office administrators ($n = 73$).

The data in Exhibit A.1 describes internal consistency and confidence for multiple administrations of *Leadership Maps*. This is particularly important to *Leadership Maps*, as it is designed for multiple administrations by leaders and leadership teams at frequent intervals within any subscription year. The second statistic addresses the question of confidence in the overall instrument and individual items.

Standard Error of Measurement

The standard error of measurement (S_{EM}) helps to establish confidence that the items and domains of *Leadership Maps* are reliable to a 95 percent probability level ($p \leq .05$). The S_{EM} is an index of accuracy that allows us to interpret a single individual's score as if multiple administrations of the assessment were made without the influence of any intervening variables. By measuring the degree of error or influence on results across seven different *Leadership Maps* assessments, the S_{EM} provides a means to establish a level of confidence for *Leadership Maps* items. Exhibit A.2 describes results for respondents across all 100 *Leadership Maps* factors for the complete 100-item assessment, across two fifty-item assessments (Form A and Form B), and across four twenty-five-item *Leadership Maps* (A, B, C, D).

EXHIBIT A.2

Standard Error of Measurement Probability Levels

Pearson Coefficient of Correlation *r*	.55
Variance	6.56
Mean Score for All Items *X*	7.68
Standard Deviation S_D	2.56
Standard Error of Measurement S_{EM}	1.68
Confidence Interval for S_{EM}	$p \leq .05$
% *Leadership Maps* Item Scores Within the S_{EM}	96

Ninety-six percent of scores in Exhibit A.2 fell within the S_{EM}, exceeding a 95 percent level of probability that results are unlikely to have been derived by chance.

Validity

Criterion-referenced validity for *Leadership Maps* was selected to analyze test items and their relationship to measures of student achievement. *Leadership Maps* compares understanding and application of antecedents (predictors) with resulting student achievement performance. Antecedent conditions or behaviors represent all 100 of the *Leadership Maps* items. Exhibit A.3 describes how *Leadership Maps* scores related to student achievement in the *Leadership Maps* field test.

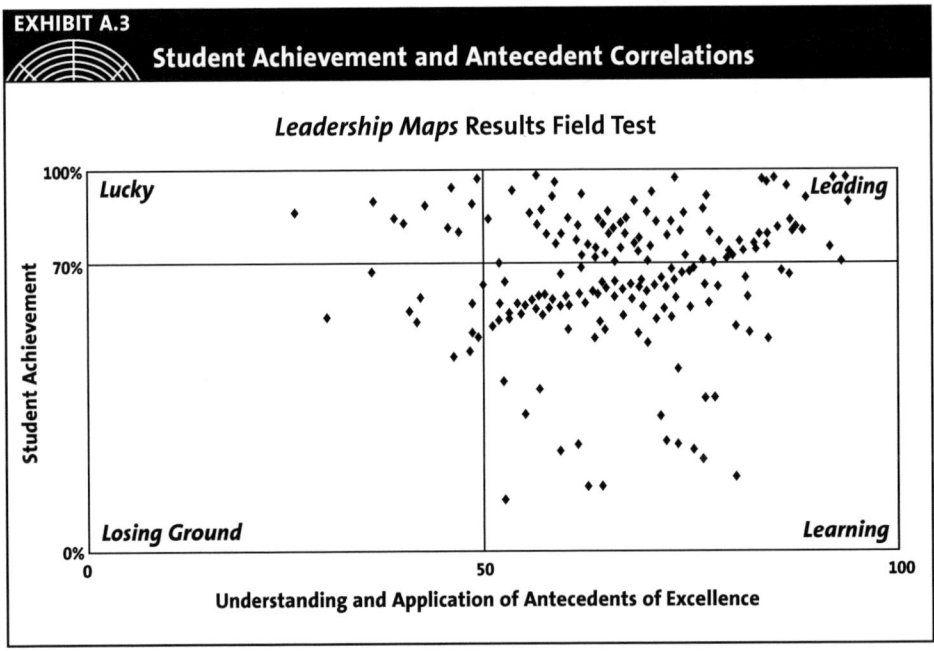

EXHIBIT A.3

Student Achievement and Antecedent Correlations

APPENDIX B: **"Wagon Wheel" Chart**

In "wagon wheel" charts, graphical representations compare performance across multiple variables. The primary purposes include: (1) to determine which issue is most critical, and (2) to compare performance across multiple dimensions.

Steps in Using "Wagon Wheel" Charts

1. Assign key variables to each of the eight spokes on the chart.
2. Collect data across key variables.
3. Establish a scale for each spoke, with the highest performance on the outer rim of the circle. Spokes have their own scales.
4. Plot the data on the spokes, color-coding the data to distinguish entities (classrooms, schools, departments, grade levels).
5. Connect the lines for each entity (spokes).
6. Identify the variables that show the largest gaps between your entity and the benchmarks represented on the outer rim.

Example Variables for "Wagon Wheel" Chart Spokes
Central Office (District)

- Multidimensional assessment of leadership. Graphically represents concise data that illustrates leaders' strengths and weaknesses. Equally useful as a self-assessment.

- Elimination of duplication of effort. Tracking processes across departments or schools.

- Budget projections. Budgeted to actual expenditures reveal degree of precision and accuracy.

- Use of technology. Degree of variability within entities (e.g., all central office) in terms of fluency with key technologies (spreadsheets, databases). Movement toward a paperless office, other dimensions of efficiency.

- Awareness of district goals, personal and departmental missions, and performance indicators for departments.

EXHIBIT B.1   "Wagon Wheel" Example Variables

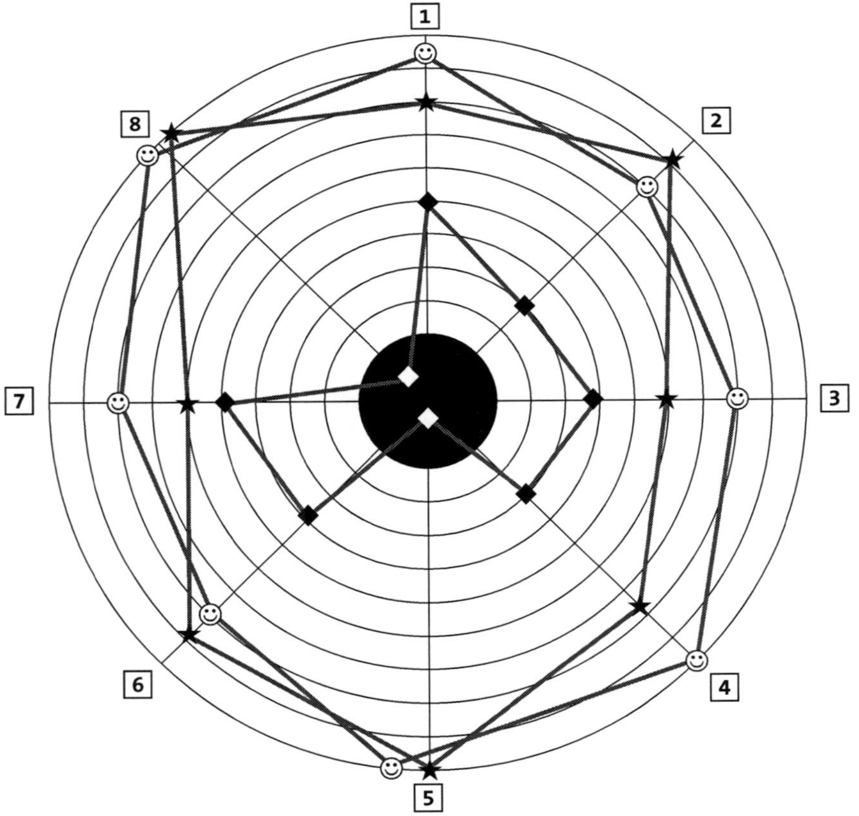

"Wagon Wheel" Example Variables

1. Percentage standards checklist in place
2. Percentage proficient in facts/opinion
3. Percentage proficient in algebraic functions
4. Number of performance assessments in place
5. Number of teachers with standards-based instructional calendar
6. Percentage proficient in writing assessment
7. 100 percent minus the gap free or reduced (F/R) lunch versus school achievement—language arts
8. Class average exceeds state average in math

Teacher A = ☺
Teacher B = ★
Teacher C = ◆

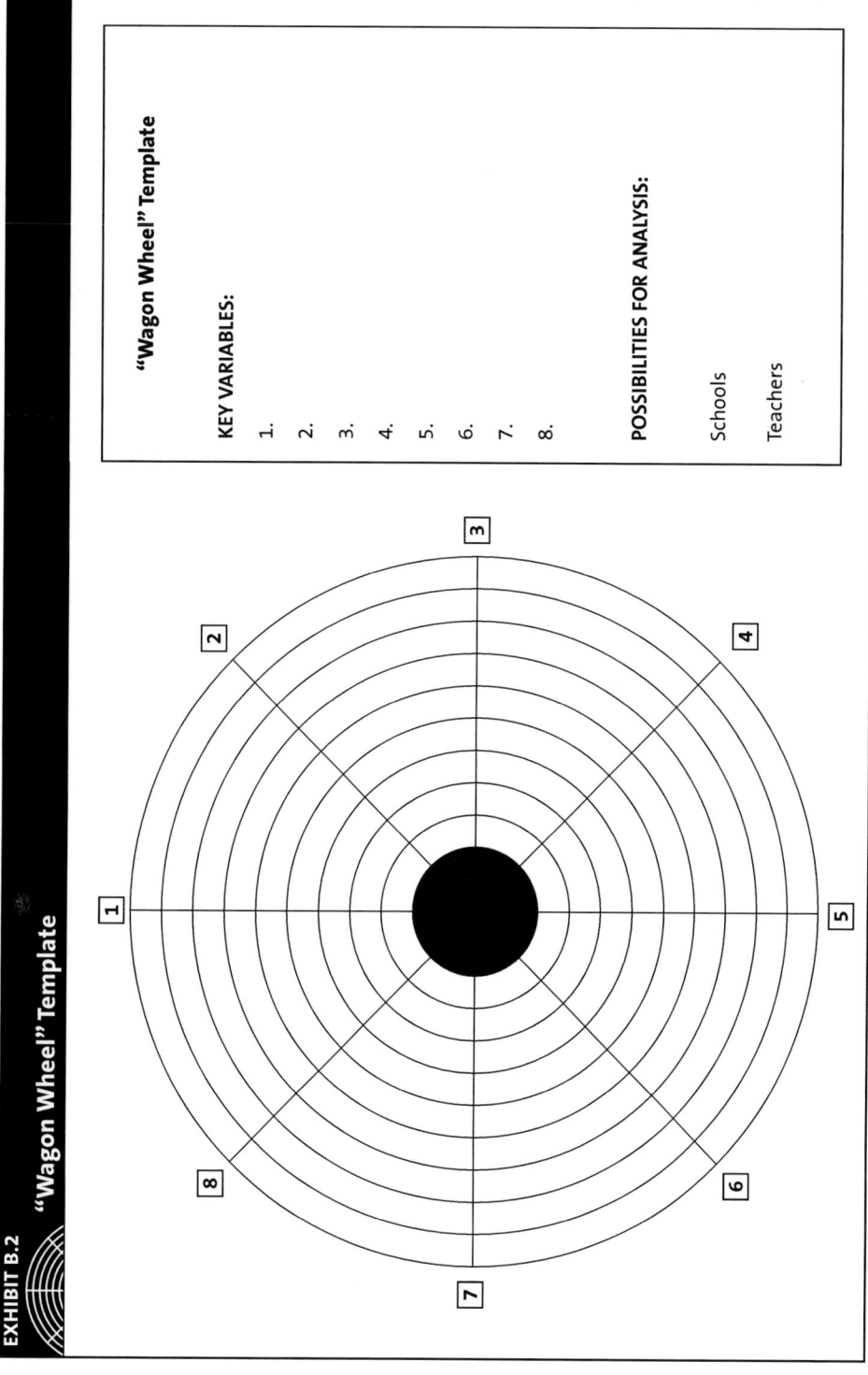

EXHIBIT B.2

"Wagon Wheel" Template

"Wagon Wheel" Template

KEY VARIABLES:

1.
2.
3.
4.
5.
6.
7.
8.

POSSIBILITIES FOR ANALYSIS:

Schools

Teachers

Site Level (Schools)

- Reduction of classroom interruptions (e.g., intercom announcements per day).

- Classroom checklist for standards implementation. "Wagon Wheel" helps monitor the percentage of items in place by the teacher.

- Leverage applied in performance assessments (number and type of standards incorporated).

- Student performance results, including behavior, attendance, and achievement.

- Time lag between identification of learning gap and intervention.

- Grade/subject level safety net (power) standards demonstrated at key times (October, March, and May).

- Percentage of total assessments delivered as performance assessments.

In Exhibit C.1, the vertical (Y) axis describes the level of achievement, and the horizontal (X) axis describes the level of understanding and application of antecedents of excellence (adult practices that make a difference in student achievement). The map also depicts a range of possible scales to create the leadership map.

Comparable Antecedent Scales

By converting selected data across a variety of scales, leaders are positioned to create a wide variety of *Leadership Maps*—for example, rubric scores for writing organization for fourth- through sixth-grade data teams, achievement on six-

EXHIBIT C.1

Scale Options for Achievement (Y) and Antecedent (X) Axes

Comparable Achievement Scales

−1 to +1	%	Likert		Rubric		*Leadership Maps*	
1.0	30	5	10	4	6	**Lucky**	**Leading**
+.8	25		9				
+.6	23	4	8		5		
+.4	20		7	3			
+.2	16	3	6		4		
0	15						
−.2	14	2	5		3		
−.4	10		4	2			
−.6	7	1	3		2		
−.8	5		2				
−1.0	0	0	1	1	1	**Losing Ground**	**Learning**

Scale −1.0 to 1.0	−1	−.8	−.6	−.4	−.2	0	.2	.4	.6	.8	1.0
Percent	<10	10+	20+	30+	40+	50	50+	60+	70+	80+	90+
Likert 0–5	0		1		2		3		4		5
Likert 1–10	1	2	3	4	5		6	7	8	9	10
Rubric 1–4	1			2				3			4
Rubric 1–6	1		2		3		4		5		6

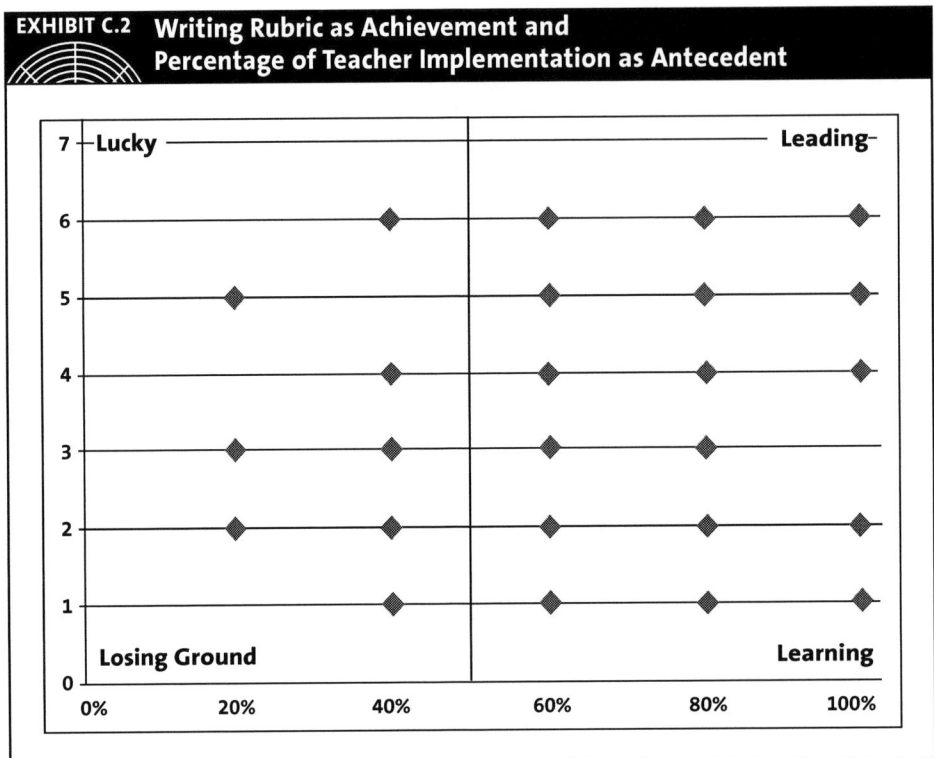

EXHIBIT C.2 Writing Rubric as Achievement and Percentage of Teacher Implementation as Antecedent

point writing-rubric monthly assessments, and antecedent data represented by the percentage of the days per week in which teachers provide daily instruction in 6+1 Traits of Writing, grades four through six.

Not only is it possible to create the map with data about implementation and

EXHIBIT C.3

Levels of Student Achievement and Levels of Implementation

Teacher	Degree of Implementation	Classroom Writing Rubric %	Teacher	Degree of Implementation	Classroom Writing Rubric %
A	69%	3.714286	E	69%	3.571429
B	74%	4.714286	F	71%	3.714286
C	49%	3.571429	G	69%	3.142857
D	80%	5.142857	H	71%	5.142857
			I	74%	5.285714

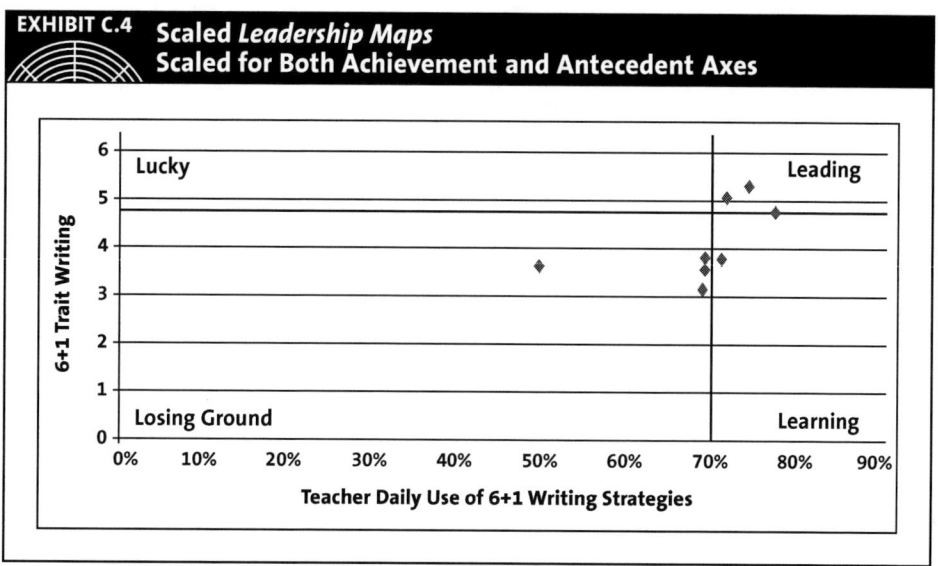

EXHIBIT C.4 Scaled *Leadership Maps*
Scaled for Both Achievement and Antecedent Axes

writing achievement, but the process also yields comparative data by teacher. Examine a second *Leadership Map* created with the same data, but this time utilizing average student scores by teacher (Exhibit C.3). Teachers A through I (nine intermediate teachers, grades four through six) reported the information depicted in Exhibit C.3.

In the *Leadership Map* in Exhibit C.4, the principal or leadership team has set the threshold for success in terms of student achievement (Y, or vertical, axis) as an average of 4.5 out of 6 possible on the scoring rubric. Note that leaders are also encouraged to establish a threshold for antecedents as well, in this case at 80 percent implementation of the strategy on four of five days weekly.

A traditional *Leadership Map* sets the antecedent level midpoint on the scale as well as at the midpoint on the scale for student achievement, where seven of eight teachers would be designated learning or leading. In Exhibit C.4, the team selected a much higher standard, revealing that only one of the nine teachers was performing at the leading level, three at the lucky level, and five at the losing ground level. Regardless of what level you select, the process allows you to tailor your map as you see fit.

Exhibit C.5 provides a blank template to help you develop your own *Leadership Map* with guiding questions to select the horizontal X axis antecedent actions by educators as well as the four achievement measurements for the Y (vertical) axis.

EXHIBIT C.5 Template *Leadership Map* with Achievement as Y Axis and Antecedents as X Axis

Lucky		**Leading**
Losing Ground		**Learning**

1. Achievement

2. Understanding and Application of Antecedents of Excellence

Achievement Variables	Understanding and Application of Antecedents of Excellence
a.	a.
b.	b.
c.	c.
d.	d.
e.	e.
f.	f.

APPENDIX D: **Sources for Academic Content Standards**

Content Area	Advocate Professional Organizations for Standards	Content Area	Advocate Professional Organizations for Standards
Reading	International Reading Association National Reading Panel National Council of Teachers of English	**Physical Education**	Academy of Kinesiology and Physical Education National Association of Sports and Physical Education National Coalition for Promoting Physical Activity President's Council on Physical Fitness and Sports
Writing	Canadian Authors Association National Council of Teachers of English National Writing Centers Association National Writing Project Northwest Regional Educational Laboratory The Association of Writers and Writing Programs	**Science**	American Association for the Advancement of Science National Science Foundation National Academy of Science National Science Teachers Association The Association for Science Education (United Kingdom)
Mathematics	Association of Mathematics Education Teachers European Society for Research in Mathematics Education National Council of Teachers of Mathematics National Science Foundation Science, Technology, Engineering, and Mathematics (STEM) Education Coalition	**Instructional Technology**	Society for Information Technology and Teacher Education SITTE) Association for Educational Communications and Technology Association for Educational Technology International Society for Technology in Education (ISTE)

Content Area	Advocate Professional Organizations for Standards	Content Area	Advocate Professional Organizations for Standards
Social Studies	Center for Civic Education Geography Education Standards Project National Council for the Social Studies Professional Organization for Social Studies Educators Society for History Education (SHE) Canada's National History Society: Education	**Special Education**	American Association on Mental Retardation (AAMR) American Council of the Blind Association for Persons with Severe Handicaps (TASH) Autism Society of America Brain Injury Association Council for Exceptional Children National Center for Learning Disabilities National Institute on Disability and Rehabilitation Research (NIDRR)
Visual and Performing Arts	Americans for the Arts Arts Education Partnership Consortium of National Arts Organizations National Arts Education Association National Arts and Education Partnership President's Committee on the Arts and Humanities	**World Languages**	Modern Language Teachers Association Association of Departments of Foreign Languages American Council on the Teaching of Foreign Languages World Language Teachers' Organizations
Career and Technical Education	Association for Career and Technical Education National Center for Career and Technical Education High Schools that Work	**Teaching and Learning**	National Board for Professional Teaching Standards National Staff Development Council National Research Council U.S. Department of Education State Departments of Education Regional Educational Laboratories Council of Chief State School Officers

APPENDIX E: *Basic Leadership Maps* Items

Leadership Maps

	Site Administrator *Leadership Maps*	Central-Office Administrator *Leadership Maps*
1	Analyzed data routinely leads to recommendations, which lead to decisions to take action for the following estimated percentage of decisions: _____ .	Analyzed data routinely leads to recommendations, which lead to decisions to take action for the following percentage of decisions: _____ .
2	School improvement goals should be written for the entire school or to close learning gaps for specific subgroups.	Department and school improvement goals should be written: to close learning gaps, reduce duplication of efforts, and improve productivity, or to measure systemwide improvements.
3	A guaranteed and viable curriculum is best represented by agreement by teams about what gets taught when or autonomy and flexibility about what topics to teach when.	Once the decision has been made to establish a schedule, select an intervention, or implement an improvement strategy, I stay the course for the entire year or I make changes if data warrants.
4	Technology promotes accountability at my school by making data more accessible to my staff or making data more transparent to staff, students, and stakeholders.	Technology promotes accountability in my area of responsibility by making data more accessible to my staff or making data more transparent to staff, students, and stakeholders.
5	Teacher assignments by classroom, grade, or courses taught are primarily determined by student needs in my school or teacher preference, experience, and tradition.	I estimate the percentage of school leaders who have aligned curriculum, assessments, and instruction to state content standards at _____ .
6	I estimate the percentage of teachers at my school who participate in mentoring, modeling, and coaching on a weekly basis at _____ .	The percentage of people whom I supervise who cite examples of how I promote replication of best practices (ideas borrowed, ideas given away, results from ideas, opportunities to identify benchmarks, learn from successful models, etc.) is estimated at _____ .

Leadership Maps

	Site Administrator *Leadership Maps*	Central-Office Administrator *Leadership Maps*
7	I estimate the percentage of teachers at my school who examine student work to determine proficiency and agree on specific characteristics of acceptable work at ____.	I estimate the percentage of staff in my department who agree on a specific standard of acceptable work at ____.
8	At my school, writing is best characterized by a common rubric with writing assignments in all content areas or lessons that include explanation, examples, practice, and feedback.	I estimate the percentage of staff who employ a defined protocol or process to complete a routine job task at standard at ____.
9	I estimate the percentage of teachers who have aligned curriculum, assessments, and instruction to state content standards at ____.	My district's vision/mission statements are visible and form the basis of decision-making in the following percent of schools: ____.
10	My school's improvement plan aligns comprehensive needs assessment to reflective inquiry about cause and effect to create goal statements, and the master plan design is monitored for quality implementation and allows for a thorough evaluation of the plan. T F	My strategic or district/department improvement plan aligns comprehensive needs assessment to reflective inquiry about cause and effect to create insightful goal statements. The master plan design is monitored for quality implementation and allows for a thorough evaluation of the plan's effectiveness. T F
11	I estimate the percentage of teachers at my school who examine both student achievement data and data about teaching practices to make decisions at ____.	I estimate the percentage of school leaders in my district who examine both student achievement data and data about teaching practices before making decisions at ____.
12	My leadership in aligning curriculum to standards is evident in links between professional development, assessment design, and lesson planning in ____ percent of classrooms.	As a leader, an effective culture is most evident when: (a) staff enjoy coming to work and are supported by colleagues, or (b) standards are well known and carried out in practice.
13	I estimate the percentage of teachers at my school who employ a defined process to engage students in every lesson (e.g., Engaging Scenario or Know, Understand, Apply, Demonstrate, Extend) at ____.	At any time, I can report with accuracy on the work production, quality, and status of key projects for the following percentage of my staff ____.

Leadership Maps

	Site Administrator *Leadership Maps*	Central-Office Administrator *Leadership Maps*
14	Leadership in monitoring is best presented by monitoring of school improvement initiatives in all classrooms or by monitoring the impact of classroom practices on student achievement.	At what level are you comfortable teaching improvement strategies to your staff (inviting them into the learning process and preparing them to implement strategies following training and practice)? I am very comfortable to I am not at all comfortable.
15	At my school, the percentage of music classes that incorporate academic content and assessment in writing, reading, mathematics, or social studies is estimated at _____.	The percentage of those whom I supervise, and who demonstrate a relentless focus on performance results by displaying quality work, graphing progress toward goals, or analyzing data, is estimated at _____.
16	Professional development at my school is referenced in the supervision process.	As a supervisor, the relationship I have with those whom I supervise is best characterized as friend or coach.
17	Each observation and supervision conference narrative references how teaching performance impacts schoolwide goals or references lessons observed.	Communication with vendors, clients, suppliers, and stakeholders (e-mail, Web site, focus groups, and newsletters) is: (a) something best delegated to staff, or (b) part of my leadership responsibility.
18	My school's vision/mission statements are visible and form the basis of decision-making in the following percentage of classrooms _____.	Goals and objectives at my school are: (a) developed on the basis of student achievement needs, or (b) aligned to district goals.
19	Professional development in my school is differentiated by modality, readiness and the match between student needs and staff competency the following percentage of the time _____.	I estimate the percentage of my staff who utilize a continuous improvement cycle for data-driven decision-making (e.g., treasure hunt, analyze, prioritize, set SMART goals, select instructional strategies, develop results indicators, and reflect on results for lessons learned) at _____.
20	I estimate the percentage of teachers at my school who create classroom environments that stimulate engagement by posting standards, displaying excellent student work, and making sure Essential Questions are evident at _____.	I estimate the percentage of staff who volunteer an idea to improve the organization to me each month at _____.

Leadership Maps

	Site Administrator *Leadership Maps*	Central-Office Administrator *Leadership Maps*
21	The percentage of my faculty who participate in at least one book study every year is estimated at _____.	Which characteristic of decision-making is more important for you as a leader to communicate within your department, district, or area of responsibility: Clarity or Certainty?
22	At my school, high-yield strategies are supported with professional development, observed practice, and corrective feedback the following percentage of the time _____.	Benchmark practices and high-yield strategies are supported with professional development, observed practice, and corrective feedback for the following percentage of strategies _____.
23	At my school, art classes that incorporate academic content and assessment in writing, reading, mathematics, science, or social studies is estimated at the following percentage: _____.	At what level are you comfortable teaching your staff to better serve other staff, vendors, and the public? I am completely comfortable teaching or I am uncomfortable teaching about customer service.
24	My staff can identify specific ways I share personal and organizational mistakes in a way that guides, inspires, and teaches others. This is consistently true of my leadership practice now or not yet evident in my leadership practice.	The percentage of schools or departments that monitor progress by posting data walls in their work area is estimated at _____.
25	Communication with parents should be primarily delegated to faculty or should be an essential part of my leadership responsibility.	The number of initiatives in my department or district is limited to two or three initiatives per major goal area, or limited only by the creativity and energy of my administrators, faculty, and staff.
26	With regard to teaching the criteria for developing power standards for any curriculum area to my faculty and staff (leverage, endurance, readiness):	I estimate the percentage of my staff who utilize data tools such as the cause-and-effect "fishbone," force-field analysis, "wagon wheel," or affinity charts and other graphic organizers of data at _____.
27	Goals and objectives at my school are developed on the basis of student achievement needs or aligned to district goals.	To guide my organization, annual goals need to be: (a) fixed as the target we will measure ourselves against, or (b) flexible and adaptable to circumstances that occur.

Leadership Maps

	Site Administrator *Leadership Maps*	Central-Office Administrator *Leadership Maps*
28	As a leader, it is important that my faculty and staff understand that I trust them and am vulnerable about my mistakes or I am a solid, steady leader whose performance is predictable.	Those whom I supervise can cite examples of how I encourage them to challenge my ideas at the following level: from more than 90 percent of staff to less than 10 percent of staff.
29	At my school, feedback to staff and students is expected, monitored, measured, and analyzed in the following percentage of classrooms ____.	I estimate the percentage of staff in my work unit or department who implement at least one project requiring cross-training quarterly at ____.
30	The percentage of science teachers who emphasize inquiry, connections to other subjects, goal setting, project planning, and wide application of the scientific method in classroom instruction is estimated at ____.	Collaborative review of work produced in my department or district occurs at a rate of: (a) more than 90 percent of staff currently participate (b) less than 10 percent of staff currently participate.
31	My school probes to determine parental satisfaction each school year by inviting feedback through a focused survey that is carefully reviewed and analyzed, or through or several written or online surveys, focus groups, and 1:1 teacher conferences.	I have evidence to support my staff's decision-making and leadership style as committed or compliant.
32	My management of time and tasks reflects attention to the organization's priorities, and daily tasks and activities directly relate to and influence those priorities. This is consistently true of my leadership practices now or is not yet evident.	The percentage of teams in my department or district that utilize Essential Questions and Big Ideas in project planning is estimated at ____.
33	I triangulate (simultaneously analyze) multiple types of data to inform decision-making about teaching and learning (collaboration data such as the frequency of DT meetings, accountability data such as the number of classroom walk-throughs, or instructional strategies such as the percentage of teachers who implement with fidelity). This is consistently true of my leadership practices now or is not yet evident.	I triangulate (simultaneously analyze) multiple types of data to inform decision-making about teaching and learning (collaboration data such as the frequency of DT meetings, accountability data such as the number of classroom walk-throughs, or instructional strategies such as the percentage of teachers who implement with fidelity). The practice is routine for me now to I do not currently triangulate data.

Leadership Maps

	Site Administrator *Leadership Maps*	Central-Office Administrator *Leadership Maps*
34	The number of initiatives at my school is limited to two or three initiatives per major goal area or is limited only by the creativity and energy of my teachers.	Staff assignments are primarily determined in my area of responsibility by: (a) performance gaps or strengths matched to project needs, or (b) staff choices, experience, and traditions.
35	I estimate the percentage of teachers at my school who use the concept of Big Ideas as part of unit or lesson planning at ____.	In my department/district, flexible schedules to allow greater time to focus on core tasks are present in the following percentage of offices, departments, or schools ____.
36	Collaborative scoring of student work in my school occurs with the following percentage of teachers participating ____.	How do you best advance an important change initiative in your department, district, or work unit: (a) through the chain of command, relying on administration to ensure implementation, or (b) through highly respected, non-administrative personnel who can influence colleagues?
37	I estimate the percentage of my faculty who employ the use of metaphors, similes, and analogies regularly enough to observe the practice daily in my school at ____.	In my department/district, feedback to staff and students is expected, monitored, measured, and analyzed in the following percentage of schools ____.
38	A wide variation in performance is best described as the result of staff and student readiness or variation in leadership practices.	The percentage of teachers in my district who would report that their supervising administrator understands the power standards for their academic content area is estimated at ____.
39	The percentage of physical education teachers who incorporate academic content and assessment in writing, reading, mathematics, or science in their classes is estimated at ____.	Staff whom I supervise or colleagues would characterize my leadership on a continuum as carefully aligned efforts or as fragmented.

Leadership Maps

	Site Administrator *Leadership Maps*	Central-Office Administrator *Leadership Maps*
40	Resilience in school leadership means that I openly accept responsibility for my failures and mistakes, or that I am viewed as a strong leader who gets the job done.	The percentage of supervisors or administrators in my organization who are able to identify three or more collaborative structures (learning teams, meeting norms, collaborative scoring, assessment calendars, cause-and-effect analysis, etc.) is estimated at ____.
41	I estimate the percentage of teachers at my school who regularly use scoring guides that inform instruction and are instructive to students at ____.	Observation and supervision conferences for those whom I supervise reference the following: (a) how leadership performance impacts department or district goals, or (b) how leaders perform specific activities and job tasks.
42	At what level do you monitor the frequency and quality of performance assessments by department or grade level at your school? At least ____ quarterly to not at all.	Collaboration in data analysis is planned and scheduled by collaborative teams (project teams, staff units) for an estimated ____ percentage of major tasks in my district/department.
43	I estimate the percentage of teachers at my school who use data about teaching practices to better understand student achievement at ____.	The percentage of team members in my department/district who have responsibility and authority for developing and evaluating progress toward common goals is estimated at ____.
44	At my school, flexible schedules to allow greater time in basic skills in reading, writing, and mathematics are evident in the following percentage of classrooms ____.	The percentage of those whom I supervise, and who would characterize my vision as informed by evidence and driven by specific strategies, is probably ____.
45	The percentage of my faculty who can demonstrate how note taking is utilized in their classrooms is estimated at ____.	Distributed leadership that empowers staff to assume responsibility, exercise authority, and take calculated risks within defined parameters is: (a) evident across all key functions in my department or district, or (b) not yet evident in key functions in my department or district.

Leadership Maps

	Site Administrator *Leadership Maps*	Central-Office Administrator *Leadership Maps*
46	Teachers at my school report that their supervising administrator understands the power standards for their academic content area the following percentage of the time: _____.	The percentage of my staff who apply specific, proven, standards-based strategies (collaborative review, team thinking, prioritized daily task lists, service orientation, progress monitoring, data analysis) is estimated at _____.
47	My expectation for visibility and contact with students is: (a) I expect faculty to recognize each student by name, or (b) I should not have to recognize every student but all should know me as a school leader.	Resilience in leadership means that: (a) I am viewed as a strong leader who gets the job done, or (b) I openly accept responsibility for my failures and mistakes.
48	At what level are you comfortable teaching Essential Questions to your faculty (the process of inviting students into the learning process and preparing them to answer the questions at the end of the lesson, unit, semester)? I am comfortable to I am not at all comfortable.	"Unwrapping" of policies to design and implement more focused, standards-based lessons is something I teach my team by aligning practices with policy and goal targets.
49	Collaboration in data analysis is planned and scheduled by collaborative teams (e.g. DTs, PLC teams) for an estimated percentage of meetings _____.	Quality of implementation is most effectively established by: (a) a leader's words and actions, or (b) consensus of those responsible for implementing programs or policies.
50	The percentage of my faculty who demonstrate a relentless focus on student achievement by displaying student work, graphing progress toward goals, or analyzing data to improve their practice is an estimated _____.	The percentage of my staff who can describe examples of how I recognize achievement on a regular basis (daily, weekly, monthly, or even by quarter or semester) is an estimated _____.
51	The percentage of my staff who can describe examples of how I recognize achievement at my school on a regular basis (daily, weekly, monthly, or even by quarter or semester) is an estimated _____.	My staff would characterize my leadership in supporting them with data as:

Leadership Maps

	Site Administrator *Leadership Maps*	Central-Office Administrator *Leadership Maps*
52	The percentage of my reading teachers who are fluent with guided reading, mini-lessons, and at least one writing trait protocol (e.g., 6+ Traits, Simple Six) is estimated at ____.	The percentage of those whom I supervise, and who organize their program of work to address district and department goals, is estimated at ____.
53	I monitor the frequency of student reading and writing assessment in the following percentage of classrooms where reading is taught ____.	The percentage of my staff who participate in at least one book study every year is estimated at ____.
54	I facilitate changes in practice or programs by considering the following realities of the change process for adults: (a) adults perceive personal loss when changes are introduced, or (b) change needs to be based on needs of students, not adults.	In my department/district, we ensure that substandard performance for all employees is supported with additional assistance within thirty days: (a) more than 90 percent of the time, to (b) less than 10 percent of the time.
55	Delegation is important at my school within the following framework: I reserve final decision-making authority on all teams, or faculty members facilitate meetings and exercise leadership on my behalf.	My expectation for visibility and contact with district staff is demonstrated by the fact that I: (a) expect those whom I supervise to recognize staff by name, or (b) do not recognize staff members, but all should be able to recognize me by name.
56	I estimate the percentage of DTs, faculty study groups, or PLC teams that routinely implement and monitor effective teaching strategies to increase student achievement at my school at ____.	It is better for my staff to fulfill their job description requirements by: (a) focusing on deep application and knowledge of a few standards, or (b) covering all standards listed.
57	At my school, the percentage of faculty who use learning logs, instructional calendars, or pacing guides to monitor curriculum and student progress is estimated at ____.	At what level do you monitor the frequency and quality of performance by department or work unit? Monitoring ranges from not currently monitoring performance assessments to monitoring at least quarterly.
58	The percentage of my faculty who provide evidence in lesson planning of strategies to generate and test hypotheses across the curriculum is an estimated ____.	The percentage of my staff that set and post clear objectives for every lesson is estimated at ____.

Leadership Maps

	Site Administrator *Leadership Maps*	Central-Office Administrator *Leadership Maps*
59	My understanding of focused, quality teaching is best characterized by detailed curriculum/instruction that includes learning objectives, proficiency standards, and progress indicators or strategies for each objective, explicit routines, and proven practices.	The percentage of those whom I supervise, and who are fluent with and able to describe our accountability system, is estimated at _____ .
60	At my school, academically deficient students (including IEP students) receive targeted instruction within thirty days of diagnosed need the following percentage of the time _____ .	The percentage of my staff who display department data through charts, graphs, and tables is estimated at _____ .
61	At my school, no student is held more accountable than adults in terms of deadlines, meeting processes, work quality, or re-work opportunities in the following percentage of classrooms _____ .	In my department/district, internal and external surveys reveal that clients, vendors, suppliers, community, and staff: (a) feel welcome more than 90 percent of the time, or (b) feel welcome less than 10 percent of the time.
62	It is important that the culture in my school or district be represented by awareness of a collective capacity to accomplish goals or diversity in knowledge, skills, and interests among staff.	Delegation is important in my district and department within the following framework: (a) I delegate but reserve final decision-making authority, or (b) my assistants facilitate meetings and exercise leadership on my behalf.
63	As an instructional leader, budgeting for me is best characterized by the following statement: (a) I often need assistance revising my budget, or (b) I assist others with budget revisions.	In my department/district, the percentage of staff who systematically identify strengths in terms of antecedent adult actions (causes) is estimated at _____ .
64	The percentage of my faculty who provide evidence of questions, cues, and advance organizers during formal observations and informal walk-throughs is estimated at _____ .	I am familiar with industry standards for best practices for my department, and I apply and communicate those leadership practices by (a) monitoring adherence to standards for processes and results, or (b) failing to monitor process or results standards at the current time.

Leadership Maps

	Site Administrator *Leadership Maps*	Central-Office Administrator *Leadership Maps*
65	At what level do you understand the relationship of Big Ideas to Essential Questions and how both relate to the "unwrapping" process: (a) I understand these related concepts fully, or (b) I don't understand these concepts at this time.	The percentage of my staff (including certified, non-certified, para-educators, part-time) who can describe our vision for the future and defend it to others is estimated at _____.
66	At my school, the percentage of grade-level and department teams that have responsibility and authority for developing and evaluating common assessments is estimated at _____.	The percentage of my staff who link professional development to the evaluation process is estimated at _____.
67	The percentage of my faculty who provide multiple opportunities for students to improve the quality of their work through re-work and diverse performance assessments to meet the same standard is estimated at _____.	The percentage of my staff who emphasize data analysis in their decision-making is estimated at _____.
68	The percentage of my faculty who integrate science and math by applying the scientific method with graphs, charts, and tables in a major written project at least quarterly is estimated at _____.	The percentage of my staff who work collaboratively with department or district team members weekly is estimated at _____.
69	I gather and disseminate results of DT minutes for data team, PLC team, or whole-faculty study group meetings for the following percentage of meetings _____.	It is important that the culture in my school or district be represented by communicating data that represents positive aspects of our schools, or by communicating bad news as readily as awards or great test scores.
70	The percentage of staff and faculty with the authority to stop obsolete or ineffective practices without consulting me is estimated at _____.	As an instructional leader, budgeting for me is best characterized by the following statement: (a) I leverage resources to achieve district objectives, or (b) I manage budgets effectively and return funds each fiscal year.

Leadership Maps

	Site Administrator *Leadership Maps*	Central-Office Administrator *Leadership Maps*
71	A wide variation in achievement at my school is best described as the result of student readiness and motivation or a variation in teaching practices.	The percentage of my staff who emphasize inquiry in goal setting (identifying cause and effect) is estimated at _____.
72	I estimate the percentage of teachers at my school who implement at least one interdisciplinary performance assessment each quarter at _____.	In my department or district, teams are accountable to meet specific improvement targets by reporting periodically on their progress and revising improvement plans at least annually. The percentage of teams that meet this standard is estimated at _____.
73	The percentage of my faculty who emphasize nonfiction writing in daily lesson plans is estimated at _____.	The percentage of those whom I supervise, and who differentiate systemwide goals from department or school goals, is estimated at _____.
74	The percentage of my faculty who understand and apply a powerful and proven standards-based writing strategy daily (6+ Traits, Step Up to Writing, Simple 6, etc.) is estimated at _____.	My department/district has: (a) defined a standard for replicating effective practices, or (b) not yet defined a standard for replicating effective practices.
75	My school has: (a) defined a standard for replicating effective practices, or (b) not yet defined a standard for replicating effective practices.	I facilitate changes in practice or programs by considering the following realities of the change process for adults: (a) adults perceive personal loss when changes are introduced, or (b) change needs to be based on needs of students, not adults.
76	I estimate the percentage of teachers at my school who utilize data tools, such as the cause-and-effect "fishbone," "force-field analysis," "wagon wheel," or affinity charts and other graphic organizers of data, at _____.	I model an inquiry approach to leadership that questions and probes for understanding about our current practice (Why? How? If, then?) that ranges from being systematic and embedded throughout the organization to not being evident at all at the current time.

Leadership Maps

	Site Administrator *Leadership Maps*	Central-Office Administrator *Leadership Maps*
77	Cooperative learning at my school is demonstrated by all teachers at least weekly or is used at the discretion of each teacher.	I routinely monitor communication (meetings, memos, directives) throughout my department or district in an estimated _____ percent of communications.
78	As a leader, my skill and knowledge regarding specific teaching protocols for English Language Learners (ELLs) is characterized by fluency in at least one strategy and use of a formal protocol for classroom observations. This protocol is (a) well established at my school, or (b) I am not yet familiar with methods designed for ELL students.	I take ethical, calculated risks to improve student achievement and employee performance by making changes in staffing, scheduling, and implementation to close achievement gaps for students and adults. I feel it is wiser to: (a) maintain my reputation than take calculated risks, or (b) take calculated risks even at risk to my reputation.
79	I model an inquiry approach to leadership and teaching that questions and probes for understanding about our current practice (Why? How? If, then). It is currently (a) used systematically with all faculty and staff or (b) not yet evident at all.	Leaders routinely face a tension between implementing needed changes and achieving consensus. What statement best represents your leadership style in practice? It is important to: (a) encourage a passionate interchange of opinions, or (b) maintain harmony and consensus.
80	Sustained professional development under my leadership is characterized by the following faculty implementation levels two or more years after they are introduced: More than 90 percent of faculty to less than 10 percent of faculty continue to implement that development in their classrooms.	I disseminate data, charts, and graphs of ideas borrowed, ideas given away, and the impact of such replication on improved performance and student achievement in meetings: (a) at least quarterly, or (b) I have yet to schedule one replication meeting.
81	The percentage of my science teachers who utilize Essential Questions and Big Ideas in lesson plans at least weekly is estimated at _____.	The percentage of my staff who routinely monitor their performance to improve the quality of work in terms of performance standards is estimated at _____.
82	At my school, departments, grade levels, and DTs are accountable to meet specific improvement targets by reporting periodically on their progress and revising improvement plans at least annually. This is true for _____ percent of teacher teams.	I gather and disseminate results of team minutes and action plans for department or district team meetings at an estimated _____ percent of meetings.

Leadership Maps

	Site Administrator *Leadership Maps*	Central-Office Administrator *Leadership Maps*
83	The percentage of teachers at my school who can describe specific standards for quality of instruction that I monitor is estimated at _____ .	My involvement in collaboration is best represented by differentiating meetings based on clearly defined objectives: (a) at least weekly, or (b) as determined by each team leader or facilitator.
84	I am familiar with math content and process standards (problem-solving, reasoning/proofs, communication in the language of mathematics, connections to math ideas and other subjects, and mathematical representations), and I (a) monitor math classrooms for all five standards, or (b) do not currently monitor math process standards.	As a leader, my role is best characterized by skill and knowledge of the details of: (a) providing corrective feedback to staff, or (b) dealing with disruptions and organizing resources for staff.
85	Adoption of new initiatives at my school is: (a) determined by teacher perceptions of student needs, or (b) made only if ineffective or obsolete practices are also discarded.	As a leader, my skill and knowledge regarding specific protocols for implementation are characterized by defined improvement cycles and use of formal protocols to monitor quality and efficiency. Practices are (a) evident in my department or district, or (b) have not yet been established.
86	It is more important that expectations I communicate to staff be: (a) clear, explicit, and in writing, or (b) open to interpretation and creativity.	As a leader, it is important that my faculty and staff understand that I: (a) am a solid, steady leader whose performance is predictable, or (b) trust my team and am willing to be vulnerable about mistakes I make.
87	The statement most representative of my leadership in facilitating staff and faculty teams is: (a) it is important to maintain harmony and consensus, or (b) it is important to encourage a passionate interchange of opinions.	Commitments I make verbally: (a) are always reduced to writing before anyone should take action, or (b) have the same weight as written commitments.
88	The percentage of my faculty who choose to emphasize essential power standards in core subjects rather than cover every subject or every topic is estimated at _____ .	Sustained professional development under my leadership is characterized by the following implementation levels two or more years after they are introduced: (a) more than 90 percent are still applying the training, or (b) less than 10 percent are still applying the training.

Leadership Maps

	Site Administrator *Leadership Maps*	Central-Office Administrator *Leadership Maps*
89	I estimate the percentage of teachers at my school who create and administer performance tasks as part of their performance assessments at _____.	I conduct staff meetings by designing discussion and action items so that the following percentage of agenda items are devoted to improving current practice _____.
90	My staff members know precisely what is expected of them in the evaluation process, including a clearly defined set of expectations that clarify the district evaluation instrument item by item. I estimate the following percentage of staff would agree _____.	Adoption of new initiatives in my department or district is: (a) determined by staff perceptions of student needs, or (b) made only if ineffective/obsolete practices are also discarded.
91	As a leader, I expect nonfiction writing lesson plans across the curriculum to be evident in the following percentage of classrooms across content areas _____.	Visible displays of data and employee work products throughout the building should: (a) provide clear evidence of challenges, growth, and achievement, or (b) not compare staff or students in any way.
92	At my school, visible displays of data and student work are evident in the following percentage of classrooms across content areas _____.	Implementation monitoring in my department or district includes standards for quality, specific actions to be taken, timelines, and methods to gather evidence. True or false as an indication of my leadership now.
93	Are you comfortable teaching the components of an engaging scenario to your faculty (scenario, challenge, roles, audience, product)? Describe your comfort level from complete to not at all.	The use of a daily prioritized list is something that: (a) I use to complete tasks, engage in leadership, and collaborate effectively, or (b) interruptions in my work make unrealistic.
94	To what degree do those who work with you every day view you as someone who creates an overall positive tone characterized by hope for the future? From more than 90 percent to less than 10 percent.	Steady, incremental change requires: (a) incremental changes in practice, or (b) dramatic, well-defined changes in practice.

Leadership Maps

	Site Administrator *Leadership Maps*	Central-Office Administrator *Leadership Maps*
95	"Unwrapping" of standards to design and implement more focused, standards-based lessons is something that I teach my faculty by identifying the concepts, skills, and context needed to master specific standards. This occurs routinely or not yet.	A wide variation in performance is best described as the result of staff and student readiness or variation in leadership practices.
96	Distributed leadership that empowers faculty to assume responsibility, exercise authority, and take calculated risks within defined parameters is (a) evident across all key functions at my school, or (b) not yet evident in key functions at my school.	Professional development in my department is chosen on the basis of: (a) gaps in student achievement or staff performance, or (b) staff preferences.
97	I estimate the percentage of teachers at my school who utilize a continuous improvement cycle for data-driven decision-making (e.g., treasure hunt, analyze, prioritize, set SMART goals, select instructional strategies, develop results indicators, and monitor results) at _____.	Staff meetings routinely invite and receive candor through alternative viewpoints in the following percentage of faculty and team meetings _____.
98	As a leader, my role is best characterized by: (a) having skill and knowledge in the details of providing corrective feedback to staff, or (b) dealing with disruptions and organizing resources for staff.	My staff know precisely what is expected of them in the evaluation process, including a clearly defined set of expectations that clarify the district evaluation instrument item by item. More than 90 percent would agree to less than 10 percent would agree.
99	The use of common formative assessments (CFAs) administered before and during the teaching process to guide teaching and learning and determine the degree to which students know the material is: (a) not yet established in any departments or grade levels, or (b) established schoolwide in all departments and at all levels.	It is more important that expectations I communicate to staff be: (a) clear, explicit, and in writing, or (b) open to interpretation and creativity.
100	Staff meetings routinely invite and receive candor through alternative viewpoints from the following percentage of faculty and staff team meetings _____.	To what degree do those who work with you every day view you as someone who creates an overall positive tone characterized by hope for the future? From more than 90 percent would agree to less than 10 percent would agree with this statement.

References

Ainsworth, L. 2003. *Power standards: Identifying the standards that matter the most.* Englewood, CO: Advanced Learning Press.

———— 2003a. *Unwrapping the standards: A simple process to make standards manageable.* Englewood, CO: Advanced Learning Press.

Ainsworth, L., and Viegut, D. 2006. *Common formative assessments: How to connect standards-based instruction and assessment.* Thousands Oaks, CA: Corwin Press.

Anderson, L.W. *et al.* 2001. *A taxonomy for learning, teaching, and assessing: A revision of Bloom's taxonomy of educational objectives.* New York, NY: Longman Publishing, pages 38–62.

Andrews, R., Biggs, M., Seidel, M., *et al.* 1996. *The Columbia world of quotations.* New York, NY: Columbia University Press, #1605, #32863.

Auman, L., and Young, K. 2004. "What's happening at school?" (Unpublished manuscript on classroom walk-throughs; personal conversation with author, November 13).

Bangert-Drowns, R.L., Kulik, C.C., and Kulik, J.A. 1991. "Effects of classroom testing." *Journal of Educational Research* 85(2): 89–99.

Belmonte, J. 2006. Personal communication. Olympia, WA: Thurston Public School District, October.

Berliner, D. 1994. "Expertise: The wonder of exemplary performances creating powerful thinking in teachers and students," in *Creating powerful thinking in teachers and students.* J.N. Mangieri and C. Collins Block, editors. Fort Worth, TX: Holt, Rinehart & Winston, Chapter 7.

Besser, L., Anderson-Davis, D., Peery, A., *et al.* 2008. *Data teams.* Englewood, CO: The Leadership and Learning Center, page 63.

Borman, G.D., and Hewes, G.M. 2002. *The long-term effects and cost-effectiveness of success for all.* Washington, D.C.: Office of Educational Research and Improvement, U.S. Department of Education (Grant No. OERI–R-117-D40005).

Boyatzis, R., and McKee, A. 2005. *Resonant leadership.* Boston, MA: Harvard Business School Press, page 88.

Bradberry, T., and Greaves, J. 2003. *The emotional intelligence quick book: Everything you need to know to put your EQ to work.* New York, NY: Fireside Publishing.

Buckingham, M., and Clifton, D.O. 2001. *Now, discover your strengths.* New York, NY: The Free Press.

Casciaro, T., and Lobo, M.S. 2005. "Competent jerks, lovable fools, and the formation of social networks." *Harvard Business Review* (June): 92–99.

Collins, J. 2001. *Good to great: Why some companies make the leap . . . and others don't.* New York, NY: HarperCollins.

Council of Chief State School Officers 2008. *Educational leadership policy standards: ISLLC 2008.* Washington, D.C.: Council of Chief State School Officers.

Covey, S. 1989. *The seven habits of highly effective people.* New York: Simon & Schuster, pages 188–190.

Culham, R. 2003. *6+1 Traits of writing.* New York: Scholastic Professional Books.

Danielson, C. 1996. *Enhancing professional practice: A framework for teaching.* Alexandria, VA: Association for Supervision and Curriculum Development.

———— 2002. *Teaching evaluation.* Alexandria, VA: Association for Supervision and Curriculum Development.

Darling-Hammond, L. 1997. *The right to learn: A blueprint for creating schools that work.* San Francisco: Jossey-Bass, page 69.

———— 1999. "Reshaping teaching policy, preparation, and practice: Influences of the National Board for Professional Teaching Standards." Washington D.C.: American Association of Colleges for Teacher Education (February).

DuFour, R., Eaker, R., and DuFour, R., *et al.* 2005. *On common ground: The power of professional learning communities.* Bloomington, IN: Solutions Tree.

Eide, P.A. 2001. "Coping with change: Educational reform in literacy practice." *Primary Voices K-6* 9(3): 15–20.

Elmore, R. 2000. "Building a new structure for school leadership." In *American Educator.* Washington, DC: American Federation of Teachers, pages 1–9.

———— 2004. "The right thing to do: School improvement and performance-based accountability." Harvard University and Consortium for Policy Research in Education (CPRE). Washington, D.C.: The NGA Center for Best Practices.

Elstad, E. 2008. "Towards a theory of mutual dependency between school administrators and teachers: Bargaining theory as research heuristic." *Educational Management Administration and Leadership* 36(3): 393–414.

Epstein, J.L., and Sheldon, S.B. 2002. "Present and accounted for: Improving student attendance through family and community involvement." *Journal of Educational Research* 95: 308–318.

Evans, R. 2001. *The human side of school change: Reform, resistance, and real-life problems of innovation.* San Francisco: Jossey-Bass.

Fernandez, K.E. 2006. "Clark County School District Study of the Effectiveness of School Improvement Plans (SESIP)." Las Vegas, NV: University of Nevada at Las Vegas.

Fisher, D., and Frey, N. 2007. *Checking for understanding: Formative assessment techniques for your classroom.* Alexandria, VA: Association for Supervision and Curriculum Development.

Foster, E. 1993. "A review of invitational teaching, learning, and living." *Journal of Invitational Theory and Practice* 2(2): 97–100.

Fredricks, J.A., Blumenfeld, P.B., and Paris, A. 2004. "School engagement: Potential of the concept, state of the evidence." *Review of Educational Research* 74(1): 59–109.

Fullan, M. 2005. *Leadership & sustainability: System thinkers in action.* Thousand Oaks, CA: Corwin Press.

———— 2008. *The six secrets of change: What the best organizations do to help their organizations survive and thrive.* San Francisco: Jossey-Bass.

Fullan, M., Hill, P., and Crevola, C. 2006. *Breakthrough.* Thousand Oaks, CA: Corwin Press.

Ganz, J. 2007. *The expanding digital universe: A forecast of worldwide information growth through 2010.* Retrieved 12.3.2007 from EMC² at http://www.emc.com/about/destination/digital_universe

Gira, R. 2002. "Acceleration, not remediation: Closing the achievement gap with AVID strategies." *New Horizons Online Journal* 8(3).

Giuliani, R. 2002. *Leadership.* New York: Miramax Books, page 46.

Gonzales, P., Guzmán, J.C., Partelow, L., *et al.* 2004. *Trends in International Mathematics and Science Study (TIMSS).* Washington, D.C.: U.S. Department of Education, Institute of Education Sciences.

Gregory, G.H., and Chapman, C. 2002. *Differentiated instructional strategies: One size doesn't fit all.* Thousand Oaks, CA: Corwin Press, pages 100–103.

Grigg, W., Lauko, M., and Brockway, D. 2006. *The nation's report card: Science 2005.* Washington, D.C.: National Center For Educational Statistics, U.S. Department of Education, pages 14–21.

Hall, G.E., and Hord, S.M. 1987. *Change in schools.* Albany, NY: SUNY Press.

Hallmarks of Excellence®. 2007. *Personal results workbook.* Bloomington, IN: Chorus, Inc., pages 55–57.

Hargreaves, A., and Goodson, I. 2006. "Secondary school change and educational continuity." *Educational Administration Quarterly* 42(3): 33–35.

Haycock, K. 2008. "Dispelling the myth—online." Washington, D.C.: The Education Trust. Retrieved 7.12.2008 from http://www2.edtrust.org/edtrust/dtm/.

Heacox, D. 2002. *Differentiating instruction in the regular classroom: How to reach and teach all learners, grades 3-12.* Minneapolis, MN: Free Spirit Publishing.

Heath, C., and Heath, D. 2007. *Made to stick.* New York: Random House.

Heifetz, R.A., and Linsky, M. 2002. *Leadership on the line.* Boston, MA: Harvard Business School Press.

Hill, J.D., and Flynn, K.M. 2006. *Classroom instruction that works with English language learners.* Alexandria, VA: Association for Supervision and Curriculum Development.

Hoff, D.J. 2007. "Growth models Gaining in accountability debate." *Education Week* 27(16): 22–25.

Hoy, W.K., and Smith, P.A. 2007. "Influence: A key to successful leadership." *International Journal of Educational Management* 21: 158–167.

Hunter, M. 1985. "What's wrong with Madeline Hunter?" *Educational Leadership* 42(5): 57–60.

Kannapel, P.J., and Clements, S.K. (with Taylor, D., and Hibpshman, T.) 2005. *Inside the back box of high-performing high-poverty schools: A report from the Prichard Committee for Academic Excellence.* Lexington, KY: Prichard Committee for Academic Excellence. Available online at: http://www.prichardcommittee.org.

Keller, B. 2008. "Districts discharge unwanted faculty through buyouts." *Education Week* 27(20).

Kotter, J.P. 1990. *A force for change: How leadership differs from management.* New York: Free Press, page 21.

———— 1996. *Leading change.* Boston, MA: Harvard Business Press.

Kouzes, J., and Posner, B. 1995. *The leadership challenge: How to keep getting extraordinary things done in organizations.* San Francisco: Jossey-Bass.

———— 2002. *The leadership challenge: How to keep getting extraordinary things done in organizations.* Third Edition. San Francisco: Jossey-Bass, page 92.

The Leadership and Learning Center. 2005. Planning, implementation, and monitoring (PIM™). Retrieved 1.15.2009 from http://www.leadandlearn.com/displayPage/77.

Lencioni, P.M. 1998. *The five temptations of a CEO: A leadership fable.* San Francisco: Jossey-Bass.

———— 2000. *The four obsessions of an extraordinary executive: A leadership fable.* San Francisco: Jossey-Bass, page xiii.

———— 2002. *Overcoming the five dysfunctions of a team: A field guide for leaders, managers, and facilitators.* San Francisco: Jossey-Bass.

———— 2004. *Death by meeting.* San Francisco: Jossey-Bass.

———— 2006. *Silos, politics, and turf wars: A leadership fable.* San Francisco: Jossey-Bass.

———— 2007. *The three signs of a miserable job.* San Francisco: Jossey-Bass.

Lezotte, L. 2008. *Correlates of effective schools: The first and second generation.* Bloomington, IN: Solution Tree. Video/DVD set.

Lezotte, L., and McKee, K. 2002. "Stepping up, leading the change to our schools." Okemos, MI: Effective Schools Products Ltd.

Little, J., Gearhart, M., Curry, M., *et al.* 2003. "Looking at student work for teacher learning, teacher community, and school reform." *Kappan* 83(5): 187.

Lortie, D. 1975. *School teacher: A sociological study*. Chicago: Chicago University Press, pages 62–173.

Mangan, K.S. 2000. "Revamped library schools, information trumps books: Institutions reflect student interests and the job market." *Chronicle of Higher Education* 7 (April): A43.

Marzano, R.J. 2003. *What works in schools: Translating research into action*. Alexandria, VA: Association for Supervision and Curriculum Development.

——— 2007. *The art and science of teaching: A comprehensive framework for effective instruction*. Alexandria, VA: Association for Supervision and Curriculum Development.

Marzano, R.J., and Kendall, J.S. 1996. *A comprehensive guide to designing standards-based districts, schools, and classrooms*. Alexandria, VA: Association for Supervision and Curriculum Development, pages 19–25.

Marzano, R.J., Pickering, D., and Pollock, J.E. 2001. *Classroom instruction that works: Research-based strategies for increasing student achievement*. Alexandria, VA: Association for Supervision and Curriculum Development.

Marzano, R.J., Waters, T., and McNulty, B.A. 2005. *School leadership that works: From research to results*. Alexandria, VA: Association for Supervision and Curriculum Development.

Mattingley, R. 2008. "Effective planning for continuous school improvement." Toronto, ON: Literacy and Numeracy Secretariat. Power Point Presentation to Ontario School Boards, September, Slide 9.

Maxwell, J. 1999. *The 21 irrefutable laws of leadership*. Nashville, TN: Thomas Nelson, Inc.

——— 2001. *The 17 indisputable laws of teamwork*. Nashville, TN: Nelson Publishing, pages 17–18.

Mintrop, H., MacLellan, A.M., and Quintero, M.F. 2001. "School improvement plans in schools on probation: A comparative content analysis across three accountability systems. *Educational Administration Quarterly* 37 (April): 197–218.

Murphy, C., and Lick, D. 2001. *Whole-faculty study groups: Creating student-based professional development*. Second Edition. Thousand Oaks, CA: Corwin Press.

National Council of Teachers of Mathematics. 2006. "Professional standards for teaching mathematics." Reston, VA: National Council of Teachers of Mathematics. Retrieved 2.23.2006 from http://standards.nctm.org.

Parsley, D., and Galvin, M. 2008. "Think systemically, act systematically." *Journal of Scholarship and Practice* 4(4): 4–6.

Partnership for 21st Century Skills. 2009. "Framework for 21st century learning." Retrieved 2.1.2009 from http://www.21stcenturyskills.org/ documents/ Frameworkflyer092806.pdf.

Pfeffer, J., and Sutton, R. I. 2000. *The knowing-doing gap: How smart companies turn knowledge into action.* Boston: Harvard School Press.

———— 2006. *Hard facts, dangerous half-truths, and total nonsense.* Boston: Harvard School Press.

Piercy, T. 2006. *Compelling conversations: Connecting leadership to student achievement.* Englewood, CO: Advanced Learning Press.

Pink, D. 2006. *A whole new mind: Why right-brainers will rule the future.* New York: Penguin Press, page 218.

Popham, W. James 2003. *Test better, teach better: The instructional role of assessment.* Alexandria, VA: Association for Supervision and Curriculum Development.

Powell, A.G., Farrar, E., and Cohen, D.K. 1985. *The shopping mall high school: Winners and losers in the educational marketplace.* Boston: Houghton-Mifflin, Chapter 3.

Quinn, R.E. 2004. *Building the bridge as you walk on it: A guide for leading change.* San Francisco: Jossey-Bass.

Reeves, D.B. 2002. *The daily disciplines of leadership: How to improve student achievement, staff motivation, and personal organization.* San Francisco: Jossey-Bass, page 83.

———— 2002a. *Making standards work: How to implement standards-based assessments in the classroom, school, and district.* Third Edition. Denver, CO: Advanced Learning Press.

———— 2002b. *Reason to write: Helping your child succeed in school and in life through better reasoning and clear communication.* New York: Kaplan Publishing.

———— 2003. "High performance in high poverty schools: 90/90/90 and beyond." Englewood, CO: Center for Performance Assessment. Retrieved 10.14.2008 from http://www.sabine.k12.la.us/online/leadershipacademy/high%20performance%2090%2090%2090%20and%20beyond.pdf.

———— 2004. *Accountability in action: A blueprint for learning organizations.* Second Edition. Englewood, CO: Advanced Learning Press.

———— 2004a. *Assessing educational leaders: Evaluating performance for improved individual and organizational results.* Thousand Oaks, CA: Corwin Press.

———— 2006. *The learning leader.* Thousand Oaks, CA: Corwin Press.

———— 2007. *Ahead of the curve.* Edited by D.B. Reeves. Bloomington, IN: Solution Tree.

———— 2008. "Leading to change: Effective grading." *Educational Leadership* 65(5): 85–87.

Rogers, E.M. 1995. *Diffusion of innovations.* Fourth Edition, New York: The Press.

Rosenshine, B., and Meister, C. 1994. "Reciprocal teaching. A review of the research." *Review of Educational Research* 64: 500–511.

Rushkoff, D. 2005. *Get back in the box: Innovation from the inside out.* New York, NY: HarperCollins.

Sanders, W.L., and Horn, S.P. 1998. "Research findings from the Tennessee Value-Added Assessment System (TVAAS) database: Implications for educational evaluation and research. *Journal of Personnel Evaluation in Education* 12(3): 247–256.

Sarason, S.B. 1996. *Revisiting the culture of the school and the problem of change.* New York: Teachers College Press.

Scheeler, M.C., Ruhl, K.E., and McAfee, J.K. 2004. "Providing performance feedback to teachers: A review." *Teacher Education and Special Education* 27(3).

Schlechty, P. 2000. *Shaking up the schoolhouse: How to support and sustain educational innovation.* San Francisco: Jossey-Bass.

Schmoker, M. 2001. *The results fieldbook.* Alexandria, VA: Association for Supervision and Curriculum Development.

———— 2006. *Results now: How we can achieve unprecedented improvements in teaching and learning.* Alexandria, VA: Association for Supervision and Curriculum Development.

School Matters. 2008. A Website for parents researching information about public schools. New York, NY: Standard & Poor's. Retrieved 2.14.2008 from http://www.schoolmatters.com/.

Senge, P.M. 2000. *Schools that learn: A fifth discipline fieldbook for educators, parents, and everyone who cares about education.* New York: Doubleday.

Sizer, T.R. 1992. *Horace's compromise: The dilemma of the American high school.* New York: Houghton-Mifflin, pages 71–82.

———— 2004. *The red pencil: Convictions from experience in education.* New Haven, CT: Yale University Press.

Sparks, D. 2004. "Closing the knowing-doing gap requires acting on what we already know." In *Results* (March). Oxford, OH: National Staff Development Council.

Stiggins, R.J. 1987. "Design and development of performance assessments." *Educational Measurement: Issues and Practice* 6: 34.

Surowiecki, J. 2004. *The wisdom of crowds: Why the many are smarter than the few and how collective wisdom shapes business, economies, societies and nations.* New York: Doubleday.

Thinkexist.com. 2009. " Dwight David Eisenhower quotations." Retrieved 2.1.2009 from http://thinkexist.com/quotes/dwight_david_eisenhower/2.html.

Viadero, D. 2004. "Achievement-gap study emphasizes better use of data." *Education Week* 23(19): 9.

———— 2006. "Cognition studies offer insights on academic tactics." *Education Week* 26(1): 12–13.

Virginia Department of Education, 2003. *Science standards of learning curriculum framework.* Richmond, VA: State Board of Education. Retrieved 1.16.2006 from http://www.pen.k12.va.us/VDOE/Instruction/Science/sciCF.html

Weick, K.E. 1976. "Educational organizations as loosely coupled systems." *Administrative Science Quarterly* 21:1–19.

Weiss, H. 1995. *Maps: Getting from here to there.* New York: Houghton Mifflin, page 6.

Wenglinsky, H. 2002. How schools matter: The link between teacher classroom practices and student academic performance. *Education Policy Analysis Archives* 10(12): 6–31.

White, S.H. 2005. *Beyond the numbers.* Englewood, CO: Advanced Learning Press.

———— 2005a. *Show me the proof!* Englewood, CO: Advanced Learning Press.

———— 2006. "Don't wait to replicate." *Maryland ASCD Journal* (Spring): 19–25.

———— 2007. "Data on purpose: Due diligence to increase student achievement." In Reeves, D.B., Editor, *Ahead of the curve.* Bloomington, IN: Solution Tree, pages 207–225.

Wiggins, G. 1993. *Authentic education.* San Francisco: Jossey-Bass, page 229.

Wiggins, G., and McTighe, J. 1998. *Understanding by design.* Alexandria, VA: Association for Supervision and Curriculum Development.

Zemelman, S., Daniels, H., and Hyde, A. 2005. *Best practice: New standards for teaching and learning in America's schools.* Third Edition. Portsmouth, NH: Heinemann Publishing.

Recommended Reading

Antunez, B. 2002. *English language learners and the five essential components of reading instruction.* Newark, DE: International Reading Association.

Arens, A., Loman, K., Cunningham, P., and Hall, D. 2005. *The teacher's guide to big blocks.* Los Angeles: The Four Blocks Literacy Model.

Bernhardt, V.L. 1998. *Data analysis for continuous school improvement.* Second Edition. Larchmont, NY: Eye on Education.

Bowen, E.R. 2003. "Student engagement and its relation to quality work design: A review of the literature." *Action Research Exchange (ARE)* 2(1): 8.

Buchanan, J., and Khamis, M. 1999. "Teacher renewal, peer observations and the pursuit of best practice." *Issues in Educational Research* 9(1).

Calhoun, E. 2002. "Action research for school improvement. *Educational Leadership* 59(6): 18.

Calkins, L. 1994. *The art of teaching writing.* Portsmouth, NH: Heinemann Publishing.

Connecticut Department of Education 2004. "Position statement on science education." Hartford, CT: Connecticut State Board of Education. Retrieved 1.13.2006 from http://www.state.ct.us/sde/DTL/curriculum/currsci.htm.

Cotton, K. 2003. *Principals and student achievement: What the research says.* Alexandria, Virginia: Association for Supervision and Curriculum Development.

Ferrero, D.J. 2006. "Having it all." *Education Leadership* 63(8): 8–14.

Finn, P. 1999. *Literacy with an attitude: Educating working-class children in their own self-interest.* Albany: State University of New York Press.

Goleman, D. 1997. *Emotional intelligence: Why it can matter more than IQ.* New York: Bantam Books.

Horine, J.E., Frazier, M.A., and Edmister, R.O. 1998. The Baldrige as a framework for assessing leadership practices. *Planning and Changing,* 29(1), 2–23.

Hunter, M. 1985. What's wrong with Madeline Hunter? *Educational Leadership* 42(5): 57–60.

Marks, H.M. 2000. Student engagement in instructional activity: Patterns in the elementary, middle, and high school years. *American Educational Research Journal* 37: 153–184.

Martin, M.O., Mullis, I., Gregory, K. D., *et al.* 2000. *Effective schools in science and mathematics.* Chestnut Hill, MA: TIMMS International Study Center.

National Research Council. 1998. *National science education standards.* Washington, D.C.: National Academy Press.

Newmann, F., Wehlage, G.G., and Lamborn, S.D. 1992. "The significance and sources of student engagement." In F. Newmann, Editor, *Student engagement and achievement in American secondary schools* (pages 11–39). New York: Teachers College Press.

Office of Superintendent of Public Instruction. 2006. *Washington state K-12 reading model 2006 implementation guide.* Olympia, WA: OSPI. Retrieved 1.29.2006 at http://www.k12.wa.us/CurriculumInstruct.

Saphier, J., Bidga-Peyton, T., and Pierson, G. 1989. *How to make decisions that stay made.* Alexandria, VA: Association for Supervision and Curriculum Development.

Schlecty, P. 2002. *Working on the work: An action plan for teachers, principals, and superintendents.* San Francisco: Jossey-Bass, pages 11–13.

Schwartz, P. 1991. *The art of the long view: Planning for the future in an uncertain world.* New York: Doubleday, pages 60–61.

Wheatley, M.J. 2005. *Finding our way: Leadership for an uncertain* time. San Francisco: Berrett-Koehler Publishing, page 108.

Index

Academic content standards
  administrators' fluency with, 115, 182
  incorporated in art classes, 116exh
  parents' understanding of, 181
  sources/advocates for, 195–196ap
Accountability in action (AIA)
  evidenced by assigned responsibilities, 59exh
  as leadership domain, 11, 13, 88exh
  and specificity, 52
Accountability systems, 51–61
  challenged by schools as loosely coupled, 44–46
  effectiveness examined in data analysis, 27
  growth models described, 47
  as holistic. See Holistic accountability
  multiple levels for schools, 68
  universal structure throughout schools/districts, 58–59
Achievement data
  for comprehensive needs assessments, 141
  as inadequate for decision-making, 17
  multiple measures used for diversity, 57
Achievement gaps
  closed by increasing opportunities, 69
  closed by making changes, 173exh
  closed for targeting students, 146
  and intervention time lag, 190ap
  reduced by midcourse corrections, 69
  reduced by timelines for intervention, 98exh
  and SMART goals, 148
  for students receiving lunch, 146, 153exh, 188ap
  and targeted research-based strategies, 153–154
Achramovitch, Steven, 178
Action research
  findings, 93exh, 96exh, 98exh
  foundation designed for, 25exh
  opportunities for, 102
Acts of leadership
  by analyzing standards, 33–35
  as change, empowering others to change, 64–82. See also Collaboration
  and clarity of purpose, promise, protocols, 79–81
  by creating opportunities for success, 39, 40exh
  data analysis, 21
  domains, 11

focusing on the essential, 32
monitoring of, 23
as platform for risk-taking, 183
related to improved student achievement, 10–11
Administrative structures
  as antecedents promoting student achievement, 5exh, 142
  as antecedents to math achievement, 103, 106
Administrators or site administrators. See also Central-office administrators
  best practices in distinct content areas, 115–117
  instructional challenges in specific disciplines, 113exh
  limited involvement with classroom practice/teachers, 21
  maps analyzed applying Pearson's r, 184ap
  needing content expertise, 108–110, 113exh
  potential retirees percentage, 96exh
  self-assessment, 10, 197–212ap
Adult actions distinguished by antecedent type, 4–6
Adult science fairs, 61–62
Advanced organizers, 102, 133
Advanced-placement (AP) programs. See also Honors classes
  open-access to, 40–41
  students passing exams, 92
Advancement Via Individual Determination (AVID), 41
Advocacy organizations for content standards, 114, 195–196ap
Ahead of the Curve (Reeves), 23
Ainsworth, Larry, 34
Alignment of curriculum, instruction, and assessments, 17
  to standards, 12, 33exh, 50, 52
Anchor papers displayed, 100, 104, 105exh, 106
Antecedents
  adult actions defined, exemplified, 5exh
  correlated to improved student achievement, 99–100
  structures across content areas, 117–120
  success thresholds, for mapping, 193ap
Antecedents of excellence
  applied, profiled by school, 6–7
  instructional strategies as, 101–102, 127
  introduced, described, 2, 4